History

for the IB Diploma

PAPER 3

Italy (1815–1871) and Germany (1815–1890)

SECOND EDITION

Mike Wells

Series editor: Allan Todd

CAMBRIDGE
UNIVERSITY PRESS

University Printing House, Cambridge cb2 8bs, United Kingdom

One Liberty Plaza, 20th Floor, New York, ny 10006, USA

477 Williamstown Road, Port Melbourne, vic 3207, Australia

4843/24, 2nd Floor, Ansari Road, Daryaganj, Delhi – 110002, India

79 Anson Road, #06–04/06, Singapore 079906

Cambridge University Press is part of the University of Cambridge.

It furthers the University's mission by disseminating knowledge in the pursuit of
education, learning and research at the highest international levels of excellence.

www.cambridge.org
Information on this title: www.cambridge.org/9781316503638

© Cambridge University Press 2017

First published 2013
Second edition 2017
20 19 18 17 16 15 14 13 12 11 10 9 8 7 6 5 4 3 2 1

Printed in Malaysia by Vivar Printing

A catalogue record for this publication is available from the British Library

isbn 978-1-316-50363-8 Paperback

....

This material has been developed independently by the publisher and the content is in no
way connected with nor endorsed by the International Baccalaureate Organization.

Contents

Introduction

1

This book is designed to prepare students for the Paper 3, Topic 11, *Italy (1815–1871) and Germany (1815–1890)* (in HL Option 4, History of Europe) in the IB History examination. It will provide an introduction to 19th-century Italy, describing the impact of Napoleon Bonaparte and the rise of nationalism, the attempts to free Italy from foreign control between 1815 and 1848, and the causes, course and consequences of the 1848 Revolutions in Italy. You will consider the rise of Piedmont in the 1850s and Cavour's leadership, as well as the alliance with France and the war with Austria in 1859 that led to an enlarged Piedmont in 1860. You will learn about the dramatic events of 1860 that resulted in Naples, Sicily and central Italy (excluding Rome) becoming part of a new Italian kingdom, the extension of unification by 1871, and the progress and problems of the new Italian state by 1890.

Following an introduction to Germany in the 19th century, the book explores the impact of Napoleon I on Germany, the unrest in Germany under Austrian domination and the rise of Prussia, and the economic unity in Germany after 1818. You will consider the causes, course and consequences of the 1848 Revolutions in Germany, along with the role of Bismarck in bringing about unification between 1852 and 1871. Finally, the book describes the progress and problems of the new German empire and explores whether it was a true federal and parliamentary state, with comparisons drawn between Italy and Germany.

ACTIVITY

Research what is meant by the term 'nationalism'. Try to establish the reasons for the development of the desire for national unity in the 19th century.

Themes

To help you prepare for your IB History exams, this book will cover the main themes and aspects relating to *Italy (1815–1871) and Germany (1815–1890)* as set out in the *IB History Guide*. In particular, it will deal with Italy and Germany in terms of these major areas:

* unrest in Italy from 1815 to 1848 – the historical background to the unrest and Napoleon's legacy; including the settlement of 1815

and the impact of the Congress of Vienna; Austrian dominance and the role of Metternich; the revolts that took place before 1848; and the causes, course and reasons for failure of the revolutions of 1848–49

- the Risorgimento, including the changing role of Piedmont, Cavour's diplomacy, Mazzini, Garibaldi and the events of 1859–61 and the role of foreign influence
- Italy between 1861 and 1890, including the problems of the 1860s, the extension of the Italian kingdom and Italy's development by 1890
- Germany between 1815 and 1862, with consideration of Germany before 1815, the Vienna Settlement, forces for change and reaction in the Bund, the Zollverein and the growth of nationalism
- the causes, events and outcome of the 1848 Revolutions and the political and economic rise of Prussia and the decline of Austria
- Germany and unification between 1862 and 1871, including the rise of Bismarck and events to 1866, the role of Denmark and Austria, the North German Confederation, the war with France and the forging of the German empire
- Germany under Bismarck, including domestic policy between 1871 and 1890, the Kulturkampf and the anti-socialist campaign, how liberal the German empire was, political change, the problems of foreign policy, Bismarck and colonial policy, and Bismarck's fall and the situation by 1890.

Key Concepts

Each chapter will help you focus on the main issues, and to compare and contrast the main developments that took place in the history of Italy and Germany from 1815 to 1890. In addition, at various points in the chapters, there will be questions and activities which will help you focus on the six Key Concepts. These are:

- change
- continuity
- causation
- consequence
- significance
- perspectives.

Theory of Knowledge

In addition to the broad key themes, the chapters contain Theory of Knowledge (ToK) links to get you thinking about aspects that relate to history, which is a Group 3 subject in the IB Diploma. The *Italy and Germany* topic has several clear links to ideas about knowledge and history. The subject is highly political, as it concerns aspects of ideology. The term 'ideology' means a logically connected set of ideas that forms the basis of a political belief system or a political theory. As far as this book is concerned, the main relevant ideology is that of nationalism.

At times, the deeply political nature of this topic has affected the historians writing about these states, the leaders involved, and the policies and actions taken. Questions relating to the selection of sources, and the way historians interpret these sources, have clear links to the IB Theory of Knowledge course.

For example, when trying to explain aspects of particular policies, political leaders' motives, and their success or failure, historians must decide which evidence to select and use to make their case and which evidence to leave out. You will need to reflect on the extent to which historians' personal political views influence them, both when selecting what they consider to be the most relevant sources and when making judgements about the value and limitations of specific sources or sets of sources.

You will need to consider: Is there such a thing as objective 'historical truth'? Or is there just a range of subjective historical opinions and interpretations about the past, which vary according to the political interests of individual historians?

The assumptions made by earlier historians and writers about nationalism in Europe after 1815 have been challenged by recent research. There is also a great deal of historical controversy – for example, about the role of Bismarck in relation to other factors, such as economic growth and whether he was in control of events or merely an improviser in the face of change. You will discover there is a range of different interpretations and several historical debates surrounding Bismarck's policies and actions. (For more on the historical debate surrounding Bismarck, see 6.7, 'How did Bismarck do it?' and Chapter 7.)

You are therefore strongly advised to read a range of publications giving different interpretations of the theory and practice, and the various economic, political and social policies covered by this book, in order to gain a clear understanding of the relevant historiographies (see Further reading).

IB History and Paper 3 questions

Paper 3

In IB History, Paper 3 is taken only by Higher level students. For this paper, IB History specifies that three sections of an Option should be selected for in-depth study. The examination paper will set two questions on each of the eighteen sections – and you have to answer three questions in total.

Unlike Paper 2, where there are regional restrictions, in Paper 3 you will be able to answer *both* questions from one section, with a third chosen from one of the other sections. These questions are essentially in-depth analytical essays. It is therefore important to ensure you study *all* the bullet points set out in the *IB History Guide*, in order to give yourself the widest possible choice of questions.

Exam skills

Throughout the main chapters of this book, there are activities and questions to help you develop the understanding and the exam skills necessary for success in Paper 3. Your exam answers should demonstrate:

- factual knowledge and understanding
- awareness and understanding of historical interpretations
- structured, analytical and *balanced* argument.

Before attempting the specific exam practice questions that come at the end of each main chapter, you might find it useful to refer *first* to Chapter 9, the final exam practice chapter. This suggestion is based on the idea that, if you know where you are supposed to be going (in this instance, gaining a good grade), and how to get there, you stand a better chance of reaching your destination!

Questions and mark schemes

To ensure that you develop the necessary skills and understanding, each chapter contains comprehension questions and examination tips. For success in Paper 3, you need to produce essays that combine a number of features. In many ways, these require the same skills as the essays in Paper 2.

However, for the Higher level Paper 3, examiners will be looking for greater evidence of *sustained* analysis and argument, linked closely to the demands of the question. They will also be seeking more depth and precision with regard to supporting knowledge. Finally, they will be expecting a clear and well-organised answer, so it is vital to do a rough plan *before* you start to answer a question. Your plan will show straight away whether or not you know enough about the topic to answer the question. It will also provide a good structure for your answer.

It is particularly important to start by focusing *closely* on the wording of the question, so that you can identify its demands. If you simply assume that a question is *generally about this period/leader*, you will probably produce an answer that is essentially a narrative or story, with only vague links to the question. Even if your knowledge is detailed and accurate, it will only be broadly relevant. If you do this, you will get half-marks at most.

Another important point is to present a *well-structured* and *analytical argument* that is clearly linked to *all the demands of the question*. Each aspect of your argument/analysis/explanation then needs to be supported by carefully selected, precise and relevant own knowledge.

In addition, showing awareness and understanding of relevant historical debates and interpretations will help you to access the highest bands and marks. This does not mean simply repeating, in your own words, what different historians have said. Instead, try to *critically evaluate* particular interpretations. For example, are there any weaknesses in some arguments put forward by some historians? What strengths does a particular interpretation have?

Examiner's tips

To help you develop these skills, most chapters contain sample questions, with examiner tips about what to do (and what *not* to do) in order to achieve high marks. These chapters will focus on a specific skill, as follows:

* Skill 1 (Chapter 2) – understanding the wording of a question
* Skill 2 (Chapter 3) – planning an essay

- Skill 3 (Chapter 4) – writing an introductory paragraph
- Skill 4 (Chapter 5) – avoiding irrelevance
- Skill 5 (Chapter 6) – avoiding a narrative-based answer
- Skill 6 (Chapter 7) – using your own knowledge analytically and combining it with awareness of historical debate
- Skill 7 (Chapter 8) – writing a conclusion to your essay.

Some of these tips will contain parts of a student's answer to a particular question, with examiner's comments, to give you an understanding of what examiners are looking for.

This guidance is developed further in Chapter 9, the exam practice chapter, where examiner's tips and comments will enable you to focus on the important aspects of questions and their answers. These examples will also help you avoid simple mistakes and oversights that, every year, result in some otherwise good students failing to gain the highest marks.

For additional help, a simplified Paper 3 mark scheme is provided in Chapter 9. This should make it easier to understand what examiners are looking for in examination answers. The actual Paper 3 IB History mark scheme can be found on the IB website.

This book will provide you with historical knowledge and understanding to help you answer all the specific content bullet points set out in the *IB History Guide*. Furthermore, by the time you have worked through the various exercises, you should have the skills necessary to construct relevant, clear, well-argued and well-supported essays.

Background to the period

The 18th century was dominated by kings and empires. Most European monarchs believed in the 'divine right of kings' (the idea that monarchs were appointed by God and so were answerable only to God). They therefore ruled as absolute monarchs, with little interference from parliaments. The chief exceptions to this rule were:

- The United Provinces (the Netherlands), Venice and Switzerland. These were the only republics of any importance in Europe and conservative in nature. Both the United Provinces and Venice had overseas empires.

1

- In Britain, the kings were constitutional monarchs and there was a parliament that was partly elected, though only by a relatively small number of voters. Part of parliament consisted of unelected nobles and churchmen.

The Enlightenment

Some monarchs – for example, the rulers of Austria, Prussia, Russia and Spain – have been described as 'enlightened despots'. They aimed to modernise their lands while keeping control of their people. They were considered 'enlightened' because they tried to put into practice some of the new reforming ideas that spread across Europe in the 18th century (a period known as the Enlightenment). They were considered 'despots', or absolute rulers, because they had unlimited power and allowed no democratic voting.

However, there were forces for change in the 18th century:

- The intellectual movement known as the Enlightenment gave rise to theories that questioned the power of kings. Some writers attacked the old privileges of king, lords and Church. For instance, Jean-Jacques Rousseau suggested that there was a contract between ruler and ruled, rather than simply an obligation to obey.

- The revolution of the American colonies against British rule, starting in 1774 and ending with American independence in 1783, encouraged the spread of ideas about representative government. These included the view that those who were taxed had a right to discuss laws and have a say in how their country should be run.

The spread of revolutionary ideals

In 1789, there was revolution in France after the king attempted to introduce a new body, the Estates-General, to discuss public affairs during a financial crisis. French people began making political demands, including calling for a new constitution, new freedoms of speech and new rights. They demanded the overthrow of the monarchy and the establishment of a French republic.

The revolution put the people of France at war with the French monarchy, and the king became a virtual prisoner of the Paris crowds. The Republic of France was proclaimed in 1792 and the French king, Louis XVI, was executed in January 1793.

Revolutionary ideas from France quickly spread into Europe, taken by successful French generals into Italy and Germany. These new ideas included those of 'liberty, equality and fraternity (brotherhood)' and the Declaration of the Rights of Man, which saw 'citizens' (rather than 'subjects') as having a right to vote for those who ran the state.

Prior to the 18th century, Italy and Germany were made up of many small, independent states headed by their own absolute rulers. During the Revolutionary and Napoleonic Wars (1792–1815) these states were partly unified under French rule, and so the new French ideas took hold there. This undermined the 18th century tradition of loyalty to monarchs.

Napoleon established his rule over France in 1799 and assumed the title of emperor in 1804. Under him, France became the leading power in Europe. Napoleon became a focus for nationalist feeling. He also introduced modern administration and law to Italy and Germany. In this way, he inadvertently sowed the seeds of later resistance to French rule. Revolutionary ideas from France – of the right of different nationalities to rule themselves; of the will of the people to be represented in assemblies and elected parliaments – were not forgotten after Napoleon's fall in 1814–15. These modern ideas continued to be expressed in the new Italian and German states.

Romanticism

The 18th century was characterised by a revival of classical forms in the arts and a culture based on the past. The established tradition was one of respect for authority, multinational empires and the right of kings and princes to rule. However, by 1815 romanticism spread across Europe. Romantic artists and writers aimed to express personal feeling in freer forms than were common in the formal style of the classical period, and to celebrate the wonders of nature. In the majority of art, music, literature and culture, the individual and not the community was now celebrated. Romanticism meant less respect for authority: individuality was viewed as more important, and freedom of expression and the creation of new forms to express feelings were encouraged. Dress and manners became less formal; there was renewed interest in the history of nationalities and a greater desire for nationalities to bond together. In this way, the old aristocratic world that the rulers tried to restore in 1815 was replaced by nationalism, liberalism and romanticism. All three played a significant role in the demands for German and Italian unity, as this book will show.

DISCUSSION POINT

Find out more about the French Revolution of 1789–99 and the period of Napoleonic rule up to 1815. What was the main impact of the changes between 1789 and 1815, and did they benefit Italy or Germany?

Terminology and definitions

To understand the various ideas that emerged in Germany and Italy during the period under study, you will need to be familiar with a few basic terms, including nationalism and liberalism. This is complicated by the fact that terms such as these have meant – and still mean – different things to different people, both to historians and to contemporaries.

You will also need to understand what is meant by Right, Centre and Left in politics. This will help explain, for example, the divisions of 1848–49 and the struggles after the unification of both Italy and Germany.

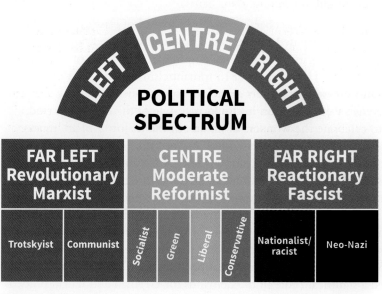

Figure 1.1: The political spectrum: Left/Centre/Right in the 19th century

Liberalism

This word comes from the Latin *liber*, meaning free. Liberalism in the period you are going to study means a belief in political freedom. This involves:

- freedom from absolute monarchs and states
- freedom under the law – the right to a fair trial
- freedom to express political views
- freedom to elect parliaments to discuss laws.

Many of these ideas originate from the American Declaration of Independence of 1776 and the French Declaration of the Rights of Man of 1789. These reflect the view that all men have the natural right to be free.

Liberalism also means economic freedom. Liberals believed that government should not interfere with people's desire to improve their lives through their own efforts. Liberals thought that taxes on internal trade restricted prosperity and should be abolished. They believed that if trade within nations were free, people's labour and profits would not need to be taxed much.

In terms of religion, liberals argued that people should be free to choose whether to believe in and practise religion or to have none – that is, the churches should not impose their beliefs.

The limit that liberals placed on this freedom was that it should not restrict the right to freedom of others. People should not be free to commit crimes, for instance.

Liberals were not necessarily democrats. Many liberals thought that only those with a share in society should vote – this excluded the poor and those who did not pay taxes. To some, democracy was flawed because it gave the 'ignorant' a voice as well as the informed, educated classes. Also, tyrants such as Napoleon had used universal suffrage (the right of all men to vote) to get support, often by falsifying election results.

Liberals did not always believe in social reforms or helping the poor, because they thought this would interfere with the people's individual responsibility for their own lives. They also were against raising taxes, as they thought people should be free to keep what they earned.

Reactionary

The reactionaries were those who were against the new liberal ideas and reacted against change. They were the defenders of established traditions and the old order.

One example of a reactionary is the Austrian statesman Clemens von Metternich. Metternich wanted to prevent discussion about change and bring back respect for traditional authority – the monarch, the aristocracy, the Church – after the French Revolution.

Nationalism

Nationalism is the belief that progress and happiness will follow if people of the same nationality live in the same state.

Nationality was usually seen in terms of a common language or culture. However, this was difficult to define in practice. Furthermore, not all nationalists believed in the same nation. For example, some believed in a *Grossdeutschland* – a 'greater Germany' made up of all Germanic peoples including those in Austria – while others believed in a smaller Germany, or *Kleindeutschland*, made up of Protestant north Germans. Similarly, some believed in a northern 'Italy' while others thought that all Italians, including those living in the south, should be included. What united nationalists was a dislike of foreign rule.

Republicans

Some nationalists were also republicans. They believed in an end to hereditary monarchy and in rule by elected heads of state and assemblies.

France had set up a republic in September 1792, following a joint Austrian–Prussian invasion of France in August, and suspicions that the king was in touch with the invaders. However, a combination of French defeats, radical political ideas, popular unrest and further evidence of contacts with enemy forces, led to the king's trial for treason in December 1792 and his execution in January 1793. Republics were therefore associated with violent revolution in the 19th century.

Some republicans were also nationalists, but not all nationalists were republicans. In the end, both the united Germany and the united Italy were monarchies.

Summary

By the time you have worked through this book, you should be able to:

- understand what Italy and Germany were like before 1815, and what problems were faced by those who wished to unite them
- understand and account for the various attempts to unite Germany and Italy before and during 1848 and 1849, and the reasons for their failures
- understand why changes after 1849 made unification possible in both countries, and make a judgement about the importance of key personalities in the development of unification
- understand the developments after unification, and make a judgement about how well the rulers of Italy and Germany coped with the problems that arose because of unification
- make comparisons between developments in the two countries.

2 | The unification of Italy, 1815–48

Introduction

This chapter explains the disunity in Italy before 1815 and briefly outlines the impact of the French Revolution and the Napoleonic Wars in creating a more unified Italian nation, despite the attempts of statesmen such as the Austrian Foreign Minister, Metternich to uphold the old order and strengthen Austrian power in Italy. There was increasing interest in the creation of this 'new Italy', and the hope that greater unity would result in a moral regeneration. This idealism was particularly associated with the writer and political agitator Giuseppe Mazzini, who inspired many young Italians. However, Italy's rulers had little interest in a new state. Austria was the dominant power after 1815, and its strong armies were a barrier to Italian nationalism. The leading Italian state was Piedmont, and some nationalists saw their greatest hopes in a movement led by this northern kingdom. For a while, it even seemed that Pope Pius IX might lead a more unified Italy. However, the revolts of 1848 proved this was not to be. The king of Piedmont was an unenthusiastic nationalist and Austria defeated his armies, while the Pope turned strongly against national unity. Italian nationalists led daring revolts, but by 1849 they were defeated and the Austrians and the old rulers were back in control.

TIMELINE

1789 French Revolution begins; new ideas of liberty and progress

1792 **Apr:** French Revolutionary Wars begin; Italy becomes a battleground between France and Austria

1796 **Mar:** Napoleon leads French army and defeats Piedmont and Austria

1797 **Oct:** Peace of Campo Formio

1802 **Jan:** Republic of Italy established by France

1804 **Dec:** Napoleon becomes emperor; Italy is part of his empire

1805 **Mar:** Kingdom of Italy established

1806 **Mar:** Kingdom of Naples set up

1814 **Apr:** Napoleon abdicates; Congress of Vienna discusses peace settlement

1815 **Jun:** Treaty of Vienna; Austria dominates Italy

1820–21	A series of revolts across Italy – all fail
1831	**Jul:** 'Young Italy' republican movement founded by Giuseppe Mazzini
1846	**Jun:** Election of Pope Pius IX raises hopes of a united Italy
1848	**Jan:** Revolt in Sicily
	Mar: Revolts in Milan and Venice
	May: Invasion of Lombardy by Piedmont
	Jul: Battle of Custoza – Austria defeats Piedmont under Carlo Alberto
1849	**Apr:** French troops sent to Rome to protect the Pope
	Mar: Battle of Novara; abdication of Carlo Alberto; Vittore Emanuele II becomes king of Piedmont
	Jun: Defeat of Roman Republic
	Aug: Defeat of Venetian Republic

KEY QUESTIONS

- What was Italy like before 1815?
- What impact did the French Revolution and Napoleon have on Italy?
- What was the impact of the Congress System on Italy?
- Why was there unrest in Italy between 1815 and 1848?
- How strong was nationalism in Italy by 1848?
- Why did the 1848 Revolutions fail and how important were they?

Overview

- There was little sense of being 'Italian' in 1796, since regional loyalties, laws, dialects and customs were more important than national ideals.
- The French Revolution and France's subsequent invasions and control brought greater political unity to Italy. Napoleon Bonaparte forced Italians to live in new states with a new type of government and new laws. Italian nationalism was a consequence of this unpopular French rule.

- The Austrians were given dominance in Italy by the Treaty of Vienna and strove to uphold this in order to maintain its great power status and to act as a counterweight to Prussia in Germany. Austria was opposed to the new forces of nationalism and unity that had emerged during the Revolutionary and Napoleonic Wars.
- Some Italians were inspired to work towards increased unity after 1815, when the old order was restored and Italy once again fell under foreign control – this time by Austria.
- Some Italian nationalists formed secret societies and were idealistic writers and agitators. The most important of these was Giuseppe Mazzini.
- Piedmont was the strongest of the Italian states and there were hopes that it might lead Italy towards unification. In the 1840s, some nationalists looked to the papacy to take charge of a new Italy.
- However, Italian nationalists were a minority. When revolution broke out on a large scale in 1848, it failed because there was too much disunity in Italy and Austria was too powerful.

2.1 What was Italy like before 1815?

Italy on the eve of the Napoleonic era

Before 1796, 'Italy' was a concept rather than a country. Contemporaries referred to Italy in a similar way that we might refer to the 'Arab world' or 'the West'. It was made up of many different states with different traditions, languages and levels of economic and social development. The Austrian statesman Clemens von Metternich described Italy in 1847 as 'a geographical expression'. The different states and regions had little in common. There was no official language; no common form of government; no education system; no standard currency, weights and measures or even time measurement. There were economic barriers; difficulties in crossing frontiers; poor communications; and barriers to travel, such as mountain ranges. There was only a distant tradition of Italian unity that dated from Roman times.

Figure 2.1: Italy in 1749

Piedmont-Savoy or the Kingdom of Sardinia

The Italian state of Piedmont-Savoy developed as its rulers – the dukes of Savoy and kings of Sardinia – acquired new lands. Savoy was occupied by France in 1792 and its people considered themselves to be French. It was separated by mountains from Piedmont, which was viewed as Italian. This divided state also included the island of Sardinia, which had a dialect and culture of its own. The capital of Piedmont-Savoy was Turin (Torino).

Lombardy

The province of Lombardy, the former duchy of Milan, lay to the east of Piedmont and was ruled by Austria. It had an impressive capital in Milan and an efficient administration. Its citizens were well educated, and benefited from fair taxes and a legal system based on the principle of equal rights for all.

The Republics of Venice and Genoa

These were two self-governing states. They were ruled by heads of state, called *doges*, who were elected by the upper classes. Venice had colonies along the Adriatic coast and was one of the great cities of Europe. Genoa was a major trading centre.

Modena and Parma

These were small states ruled by dukes and duchesses and allied to the ruling family of Austria, the **Habsburgs**.

The Habsburgs:

The Habsburg family was one of the key ruling houses of Europe. They had been Holy Roman Emperors since the 15th century. The empire was a great area of land in central Europe. Although its emperors were in theory elected by certain key bishops and princes, in practice the rulers of Austria – the Habsburg family – were always chosen, from the late 15th century through to the abolition of the Holy Roman Empire in 1806 under Napoleon. After 1806, the Habsburg family ruled the Austrian empire – which included lands in Italy – from their capital, Vienna. The Austrian empire was defeated in Italy in 1860 and in Germany in 1866, and became known as the Austro-Hungarian empire from 1867 until its demise after the First World War, when it was broken up into separate states.

Tuscany

The Grand Duchy of Tuscany, with its capital Florence, was ruled by a Habsburg relative of the Austrians.

The Papal States

This was the name given to great areas of central Italy that were ruled directly by the Pope in Rome.

The Kingdom of the Two Sicilies

The southern part of Italy was called the Kingdom of the Two Sicilies because of the union of the island of Sicily with the large southern state of Naples, under a ruling family of Spanish origin. Naples was one of Europe's biggest cities, with a population of 300 000.

ACTIVITY

On a blank map of Italy, make sure you can identify the following: Turin, Venice, Rome, Naples, Sicily, Piedmont, the Papal States, Lombardy.

This knowledge is essential if you are to understand how the different parts of Italy came together.

The political situation in Italy

- There were three republics – Genoa, Venice and Lucca – but these were oligarchies (states in which decisions were made only by the wealthy).
- Piedmont was an absolute monarchy – that is, the word of the king was law. The Papal States were ruled as an absolute monarchy (with the Pope as absolute ruler), as were Naples and Sicily.
- The smaller duchies, such as Parma, had no political freedom.
- Austria, ruling Lombardy directly, was a major influence on other areas through alliances and family connections.

The economic situation in Italy

In many areas, there was little trade between regions or even between cities and their agricultural lands. Many rural areas simply grew enough food to live on. The northern agricultural lands were fertile and there was some investment and development in these areas. Piedmont and Lombardy were among the few regions of 18th century Europe to introduce modern farming techniques, such as drainage and crop rotation. Elsewhere, agricultural practices had changed little over the centuries. Outside the fertile Lombard plains, farmland was often of inferior quality. There were extensive marshes that were hazardous and difficult to cultivate, and those who lived in the mountain areas were poor.

Trade for the urban markets was limited because of poor communications. Travel was difficult – carriages encountered substandard roads and the threat of bandits was common. In most rural areas, there was no real cash economy. Many people lived in shanty towns and caves, unable to read or write. They had a low life expectancy and survived on a diet of polenta (a thick mush made from cornmeal) rather than bread. Industrial development was also limited. The landowners invested little in manufacturing, and the main industry was silk. There was some trade and a history of commercial finance, but much of Italy was economically backward.

Culture and society

Italy was famous for its cities. Culturally, Italian art, music and architecture were very influential across Europe. The villas of the architect Andrea Palladio were widely copied, and Italian opera was a major artistic export. However, these cultural achievements did not bind the Italian states together very much.

Italian literature was written in a dialect used by the educated classes of Tuscany. However, by the late 18th century there was some doubt whether this dialect would survive, as educated Italians mostly communicated in French. Across the Italian states, there were various regional dialects that made communication difficult between people from different areas. Those living in remote areas were cut off, not only by poor roads and lack of transport, but by speaking in a little-known local language. People from the more developed regions rarely, if ever, visited the south of the country.

ACTIVITY

As a class, produce a series of wall charts for a museum exhibition on Italy in the 18th century. Describe the political, economic, cultural, architectural and geographical Italy that visitors would have seen or read about in their journeys in the late 18th century.

DISCUSSION POINT

Working in pairs, each person chooses one of the following roles:

- You are a tutor to a rich young man in 1788. Explain to him why Italy is an important place to know about and what he can expect on a visit there.
- You are a young, rich man who plans to visit Italy. You need to ask some questions about your forthcoming tour.

If there are things that either tutor or visitor are unsure of, stop and do some more research. When you are ready, act out the conversation for the class.

2.2 What impact did the French Revolution and Napoleon have on Italy?

In 1789, revolution broke out in France. The French monarchy gradually lost power and was then overthrown. Initially, a constitutional monarchy was introduced, in which the king shared power with elected representatives of the people. However, in 1792 this gave way to a republic – a state without a king. In 1793, the French king Louis XVI and his queen Marie Antoinette were tried and executed. The other monarchies in Europe were shocked by this and opposed revolution, but French armies moved into Europe to spread revolutionary ideas.

The French Revolutionary Wars had a major impact on Italy. French forces invaded Savoy in 1792, in order to secure France's southern boundary. This resulted in the spread of new political ideas into Italy, with reformers in the cities giving voice to the key revolutionary ideals of 'liberty, equality and fraternity (brotherhood)'.

Napoleon

In 1794, France's Army of Italy, which had defended France's frontiers, crossed the border at Genoa. The army was inadequately supplied, poorly paid and undisciplined. It made little progress until a young general called **Napoleon Bonaparte** took charge of it. Napoleon was able to lead the army to a swift victory over Piedmont's and Austria's troops. He then imposed his own rule on Austria in 1797, effectively redrawing the map of northern Italy. Napoleon even experimented with internal reforms in the lands he conquered.

Napoleon Bonaparte (1769–1821):

Napoleon was of Italian descent. He was born in Corsica while the island was still part of Genoa, and lived there during French occupation. He trained in France as an officer, rose to be a successful artillery officer and was a commander by the age of 32. His brilliant military campaign gave France control of Italy. After a campaign in Egypt, he led a successful coup against the French revolutionary government in 1799 and became the First Consul of France. He became Emperor of France in 1804, and defeated Prussia, Russia and Austria between 1805 and 1807. Under his leadership, France dominated Europe, but Napoleon was eventually defeated by wars with Spain and Russia in 1812 and the British army and navy. He abdicated in 1814 and was exiled to the Italian island of Elba. He returned in 1815 only to be defeated again and exiled to the Atlantic island of St Helena, where he died in 1821.

Changes in Italy as a result of the campaign of 1796–97

Napoleon's campaign, 1796–97, resulted in various territorial changes:

- At the Treaty of Campo Formio in October 1797, the Austrians acquired Venice and gave Belgium and Lombardy to France.
- The king of Naples sent an army to fight the French in 1798, but this was defeated and Naples was occupied; two new republics – the Roman Republic and the Neapolitan Republic – were established here as pro-French satellite states (states that were in theory independent but were in reality ruled by France).
- French troops occupied the Kingdom of Sardinia in December 1798.

2

Italy (1815–1871) and Germany (1815–1890)

Figure 2.2: Napoleon Bonaparte

In addition, some major elements of revolutionary France were introduced into Italy. The republics acquired a constitution (a set of rules by which a country is governed) based on the French constitution, and there were elections and major changes in law and government.

In 1798, Napoleon led an army in Egypt. He then returned to France, organised a successful coup against the French government and became First Consul of the Republic in 1799. By this time, Austrian troops had entered Italy and reversed Napoleon's gains of 1796–97. Napoleon crossed the Alps once more and inflicted a humiliating defeat on Austria at Marengo in 1800. French forces once again dominated Italy, resulting in another reorganisation of states.

Napoleon introduced radical changes to Italy between 1802 and 1810:

- In January 1802, the Republic of Italy was established. In 1805, after Napoleon took the title of Emperor of France, this became the Kingdom of Italy. The Republic's original boundaries expanded so that the kingdom controlled one-third of Italy's territory and 6.5 million inhabitants.
- Venice and its Illyrian provinces on the Adriatic also became part of the French empire.
- In 1806, following Napoleon's spectacular victories in central Europe, he sent troops into Naples and established the Kingdom of

Naples. This new kingdom was not ruled by a traditional royal family but by one of Napoleon's most trusted generals, Joachim Murat.

- In addition to the two kingdoms, Napoleon annexed (brought under the control of France) several Italian territories: Piedmont became part of France in 1802, followed by Liguria (Genoa) in 1805, Tuscany in 1808, and Parma and Piacenza in 1809.
- The Papal States were gradually broken up, and the Pope was exiled in 1809 when Rome also became part of France.

Figure 2.3: French control of Italy by 1810

The significance of the changes

The French conquest of Italy meant that disparate Italian territories were now united under French control. The Italian response to this was significant: there were calls for Italians to unite against foreign domination, and among some educated Italians there emerged the desire for greater national unity led by Italians themselves.

KEY CONCEPTS ACTIVITY

Significance: Prepare a short presentation on the importance of the Napoleonic period for Italy.

2.3 What was the impact of the Congress System on Italy?

The Congress System is the name given to series of Congresses held by the Great Powers between 1818 and 1822. The aim was to maintain the common purpose that had united the powers in the final drive against Napoleon. To some extent its aim was to prevent change and prevent France and Russia from expanding. However, many historians have argued that there was no real 'system' behind the meetings that took place. Despite this, Metternich did use the meetings to discuss unrest that broke out in Italy in 1820 and agree with the other eastern powers of Russia and Prussia that it was the duty of the Great Powers to intervene with force to support governments that were overthrown by revolution. The 'system' was therefore used to ensure that Austria maintained its control over Italy and developments in its political life, crushing any semblance of revolutionary or liberal activity.

The situation in 1815

Napoleon reached the height of his powers in 1807 after defeating Austria, Prussia and Russia. He dominated Europe, although he failed to defeat Britain. However, in 1812, Napoleon was forced to abandon his attempt to conquer Russia, with heavy losses. His enemies – Britain, Russia, Austria and Prussia – now joined forces against him. France was invaded and Napoleon abdicated in 1814. Finally, in 1815, with Napoleon's defeat at Waterloo, the Napoleonic Wars came to an end and he was banished to St Helena in the Atlantic Ocean.

Discussions were held by the victorious powers to decide what to do about Napoleon's European empire. The aim of the peacemakers who met in Vienna was to return Europe to political stability, security and order and ensure that France could not dominate Europe again. The Conference was largely dominated by the Austrian Foreign Minister, Prince Klemens Metternich who saw Italy simply as a 'geographical expression' and had no intention of allowing an Italian state to emerge. He was determined to ensure that, to preserve 'the old order' of pre-revolutionary Europe, liberalism and nationalism should be crushed and a conservative settlement imposed.

The settlement, known as the Treaty of Vienna, was a triumph for the aims of Austria:

- Austria took control of an enlarged Lombardy and Venetia.
- Piedmont took control of the Genoese Republic, Nice and more land in Savoy.
- The Pope was restored to his lands in central Italy.
- The King of Naples was restored to Sicily and Naples.
- Tuscany came under the control of an Austrian archduke.
- An Austrian archduke took control of Modena.
- Parma came under the rule of an Austrian-born duchess.

The old ruling families, the Austrian emperor and the Pope now dominated Italy. This *Ancien Régime* (the 'old regime' – the name given to the monarchies of the 18th century) was determined to resist change and was blatant 'Great Power' politics designed to strengthen Austria so that it could act as a counterweight to Prussia in Germany. Most rulers sympathised with the king of Piedmont, who insisted on wearing an old-fashioned wig and preventing any modernisation – even the building of new roads and bridges. This traditionalist approach went against the idea of a united Italy and in many ways the old pre-war system was restored.

However, it was not possible for life to return to how it had been in 1789. The Italians' experience of collective rule under France, and of the modernisation that the French had introduced, could not simply be forgotten. Napoleon had shown that there was an alternative to the authority of the Pope and Italy's traditional rulers. Underpinning the French victories was a strong belief in ideals, charismatic leadership and the whole nation supporting the war effort (with the French army loyal to the nation rather than simply its ruler). Art, music and literature celebrated these big changes in the old order, and the turmoil that accompanied them. As the Holy Roman Empire, the Spanish empire in South America and the French empire fell, there was a sense of new possibilities that increased people's enthusiasm for change.

Forces for change in 1815	Forces for stability in 1815
By 1815, the idea existed among Piedmont's ruling class that Piedmont could become a strong Italian state in northern Italy and fill the power vacuum left by France.	There was no organised and effective movement for Italian unification.
Many merchants, administrators and landowners had benefited from the more unified rule imposed by France and access to wider markets in the French empire. In this way they had experienced the material benefits of change.	The peasantry were conservative, so they were not enthusiastic for change. They were traditionally loyal to their local rulers and to the Church, so they opposed French rule. The ideas of the French Revolution appealed far more to the urban population and to the middle classes.
Changes during the Revolutionary and Napoleonic period meant that Europeans in general, and Italians in particular, were reluctant to return to the ways of the old regime. There was a rise in the number of secret societies that wanted a more united Italy.	The monarchs of Europe preferred to rule Italy as a series of independent states – and had the power to maintain this system. There remained deep divisions in Italy. Regional identity was far stronger than any desire to be a united nation. Differences in language and history between the various parts of Italy were a serious barrier to revolutionary change.

KEY CONCEPTS ACTIVITY

Change and continuity: Work in pairs. One of you should defend the view: 'In 1815 there was little prospect of change in Italy and the old regimes were strongly reasserted.' The other should defend the view: 'Too much had changed in 1815 to make the restoration of the old regimes permanent.'

Write down six points for each view. Write each point on a separate card. Then, on the back of each card, write down evidence to support that point. Practise making your points in pairs, then share your views in a class debate.

2.4 Why was there unrest in Italy between 1815 and 1848?

There were three sets of revolutions in Italy. These occurred in 1820–21, 1831–32 and 1848–49. The demands of the rebels in both 1820 and 1831 suggest that they were protesting against harsh rule and were not attempting to bring about unity. However, the revolutions of 1848–49 did have more of nationalist element to them. However, they all ultimately failed, although the revolutions of 1848–49 did enjoy some initial success. The rebels were often divided among themselves, lacked mass support and were crushed by the power of the Austrian army.

Secret societies and rebellions, 1815–48

The period after 1815 saw an increase in the number of secret societies and illegal organisations pushing for change. Influential figures emerged, the most famous of whom was **Giuseppe Mazzini**, and various rebellions failed. There was a significant movement for change in 1848, which became part of a European revolutionary movement. Yet, by 1850 the situation in Italy was much as it had been in 1815, and so prospects for unity were limited.

Giuseppe Mazzini (1805–72):

Mazzini came from a middle-class family in Genoa. He was inspired by the sight of the revolutionaries of 1821 waiting to go into exile in Spain. He joined the Carbonari and went into hiding, forming the underground group 'Young Italy' in 1831 and taking part in whatever unrest occurred in Italy subsequently. Through his passionate writings, Mazzini became an inspirational figure for many Italians who wanted freedom from Austrian rule and a new unified Italy.

Figure 2.4: Giuseppe Mazzini, the 'Soul of Italy'

The Revolutions of 1820–21

The Naples uprising

The Carbonari, or 'charcoal burners', were the most famous of a number of secret organisations to emerge in this period. This underground organisation adopted terms used in charcoal burning to develop a sort of secret code. Their aims included republicanism and support of 'the people', although their actual policies were often obscure. The Carbonari originated in Naples, but their influence later spread into the Papal States.

In 1817, the Carbonari led a small uprising against the Pope's rule, but it had little impact. Undeterred, they planned a larger rebellion in Naples in 1820, inspired by the revolution in Spain. The 1820 revolt was led by an army unit based in the town of Nola, and was supported by a leading general and some army officers and civil servants. The unexpected result of the revolt was that the king of Naples agreed to a constitution

– a distinct set of rules by which Naples would be run and which prevented the king from simply acting as he wished.

Revolution in Sicily, 1821

The Carbonari's revolt spread to Sicily, with unrest in the capital. Led by workers, the aim was to bring about a new constitution. There was little evidence of any nationalist support and the unrest was largely confined to Palermo, and Sicily showed little interest in the action of their neighbours in Naples. However, the king of Naples sent troops to crush it, and they suppressed the revolt with Austrian help in 1821.

The Piedmont revolt, 1821

There was a military revolt against King Vittore Emanuele I of Piedmont in 1821, and various groups took part. Some were conspirators – different secret societies including the Carbonari – while others sought greater independence for certain regions, such as Genoa and Savoy. In addition, there were discontented army officers and some who hoped to annex Lombardy.

The officer in charge of the revolt was **Santorre di Santarosa**. In March 1821, he led army units in a march on Turin. Piedmont's regime proved surprisingly weak and King Vittore Emanuele I abdicated, appointing his cousin **Carlo Alberto** as regent before going into exile.

Under pressure from the reformers, Carlo Alberto introduced a constitution based on the Spanish constitution. However, the new king Carlo Felice was afraid of the consequences of such radical changes, and he later withdrew it. With Austrian help, the rebel units were defeated during a skirmish at Novara in April 1821.

Santorre di Santarosa (1783–1825):

Santarosa was a Sardinian officer who fought in the wars against Napoleon and bitterly opposed Austrian rule. He hoped for Piedmont's support for revolts in Naples. After the rebellion in Piedmont was crushed, Santarosa fled to France and later England. He died in exile.

Carlo Alberto (1789–1849):

Carlo Alberto was heir to the throne of Piedmont, though he was not directly descended from King Carlo Felice, whom he succeeded in 1831. Alberto was educated in Geneva and France, and served as an officer in Napoleon's army. He sympathised with liberal reforms. As regent, he agreed to a constitution in Piedmont in 1821, but Carlo Felice prevented it. As king of Piedmont, Carlo Alberto introduced legal reforms and a new constitution. He fought against Austria in 1848 but was defeated, then fought again in 1849 and was defeated once more. He abdicated in favour of his son, Vittorio Emanuele, in March 1849.

The language of these revolts was poetic and powerful. Santarosa wrote movingly, 'The emancipation of Italy will occur: the signal has been given. O Italians, even if we have to wear chains, let us keep our hearts free.' However, there was little sign that the revolutions of 1820 were truly national in character. They often reflected local grievances and ideals rather than a planned programme for unification.

ACTIVITY

Find out more about the Carbonari using an internet search or your library. Why do you think the Carbonari are important? What led Italians to join secret societies such as these?

The 1831 rebellions

Throughout 1830, there was increasing unrest across Europe. The fall of the reactionary monarch Charles X in France, who abdicated on 2 August 1830, triggered revolts in Italy. Rebellions began in Modena and Parma and then spread to the Papal States, where the repressive policies of Pope Leo XIII were unpopular in the northern Legations (comprising the cities of Bologna, Ferrara, Ravenna and Forlí). Although relatively small numbers were involved, the revolutionaries succeeded in driving out the duchess of Parma.

Some rebels from Modena joined them to form a small army, but this was easily suppressed by the duke of Modena, Francesco IV. In the Papal States, there was an attempt to set up a 'government of the Italian provinces' by some middle-class nationalists, but the Pope appealed for Austrian support and the revolt was quickly repressed. A few more disturbances were crushed in 1832.

The rebellion of 1831 (if, indeed, these local protests and riots deserve that name) lasted for three weeks. However, the middle-class protestors had little sense of any national movement and were unable to act together. For instance, the people of Bologna distrusted the people of Modena and would not cooperate with them. In the end, Austrian troops decisively crushed the rebellions.

Mazzini hoped to inspire the Italian people to a national uprising, but this did not occur. However, he continued to plot – although his planned rising in Genoa was thwarted by the king of Piedmont, Carlo Alberto, in 1833. 'They cannot kill ideas', Mazzini said, but Piedmont's police and army were able to suppress the revolutionaries.

SOURCE 2.1

Why should not a new Rome, the Rome of the Italian people arise to create a vast unity, to link together and harmonise earth and heaven, right and duty? The labours, studies and sorrows of my life have not only confirmed this idea but transformed it into a faith. A mighty hope flashed before my spirit like a star. I saw regenerate Italy becoming at one bound the missionary of a religion of progress and brotherhood, far grander than any she gave to humanity in the past.

Mazzini, G. 1864. Life and Writings of Mazzini. *London.*

QUESTION

Look at Source 2.1. How would you describe the tone of this piece of writing? Do you think that Mazzini is simply concerned with Italian unification? Why do you think writing such as this might have been influential?

Underground resistance

In 1831, Mazzini set up a secret society called 'Young Italy'. It was a quasi-religious organisation, with 'apostles' providing teaching and instruction that was supposed to lead towards a final revolution. The group attracted a larger membership than older societies, but its aims were not clearly defined. While there was talk of 'the people' and 'the nation', policies of reform and equality, and ideas about what form a future unified Italy would take, were poorly thought through.

The members of 'Young Italy' were investigated by the authorities and many were forced into exile, as was Mazzini himself. There were also unrealistic attempts at risings; for example, plans to start a revolution in Genoa in 1834 failed. Later, in 1844, the Bandiera brothers – Emilio and Attilio – were inspired by Mazzini's example. The brothers were noble Venetians, and officers in the Austrian navy, who formed their own secret society called Esperia. In correspondence with Mazzini, who was then exiled in London, they led an expedition to Calabria in Naples in the hope of starting a national rising. The revolt ended when the Bandiera brothers and 17 of their followers were executed.

KEY CONCEPTS ACTIVITY

Causation: Find five reasons why the Italian risings between 1821 and 1844 achieved so little. Write them on separate cards, and then rank the reasons by importance.

2.5 How strong was nationalism in Italy by 1848?

One popular reason given for the eventual unification of Italy has been the growth of nationalism, which produced the *Risorgimento,* or national awakening or rebirth in Italy. The idea of the *Risorgimento* is that Italy came into being not because of war, diplomacy or the work of Cavour, all of which are discussed in the next chapter, but because of the growth of nationalism and the actions of Italians. While many Italian historians have argued that this re-birth played a crucial role, others have argued that nationalism was never that strong as there were divisions between nationalist groups and that without outside help in the 1850s and 1860s Italy would never have become unified.

The failure of the secret societies in the 1820s and the early revolutions led to the founding of 'Young Italy' in 1831. But, despite the work and role of Mazzini in this period, the failure of the 1848 Revolutions would suggest that national feeling was still not that strong and that

very few people in the peninsular thought in terms of the creation of
an Italian state. Mazzini wanted to see a democratic state established, but
very few supported such a view and at no time were the peasantry ever
willing to support a rising to bring this about. They were less concerned
with democratic ideals and more worried by poverty and social issues,
particularly land ownership. It was really only among the middle classes
that Mazzini's views found much appeal as they looked to gain political
rights to go with their economic power.

A sense of national feeling was further weakened by the lack of a native
language. The peninsular was made up of a range of languages and
dialects. What eventually became the Italian language came from the
Tuscan dialect and was spoken only in Florence. It was such division
that allowed Metternich to comment that Italy was a 'mere geographical
expression'. However, despite this there was some progress towards a
common language with the Italian language periodical, *Biblioteca Italiana*
founded in 1816 and the journal *Il Politecnico* produced between 1839
and 1845, both of which helped to raise the idea of a common culture.
There were also some national organisations established, such as the
Congresso degli Scienziata, which brought together people from different
parts of Italy. Yet, with all these developments their appeal was largely
limited to the educated middle class.

During the 1830s and 1840s there were also a number of cultural
developments, particularly among music and literature, which some
have suggested had an impact on the *Risorgimento*. In music the most
important was Giuseppe Verdi whose works had a clear political message,
seen perhaps most clearly in *Nabucco,* first performed in 1842, with the
'Chorus of the Hebrew Slaves', drawing a clear parallel between the
Israelites and Italians. However, it is unlikely that his view represented
the majority, even among those who went to opera. In terms of literary
works writing did encourage debate about the future and the regions
were drawn closer together by economic progress.

New ideas

There was a considerable growth in radical literature after 1815. Various
ideas for change were written about and discussed. 'Young Italy' and
Mazzini produced numerous articles and books urging change, which were
not fully censored. There was also a growth of more moderate writing.

The most famous of these moderate writers was a Piedmontese
churchman, **Vincenzo Gioberti**, whose *Il Primato Morale e Civile degli*

Italy (1815–1871) and Germany (1815–1890)

Italiani ('The Moral and Civil Primacy of the Italians') was printed in 1843. Gioberti anticipated changes in Europe and Italy under a reformed papacy, and envisioned a confederation of Italian rulers under the Pope's guidance. In this new Italian union, Piedmont would supply the military power and Rome the spiritual leadership.

Vincenzo Gioberti (1801–52):

Gioberti was initially a royal chaplain in Piedmont, and he was influenced by Mazzini's ideas. He was exiled in 1833 as a nationalist conspirator, after which time he taught philosophy in Paris. Gioberti's vision of a papal-led Italian resurgence made him famous. He returned to Italy in 1847 and became president of the Piedmontese Chamber of Deputies, and in 1848 Carlo Alberto made him prime minister of Piedmont. After the king's defeat and abdication in 1849, Gioberti retired from public life.

In 1844, Cesare Balbo published *Speranze d'Italia* ('Hopes of Italy'), in which he outlined his idea for a league of Italy free from Austrian influence. Balbo, a soldier and diplomat, also sought Italian unification under the Pope. By contrast, **Massimo d'Azeglio** sought free trade within Italy, law reform and greater freedom of speech, including more freedom for the press. He thought these aims would be achieved if the Italian princes cooperated.

Massimo d'Azeglio (1798–1866):

Azeglio was born in Turin. He moved to Milan, where he became a writer and, in the 1840s, a moderate Italian nationalist. He hoped that the Pope and the king of Piedmont would lead the movement to unite northern and central Italy. He fought in the revolutions of 1848 and was prime minister of Piedmont from 1849 to 1852. He was replaced by Count Camillo di Cavour as prime minister, whom he supported until 1860, but whose plans for taking over Naples and Sicily he opposed.

These moderate writers were mainly from Piedmont, and they proposed an Italian union of different states rather than fundamental unity. They influenced future leaders, especially Count Camillo di Cavour, as well as middle-class intellectuals and some of the educated Italian élite. For instance, Azeglio met Carlo Alberto of Piedmont in October 1845 to discuss the possibility of a 'conservative revolution' supported by the king. However, these moderate writers actually had very little impact on the Italian population as a whole.

Therefore, although ideas of national identity were more evident by the 1840s and there was some feeling that Austrian influence and interference in Italy should be removed, support for this was limited. In addition, this support was also divided over how this should be achieved, which further limited its effectiveness.

2.6 Why did the 1848 revolutions fail and how important were they?

By 1848, Italian unification still remained a remote possibility:

- Most Italian peasants had little interest in the nationalist ideas of Mazzini and the secret societies.
- Italy's rulers, supported by Austria, were strong enough to suppress the revolts.
- The secret societies were not organised effectively and sometimes their aims were not very clear.
- The educated middle classes, who were most attracted to the new ideas, were a minority.

Despite this, in 1848 there were major disturbances and significant unrest with the aim of achieving change and greater Italian unity.

The new pope

While ideas were spreading about a papal-led federation, Cardinal Mastai-Ferretti was elected pope in June 1846, taking the title Pius IX ('*Pio Nono*' in Italian). Pius had a reputation as a liberal who favoured change. This reputation seemed justified when he released some political prisoners in the Papal States. He also made changes in the way the states were ruled, so that some people who were not churchmen were allowed to participate in government.

Italy (1815–1871) and Germany (1815–1890)

The papacy had previously resisted change. The Church had lost power under the French Revolution and so, after 1815, it supported the *Ancien Régime* (see 2.3, The situation in 1815) in suppressing nationalism. Furthermore, as an international organisation, the Church had little to gain from the rise of nation states. It also considered liberalism to be ungodly.

Between 1815 and 1846, a succession of popes spoke out against political change, and the Papal States was ruled as an absolute monarchy:

- Pius VII (1800–23) had been imprisoned by Napoleon. After 1815, he reintroduced the Index (a list of banned books) and the Inquisition (a sort of religious police to investigate and punish opposition to Catholicism). He also restored the Jesuits, a powerful religious order that promoted strict discipline in religion and education.
- Leo XII (1823–29) was even more backward-looking, and restored both the powers of the landed aristocracy in the Papal States and the restrictions on Jews. He also increased the authority of the police in his lands.
- Following a decade of rule under Pius VIII (1829–30), Gregory XVI (1831–46) used Austrian military forces to suppress opposition in central Italy. He opposed the building of railways because he thought they would spread dangerous new ideas and undermine traditional rural life.

It is somewhat surprising that writers such as Gioberti and Balbo (2.5, New ideas) could hope that the papacy might actually lead a movement for Italian unification. The Popes had dominated large areas of central Italy and prevented change; they had spoken out publicly against change and nationalism; they had allied with Austria as well as backing the efforts of other rulers to stifle new ideas. So, when a more liberal and modern pope – Pius IX – was elected in 1846, many nationalists hoped that the Church might use its moral authority and influence over rural Italy and Catholic Austria to work for greater national unity.

However, Pius IX was under great pressure from the cardinals within the Church to avoid revolution. Ultimately, he reverted to the attitudes of his predecessors by failing to support nationalism:

- In 1866, he condemned liberalism and democracy in the so-called Syllabus of Errors.
- In 1870, he strengthened the authority of the papacy by introducing a decree on papal infallibility that made the Pope's 'pronouncements unchallengeable'; this effectively stated that the Pope's opinion could never be wrong.

Reforming states

In Piedmont and Tuscany, there was some interest in modernisation. For example, Piedmont's king, Carlo Alberto, introduced more liberal press laws that reduced censorship of newspapers and journals. Then, in November 1847, the grand duke of Tuscany, Alberto, agreed a customs union with the Pope that ended all taxes on trade between the two states. Shortly afterwards, in January 1848, demonstrations and unrest in Palermo forced the king of Naples to agree to a constitution for Sicily.

Peasant discontent

Economic changes also caused unrest and contributed to the revolution in 1848. There had been a continuing fall in agricultural prices since 1815. A pamphlet of 1847 outlined the woes of the peasants (Source 2.2).

SOURCE 2.2

The condition of the peasants is appalling. They dig all day for just enough to obtain bread and oil and make a soup of wild herbs. In the winter hunger forces them to ask the landlords for food; he gives it but only if they repay him twice as much or even more at harvest time and only if they let him make love to their wives and daughters. The peasant has to sell his honour for bread.

Extract from a pamphlet issued in 1847 by the Neapolitan liberal Settembrini, published anonymously.

There was also an increase in the number of day labourers, as opposed to peasants who rented or owned land. These casual workers were without work when times were hard, and this increased poverty in the countryside.

With food prices falling, landowners needed to maximise profits. To increase revenues from wheat, common pasture land was converted to cereal crops and there was more deforestation. These measures put pressure on rural workers, who relied on their traditional rights to use common land for their livestock and had little to fall back on in times of bad harvests. When their wages fell, famine and starvation led to unrest. In February and March 1848, there were food riots in Lombardy and some land seizures in Tuscany. There were also outbreaks of machine-breaking on some estates, along with rural strikes.

2

Agrarian unrest made the problems of keeping order more difficult for Italian governments at a time when they were also facing political discontent. For example, rural unrest in Lombardy in early 1848 coincided with political activity against the Austrian tax on tobacco. Those involved in rural unrest did not seek Italian unification, but the revolts undermined the authority of Italy's rulers.

Discontent among the middle classes

Economic development in the first half of the 19th century led to the rise of a larger and more prosperous middle class, and better communication between regions. In the 1840s, railways linking key cities in the north – Turin and Genoa, Milan and Venice, Florence and Pisa – were a symbol of this modernisation and change, and generated profits for investors. Banking and finance also prospered in the north, with new banks in Genoa and Turin. There was also an expansion in the textile industry.

Greater economic development created a demand for free trade. It also increased the confidence of Italy's middle classes and their desire for self-rule. There developed a belief that Italy would grow and prosper if it were not controlled by Austria and its allies. The effect of this was to encourage demands for an end to Austrian domination and a more united Italy.

1848: the main events of the revolutions

The events of 1848 began as small uprisings and built into a wider revolution:

- A revolt in Sicily gathered enough support to make Ferdinand II of Naples agree to a constitution.
- This in turn led to moves towards constitutional rule in Florence for the Grand Duchy of Tuscany, in Turin for Piedmont-Sardinia, and in Rome for the Papal States.
- There was revolution in France in February 1848.
- Unrest spread to Austria, and the Austrian foreign minister Kelems von Metternich, responsible for Austrian repression, was forced to resign.
- Revolts broke out in Hungary.
- In March 1848, a revolution in Milan was supported by the neighbouring provinces, and the Austrian army was forced into retreat.
- Venice was the next to revolt: on 22 March, Austrian forces surrendered and the Venetian Republic was restored under the patriot **Daniele Manin**.

Daniele Manin (1804–57):

Manin came from one of Venice's foremost families. He became a nationalist. He was arrested by the Austrians in January 1848, but was released two months later, after people protested to the Austrian governor. Manin and his fellow conspirators sometimes met in Venice's Caffè Florian, Europe's first coffee house. He led the Republic of San Marco, which was established when Austria was driven out of the city in 1848. He reluctantly agreed to Piedmont ruling Venice, but after King Carlo Alberto's defeat in 1848 he defended the Venetian Republic against Austria as head of a triumvirate (three-man government) and then as president. He was eventually defeated by an Austrian bombardment, and lived out his days in exile and hardship in France.

The year 1848 was a key time for Italian revolutionary movements. The high point was the invasion of Austrian territory by Carlo Alberto of Piedmont, supported by volunteers from Naples, the Papal States and Tuscany.

Figure 2.5: Carlo Alberto of Piedmont-Sardinia

There were now provisional popular governments in Venice and Milan. The king of Piedmont sought an end to foreign rule and some sort of greater Italian union. There was growing enthusiasm for greater national unity and freedom from Austrian rule. Volunteers from different parts of the Italian peninsula came to the north. Passionate ideological feeling was spread by those influenced by Mazzini, and revolutionary leaders such as Manin were emerging. France and Austria were too distracted by their own revolutions to intervene, and Britain was sympathetic to Italian nationalism.

The failure of the revolutions

However, the revolts of 1848 were not a decisive turning point. Pope Pius IX was deeply concerned by the unrest and, on 29 April, he issued a formal declaration (an 'allocution') against change. This destroyed any hope that the Pope would throw his spiritual authority behind Italian union and mobilise Italy's Catholic peasant masses.

The Pope's declaration was followed by the end of the revolution in Naples. The divisions between Sicilians and the mainland, and the king of Piedmont's inability to maintain control of his armed forces, resulted in the restoration of royal control on 15 May. This marked the beginning of the end for the revolutions in the south of Italy.

Strong leadership by Piedmont might have resulted in Austria's defeat and the creation of some unity in the north. However, Carlo Alberto was no Napoleon. His armies let the Austrians retreat into their stronghold – the famous 'Quadrilateral', which consisted of four major Austrian fortresses at Verona, Mantua, Peschiera and Legnago (see Figure 3.3) – that dominated Lombardy. This made it difficult for any army to effectively challenge Austrian power.

On 25 July 1848, Piedmont's army was defeated by the Austrian army at Custoza, and Carlo Alberto signed a ceasefire with Austria.

If Carlo Alberto was not going to lead a movement for Italian unity, there was always the possibility of a popular democratic assembly. Mazzini pushed for this and, in October 1848, a nationalist government was elected in Tuscany that was ready to support an Italian parliament in resisting Austrian rule. The grand duke fled and on 15 November 1848 the Pope's minister, Rossi, was murdered during an uprising in Rome. The Pope also fled the city, and the revolutionaries declared a Roman republic. In February 1849, Carlo Alberto broke his truce and resumed the war against Austria.

By now, however, there was less chance of unification than there had been in March 1848:

- The Roman and Florentine republics were too extreme for many Italians – they were too democratic, too opposed to the Pope and too hostile to traditional authority; the language used by Mazzini was too revolutionary.

- In Piedmont, there were divisions within the government and the ruling classes about whether to support Italian unity.
- Naples was once again under the king's control.
- The revolutions in France, Germany, Hungary and Austria were clearly failing.

A decisive military victory might have turned the situation in the nationalists' favour. However, once again the Piedmont army was defeated by the Austrians, at Novara on 23 March 1849. After the defeat, Carlo Alberto abdicated in favour of his son, Vittorio Emanuele II.

Following the defeat of Piedmont's army:

- Austria occupied Lombardy and the Venetian mainland.
- Ferdinand II of Naples took control of Sicily, in March 1849.
- The grand duke of Tuscany was restored by Austrian forces, in May 1849.
- The Roman republic, led by Mazzini and defended by his idealistic commander Giuseppe Garibaldi (see 3.4 What was the importance of Garibaldi in moving Italy towards greater unification?), was attacked by French troops sent in by the new president Louis Napoleon (a nephew of Napoleon Bonaparte who would become Emperor Napoleon III in 1851).
- French Catholics were anxious to restore the Pope to Rome and ensure his protection; although the French forces were fiercely resisted, the Roman republic fell on 3 July 1849.
- The last revolutionary stronghold, Venice, was forced to surrender to Austria on 24 August 1849.

Figure 2.6: Piedmontese troops at Novara in 1849

Causation and significance: As a class, decide on at least five elements that were essential to the success of the Revolutions of 1848. For example, was there a strong and charismatic national leader? Add notes to a table like the one below.

(The table gives an example, but you need not start with this – discuss the order in which to put the factors.)

Precondition for success	Did this exist in 1848?	How important was this element?
A successful and charismatic national leader	No – Carlo Alberto was not a successful military leader and was inconsistent. The Pope would not take on the role of national leader. Although there were heroic figures, such as Manin and Mazzini, they were not strong national leaders. There were too many divisions and no single figure to unite them.	

Next, work in groups to prepare posters on each of the five elements. You will need to organise the posters for a mini-exhibition to explain the failures of 1848. Think carefully about the order in which the posters will appear.

The reasons for failure

The most obvious reason for the failure of the revolutions of 1848–49 was the strength of the Austrian army under its military leader Josef Radetzky. Although the Austrian government was forced out, its army could rely on the effective defence provided by the Quadrilateral (see Figure 3.3) and the discipline of its soldiers, who were drawn from across the empire and were unsympathetic to revolutionary nationalism. Against these forces, Piedmont's army was ineffective.

Had Piedmont's army been supported by a national uprising, then the outcome might have been different. However, the papal allocution and the flight of Pope Pius IX from Rome reduced Catholic support for Italian unification. Furthermore, the majority of Italian peasants did not seek political change. Although rural discontent had contributed to the initial unrest in early 1848, this was not the same as popular mass support for a united Italy. There was also little backing for an Italian assembly and, with the exception of Piedmont's ruling élite, little interest in greater rule by Piedmont.

The various forces for change of the previous 50 years did not come together effectively enough for the Revolutions of 1848 to succeed:

- Most Italians did not share the desire of Piedmont's military and aristocracy for dynastic expansion, and there was insufficient military power and diplomatic influence to gain control of Lombardy.
- The Mazzinians were admired by some for their heroic defence of Rome, yet many others were appalled by these 'extreme republicans', who reminded them of the terrors of the French Revolution. Rome and Venice remained isolated centres of resistance.
- Many northern liberal Italians saw the Sicilian revolt as simply an expression of the island's restlessness and desire for independence.
- Furthermore, the foreign powers were too strong. Although threatened by revolution, Austria remained powerful enough to reassert its authority over Italy, Germany and Hungary – at least for the time being. Austria had a strong army and its opponents in all three areas were divided.
- The French were no longer the liberal bringers of revolution; instead, they protected the Pope against it.
- The tsarist monarchy in Russia was untouched by revolution and encouraged the restoration of reactionary regimes.

KEY CONCEPTS QUESTION

Causation: 'The 1848 Revolutions failed because Italians were too divided.' How far do you agree with this view?

Make a plan to answer this question. Start with points that might support this view. Then make a list of points that do not support this view but explain the failure in other ways.

Which viewpoint do you think is most convincing and why?

SOURCE 2.3

The defeat of the 1848 movement was certainly a grave blow to the cause of Italian independence and liberty; but this had by now gone too far on its way to be stopped.

Procacci, G. 1970. **History of the Italian People.** *London. Weidenfeld & Nicolson. p. 248.*

SOURCE 2.4

As the revolutionary movement collapsed, everywhere in Italy except in Piedmont the clocks were turned back. The liberal reforms had not brought the princes respect and support. Instead the floodgates had been opened and a dangerous tide of social and political unrest unleashed. In Piedmont the new king was eager after his father's defeat to revoke the constitution, but the Austrians made him keep it.

Adapted from Duggan, C. 2007. **The Force of Destiny.** *London. Penguin. pp. 181–82*

DISCUSSION POINT

Some historians believe that after 1848, unification was assured (Source 2.3). However, other historians take an opposing view (Source 2.4). Which view do you agree with and why?

Theory of Knowledge

History and opinion:

Why do historians have different views about events in the past? Does this make history more or less valid as an academic discipline if what happened in the past is a matter of opinion?

KEY CONCEPTS QUESTIONS

Significance: What do you think was the impact of Napoleon's rule of Italy for the development of nationalism?

Consequence: What do you think were the consequences of the revolutions of 1848–49 for the development of Italian nationalism?

Paper 3 exam practice

Question

Assess the **causes** and **results** of the 1848 **Revolutions** in Italy.
[15 marks]

Skill

Understanding the wording of a question

Examiner's tips

Though it seems almost too obvious to need stating, the first step in producing a high-scoring essay is to look **closely** at the wording of the question. Every year, students throw away marks by not paying sufficient attention to the demands of the question.

It is therefore important to start by identifying the **key** or **'command'** **words** in the question. In the question above, the key words are as follows:

- assess
- causes
- results
- revolutions.

Key words are intended to give you clear instructions about what you need to cover in your essay – hence they are sometimes called 'command' words. If you ignore them, you will not score high marks, no matter how precise and accurate your knowledge of the period.

- **Assess** is not the same as describe – it asks for some analysis and judgements about relative importance and not just a list.
- **Causes** – this is not the same as a general account of the background and events of 1848. While you need to isolate and explain different causes, for higher marks you will need to assess their relative importance.
- **Results** can be long- or short-term, and your assessment will involve some discussion of how important the results were.
- **Revolutions** – Italy was made up of several disparate nations in 1848, and you will need to demonstrate an awareness of these different areas.

For this question, you will need to cover the following aspects:

- **the long-term influences behind the events of 1848:** the growth of anti-foreign feeling, including resentment of foreign rule; the revolts and risings, and the influence of 'Young Italy' and Mazzini
- **the changes in the 1840s:** the hopes encouraged by the accession of Pius IX and ideas of a papal-led Italian confederation
- **the short-term economic crisis:** how this led to popular discontent
- **the Sicilian rebellion:** why Sicily was particularly restless
- **the European context:** the effects of unrest in France and the spread of revolution to Austria
- **the importance of Piedmont:** the decision of Carlo Alberto to lead the movement for change
- **the short-term results:** the failures and the restoration of foreign and monarchical rule, and the presence of French troops in Rome
- **the longer-term results:** the example of a Piedmontese-led movement for expansion; the emergence of heroic figures such as Manin and Garibaldi; the rise of moderate nationalism and modernisation such as that typified by Cavour's modernisation in Piedmont; the understanding that Italy was unlikely to be able to be unified by its own efforts alone and needed foreign support.

Common mistakes

Under exam pressure, two types of mistakes are particularly common.

One is to begin by giving some pre-1848 context but then simply to describe the situation in Italy – the different provinces, the linguistic and social differences and so on, without really linking this information to why revolutions broke out in 1848.

The other mistake is to focus entirely on a description of what happened, rather than isolating the results. This type of narrative-based account will not score highly, as it will not explicitly address the question. Also, a list of causes and results is not enough to achieve higher-level marks – this will depend on estimating the **relative importance** of long- and short-term factors and discussing the issues that historians have raised. The question you need to answer is: How important was nationalism before 1848, and did the revolutions make unity more or less achievable?

While it is helpful to have revision notes, spider diagrams and lists, it is important that you use these as aids to thinking about **the significance of the issues** and to help you address the command 'assess', which is different to 'describe' or 'explain'.

Activity

In this chapter, the focus is on understanding the question and producing a brief essay plan. So, look again at the question, the tips and the simplified mark scheme in Chapter 9. Now, using the information from this chapter, and any other sources of information available to you, draw up an essay plan (perhaps in the form of a spider diagram), which has all the necessary headings for a well-focused and clearly structured response to the question.

Paper 3 practice questions

1   Compare and contrast the causes and results of any two revolutions of 1848.

2   Evaluate the reasons for the revolutions in Italy in 1848.

3   'The 1848 Revolutions in Italy were bound to fail.' To what extent do you agree with this statement?

4   To what extent was the cause of Italian unity helped or hindered by the events of 1848–49?

5   Examine the development of nationalism in Italy between 1815 and 1859.

6   Discuss the degree to which Austria was able to maintain its influence in Italy in the period from 1815 to 1849.

3 The *Risorgimento* and the establishment of the Kingdom of Italy 1849–61

Introduction

This chapter deals with the formation of the new Kingdom of Italy. After attempts to unite Italy in 1849 failed, Piedmont became the strongest Italian state. Piedmont's prime minister, Count Camillo di Cavour, introduced important economic changes and took advantage of events abroad to gain French support against Austria. Piedmont gained new territories during the war with Austria, and the patriotic adventurer Giuseppe Garibaldi led a revolution in the south. Both of these events led to greater Italian unity. Consequently, Cavour was forced to extend his new state in the north to include most of Italy, though Rome and Venice were excluded. This period is known as the *Risorgimento*, which means the resurgence of Italy.

TIMELINE

1850 Mar: Catholic Church's powers reduced by introduction of Siccardi Laws

Oct: Cavour becomes minister of trade in Piedmont

1852 Nov: Cavour becomes prime minister of Piedmont

1853 Feb: Revolt breaks out in Milan, inspired by Mazzini

Oct: Start of Crimean War

1855 Jan: Piedmont joins Crimean War on side of Britain and France

1856 Piedmont raises 'Italian question' at Paris peace negotiations

1857 Revolt in Naples; National Society founded

1858 Jan: Felice Orsini attempts to assassinate Napoleon III

Jul: Cavour and Napoleon III meet at Plombières

1859 Apr: Austria declares war on Piedmont; France supports Piedmont

Jul: Napoleon agrees to Peace of Villafranca with Austria

Nov: Peace of Zurich ends war

1860 Mar: Treaty of Turin; Cavour gives Nice and Savoy to France

Apr: Revolt in Sicily

May: Garibaldi and 'the Thousand' land in Sicily

Aug: Garibaldi crosses to Naples

Sep: Piedmont's armies invade Papal States

Oct: Garibaldi meets Vittore Emanuele II at Teano

3   Italy (1815–1871) and Germany (1815–1890)

KEY QUESTIONS

- What were the immediate consequences of the 1848–49 Revolutions?
- How did Cavour move Italy towards unification?
- What was the role of foreign influences in bringing about Italian unification?
- What was the importance of Garibaldi in moving Italy towards greater unification?

Overview

- After some initial success, the Revolutions of 1848–49 were crushed and many of the old regimes were restored, aided in many instances by Austrian forces.
- Although Austria continued as the dominant force in Italy, its confidence had been shaken. Piedmont had the economic potential to develop, but it lacked the military strength to remove Austria and realised that it would need foreign help to achieve this.
- The unification of Italy between 1859 and 1861 is known as the *Risorgimento*, or resurgence of Italy. The term was probably first used in the 1780s in the writings of Vittorio Alfieri. It was adopted by historians to describe the emergence of the Kingdom of Italy in 1861.
- Italian unification was largely the work of the prime minister of Piedmont, Count Camillo di Cavour. Cavour modernised his country and won the support of Emperor Napoleon III of France. Austria defeated the French military in war in 1859, and this allowed Cavour to create a new state in the north of Italy.
- Giuseppe Mazzini and his followers won popular support for a new Italian kingdom. Italians were also inspired by the daring exploits of Giuseppe Garibaldi, who led a thousand men to join a rebellion in Sicily. The Sicilian revolt spread to mainland Naples, and as Garibaldi advanced through the south, Cavour had little option but to take control of the revolution by sending forces to support Garibaldi. As a result, Naples and the Papal States were included in the enlarged Italian state, although it did not include Rome.

- Rapid and dramatic events led to a new Kingdom of Italy, but this was not a nation that all Italians accepted. As Cavour said, 'We have made Italy; now we must make Italians.'

3.1 What were the immediate consequences of the 1848–49 Revolutions?

In the immediate short-term, the Revolutions appeared to be successful almost everywhere in the Italian peninsular:

- A provisional government was established in Milan as Austrian forces were forced to retreat.
- The Austrians surrendered in Venetia and the Independent Venetian Republic of St Mark was proclaimed under Daniele Manin.
- The revolt in Sicily forced Ferdinand II of Naples to agree to a constitution.
- The Piedmontese army under Charles Albert defeated the Austrians at the end of May 1848.

However, events soon began to change. The Pope, Pius IX, refused to join the war against Austria and also announced that he would not head an Italian federation of states. The loss of Catholic support was a major blow and forced people to choose between their political views and religious beliefs. It was the arrival of Radetzky in Italy with reinforcements that completely changed the situation. He defeated Charles Albert's army at Custoza, and signed an armistice with Piedmont who withdrew from Lombardy. The Venetians ended their recent union with Piedmont and prepared to continue the fight against Austria on their own.

In Rome, the Pope was forced to flee and Mazzini established a Republic, but this was also short lived as the Pope appealed for foreign help to restore him, which a French army did, with the Pope returning to Rome in April 1850.

The Venetian Republic was also under attack, besieged by the Austrian navy and shelled in the summer of 1849, it was forced to surrender in

August. However, Piedmont decided to re-enter the struggle against Austria, but it was defeated again at the battle of Novara and Charles Albert abdicated in favour of his son, Victorio Emanuele II. In Tuscany, the Grand Duke had granted a constitution at the start of 1848, but extremists had demanded a republic and the Grand Duke had fled. However, the Austrians, having defeated Piedmont, were now able to crush the Revolution and restore him. In both Modena and Parma the rulers who had fled were also restored by the Austrians.

It was therefore clear that by the late summer of 1849 the revolutions had failed. Neapolitan rule had been restored in Sicily, the Pope was restored in Rome and in most other states the Austrian grip on power appeared even stronger, with none of the states that had attempted to achieve independence being able to retain it for long. Moreover, Piedmont had suffered humiliating defeats against Austria. Even the constitutions that had been established, with the exception of the Statuto in Piedmont, had been overturned. It appeared as if the revolutions had achieved nothing. However, their failure did not destroy nationalism and many now wanted revenge for the brutal Austrian suppression. Moreover, the revolutions had created a series of myths that would be inspirational in the future. Many remembered the heroic events in Venice or the defence of the Roman Republic.

Cavour and Piedmont also learned important lessons from the events of 1848–49:

- Piedmont should only use moderate action to assert its cause in northern Italy. Mazzini's Roman Republic and the Venetian Republic failed in 1848 because their extremism alienated too many influential people, both inside and outside Italy.
- Piedmont's army was not strong enough to defeat the Austrian army on its own.
- In order to become the leading Italian state, Piedmont needed to modernise.
- Foreign support would be vital in removing the Austrians from Italy.

Although Piedmont was controlled by Austria, it was a stable state with an Italian ruler, a constitutional government and ample resources. Its fertile land and rich port of Genoa meant it had the potential for economic progress. In a confident speech of 7 March 1850, Cavour expressed his faith in Piedmont's potential to lead Italy: 'Piedmont, gathering to itself all the living forces of Italy, would be soon in a position to lead our mother-country to the high destinies to which she is called.'

Furthermore, although Austria had ultimately emerged victorious its domination of the smaller states, and of Lombardy and Venetia, was shaken by revolution.

3.2 How did Cavour move Italy towards unification?

Cavour and the development of Piedmont

Count Camillo Benso di Cavour has been credited with:

- establishing Piedmont as the leading economic power in Italy
- building good relations with France and Britain so that these two great powers supported Piedmont's cause
- defeating Austria in war.

While Cavour was prime minister, Piedmont became the main power in northern Italy. This enlarged state was then able to take advantage of the rapid turn of events and unite Italy in 1861.

Cavour (1810–61):

Cavour was born in Turin on 1 August 1810. He belonged to Piedmont's aristocratic élite and was descended from medieval nobility. Marquis Michele, Cavour's father, was in the household of Prince Borghese – the governor of Piedmont under Napoleon.

In 1820, Cavour entered the Royal Military Academy and trained as an engineer. He studied hard and was drawn to the liberal views typical of young officers. His family had done well under the French, and Cavour admired the efficient administration and progress of Napoleonic France, seeing it as an improvement on Piedmont's old-fashioned regime. He particularly resented the power of the Catholic Church, but he was not attracted to the ideas of Mazzini or to the secret societies (see 2.4, Secret societies and rebellions, 1815–48), nor did he support the revolutions of 1831. He left the army in 1831 to continue with his studies.

Figure 3.1: Count Camillo Benso di Cavour

Cavour's development

Cavour studied social and political theory. He was impressed by the economic progress made in Britain and France under parliamentary rule. In Britain especially, free trade and a liberal political system resulted in large-scale industrial development, technological innovation, the growth of cities, a railway system, and a diverse and generally well-educated society. Cavour visited both Britain and France regularly.

Indeed, he was more at home in Paris and London than in his own country – his travels did not include Italy and he never visited the south. French, not Italian, was Cavour's preferred language.

Cavour disliked the Austrian domination of northern Italy, and he wanted Piedmont to have a constitution. However, there is little to suggest that he sought complete Italian unity, which would include the backward and agrarian south. Rather, his aim was a modern and united northern Italy.

Cavour was passionate about improving agriculture, and he introduced modern systems of management to his father's estates. He supported the idea of free trade, which was developed by the British economist Adam Smith in the 18th century. Smith argued that peace and progress would follow if customs duties and restrictions on trade and economic activity were lifted. Italy was divided by trade barriers and did not seem to share in Britain's prosperity. It seemed obvious to Cavour that Piedmont's modern reforms should be modelled on Britain's constitution. Cavour also saw the building of railways as essential to progress.

Cavour and politics

Cavour worked with the pro-papal nationalist Cesare Balbo at a newspaper in Turin called *Il Risorgimento* ('The Resurgence'), and the newspaper became important and influential. The 'resurgence' of Italy was seen by Cavour in terms of constitutional freedom and economic progress. When Balbo became prime minister of Piedmont in March 1848, Cavour's political influence increased. He urged the king of Piedmont, Carlo Alberto, to support the revolts in Milan and declare war on Austria. His advice may have influenced the king's decision to go to war with Austria on 25 March 1848. If so, this came at great personal cost, as Cavour's nephew was killed in Piedmont's unsuccessful campaign.

In June 1848, Cavour was elected to the new Piedmont assembly. He supported Piedmont's constitutional monarchy, and was not a revolutionary or nationalist. Lack of fluency in Italian made him a poor parliamentary speaker, and he was not re-elected in January 1849.

Carlo Alberto restarted the war with Austria in 1849, was defeated and then abdicated. The new king, **Vittore Emanuele II**, kept Piedmont's constitutional government. In July 1849, Cavour was once again elected to parliament.

> ### Vittore Emanuele II (1820–78):
>
> Vittore Emanuele was king of Piedmont-Sardinia from 1849 until 1861. He was known for his blunt manner and lack of tact. He maintained Piedmont's constitutional government and appointed Cavour as his chief minister. He encouraged Italy's participation in the Crimean War and welcomed Piedmont's territorial expansion. He was less enthusiastic about the new Kingdom of Italy, however, as he knew little about southern and central Italy.

The reform of Piedmont in the 1850s

Even before Cavour became prime minister in 1852, there were reforms in Piedmont under Vittore Emanuele II. The king had little sympathy with the constitutional government; however, he did not abolish it once it became clear that elections in 1849 would result in a moderate assembly. Piedmont had a very restricted electorate – only 2% of the population – but it could nevertheless appear to Europe as a parliamentary state, as it had an elected assembly and a formal constitution.

Until this time, Piedmont had been dominated by the army, bureaucracy and the Church. This hierarchy began to change when the king appointed a moderate reforming minister, Massimo d'Azeglio, to the post of minister of agriculture, industry and commerce (he later became prime minister). Then, in 1850, the Siccardi Laws reduced the power of the Church. These laws were named after Giuseppe Siccardi (1802–57), an academic lawyer and the minister of justice under d'Azeglio, who was responsible for anti-clerical legislation. The new laws abolished Church courts and the rights of sanctuary, which had enabled criminal suspects to avoid arrest by sheltering in a religious building. The laws also prevented clerics from asking for cases to be held in Church courts. This ensured that the Church was no longer outside the law of the state and could not act as an independent body.

In 1852, d'Azeglio resigned, and Cavour took his place as prime minister. Cavour had already negotiated an alliance between the centre left in the assembly and the centre right (the so-called *connubio*). This limited the impact of the Mazzinian republicans and the ultra-right group – the *municipali* – who wanted an absolute monarchy in which the king ruled with no parliament. With this stability in parliament,

Cavour started to introduce changes to make Piedmont more modern and liberal.

Cavour had already discussed commercial agreements to end customs duties with France, Britain, Belgium and Austria in order to introduce free trade. Now he developed Piedmont's economic infrastructure. He introduced the National Bank, the forerunner of the bank of Italy; he financed public works, such as the Cavour Canal and the irrigation of the land around Novara and Vercelli. He also developed railways and built the Fréjus rail tunnel. By 1859, Piedmont had 850 km (528 miles) of railways, at a time when there were only 986 km (613 miles) of railways in the whole of Italy. Piedmont also benefited from a growth in foreign trade, and was the only part of Italy to have anything similar to a modern capitalist economy.

As prime minister, Cavour worked to turn Piedmont into a modern, middle-class state. He also persisted with reform of the Church, although his reforms were met with resistance from the king and conservatives within the government.

Piedmont was the only part of Italy to have freedom of the press, the right to form political parties and academic freedom. In this liberal environment, the National Society was founded with members including veterans of the 1848–49 Revolutions, such as Daniele Manin (see 2.6, 1848: the main events of the revolutions). This middle-class patriotic association wanted an Italian kingdom led by Piedmont, seeing this as a more moderate and practical alternative to Mazzini's radical republicanism. Piedmont's capital city, Turin, became a centre for exiles from other, more repressive, parts of Italy. These exiles included eminent economists, educationalists and even military men.

What was the significance of these developments?

- Piedmont had become a working constitutional state and was making progress. This was something it shared with the economically and socially 'advanced' Britain.
- The increase in industry, trade and transport improved Piedmont's status and helped its military development.
- Piedmont's modernisation – both in terms of the reduction of clerical power and the greater political freedom – put it ahead of other Italian states and marked it as a potential leader. By contrast,

the clerical, absolutist, reactionary and foreign regimes in the rest of Italy were old-fashioned and unstable.

- Piedmont was increasingly admired in British and French governing circles, and this laid the basis for the essential diplomacy that was to lead to unification.

In 1849, few would have imagined that Piedmont, defeated in war and its king forced to abdicate, would in fact lead the unification of Italy ten years later. Internal change was one key element in this transformation, but a major factor was Cavour's diplomacy.

ACTIVITY

Complete one of the following activities:

- Answer the question 'If a foreign businessman or woman visited Piedmont in 1846, and then returned in 1859, what changes might he or she observe?'.
- Write a letter from this person to his or her company, to inform them of the changes.
- In pairs, create a poster showing the major changes in Piedmont under Cavour. Then give a short presentation to the class to explain the importance of these changes.

Cavour's diplomacy

Cavour recognised that Piedmont would only be free to control northern Italy if the Austrians were defeated in war. This would end Austrian interference, and Piedmont would be powerful enough to dominate the region as an extended state that included the valuable lands of Lombardy.

To achieve this goal, Cavour carefully cultivated allies in the Crimean War (see 3.3, The Crimean War and Italian unification). He also skillfully used the Paris peace conference of 1856 to draw attention to Italy. Cavour's aim was to gradually build on this attention in order to ally with France. He realised that France had the necessary military power to fight a war against Austria, and that Piedmont had something France wanted – border lands. Furthermore, Louis Napoleon (the future Napoleon III) was willing to follow in the footsteps of his uncle, Napoleon I, and fight Austria in Italy.

Figure 3.2: Louis Napoleon, nephew of Napoleon Bonaparte, who became Emperor Napoleon III

However, war was dangerous for France. It would alarm Europe, sparking fears of a French-dominated Italy. It would also alienate French Catholics and conservatives and threaten Napoleon's claim that '*L'empire, c'est la paix*' ('the empire represents peace'). So, although circumstances were favourable to Cavour, he had to be careful in the way he sought to gain French support.

On 21 July 1858, Cavour and Napoleon III plotted a war against Austria. Cavour was motivated primarily by the interests of the House of Savoy, but he was also prepared to use the more 'moral' cause of Italian unification to take up arms. France had a history of radical support for nationalist causes – Napoleon I supported nationalism and Napoleon III had been a member of the Carbonari (see 2.4 The Revolutions of 1820–21). However, Napoleon also had French interests firmly in mind.

The negotiations between France and Piedmont were therefore characterised by a mixture of nationalist idealism and dynastic self-interest. Cavour and Napoleon had to bring about, in the words of historian Arnold Blumberg, 'a carefully planned accident' (1990). It had to appear that France had not deliberately planned a war. Cavour had a long-term aim of reviving the war against Austria, while Napoleon III wanted to increase his popularity at home, so a short and successful war in Italy suited him best. This would also give France influence over a new Italian state, which was a traditional French foreign policy aim.

Thus, the turnaround in Piedmont's fortunes was the result of three key elements:

- Cavour's single-minded determination:
  - that Austria would be defeated in war
  - that Piedmont would not have to face Austria on its own
  - that Piedmont would seize every opportunity from events and developments in Europe
  - that France alone would ally with Piedmont in order to defeat Austria.
- the emergence of an unstable French regime that was attracted to the idea of fighting Austria in Italy
- the development of a major European war in 1854 – the Crimean War – that allowed Cavour to gain France's and Britain's friendship and weakened links between Austria and Russia and between Austria, France and Britain.

Without these external developments – over which Cavour had little control – no amount of good works or clever diplomacy would have improved Piedmont's international standing after 1849. Cavour's ability to make the most of developments outside Piedmont turned events in his favour, and this makes his diplomatic policies so critical in explaining Italian unification.

Analysis: the options open to Cavour

When Cavour became prime minister of Piedmont, he was faced with various options in foreign policy.

- He could do nothing, and simply extend the commercial treaties with foreign powers and develop Piedmont. However, this was not really an option. Cavour was committed to an Italian 'resurgence', as his newspaper indicated. Following the events of 1848–49, radical figures and organisations in Piedmont sought an end to Austrian rule and greater Italian unity. So, if Cavour and his moderate centrist supporters did not act, then it was likely there would be more revolution and disorder.

- He could engage in a war of liberation similar to Carlo Alberto's war of 1848 (see 2.6, 1848: the main events of the revolutions). However, Cavour knew that Piedmont's army could not defeat Austria, no matter how much Piedmont's economy and infrastructure, such as the railways, improved. This was the lesson of the events of 1848–49. Also, Piedmont would have to overcome the cooperation between the absolute monarchies of Austria and Russia. Furthermore, France had not supported Italian nationalism previously; the forces of the Second Republic under its president, Louis Napoleon Bonaparte, had defended Rome and supported the papacy.
- Cavour could gain allies to help Piedmont go to war with Austria, with the short-term aim of ending foreign rule in northern Italy and expanding Piedmont's territories there, and the long-term aim of a more unified Italy.

It is extremely unlikely that foreign policy was a priority for Cavour before 1855, since he was busy with domestic policy. He also had little experience of foreign affairs, and there were few European powers that supported the idea of *Risorgimento*:

- Russia was a firm supporter of the post-1815 *Ancien Régime* (see 2.3, The situation in 1815) and hated nationalism, which it viewed as a threat to the Russian empire.
- Austria opposed change and relied on the absolute authority of its emperor, the young **Franz Josef II**.

Franz Josef II (1830–1916):

Franz Josef was a Habsburg prince who ruled Austria from 1848 to 1916, during a long period of crisis. He was determined not to give in to liberal demands. His armies were defeated in 1859 in Italy and then again by Prussia in 1866. Deeply traditional, Franz Josef saw it as his duty to maintain his empire. He shared power with Hungary in 1867 and allied with Germany in 1879. He agreed to war in 1914 to destroy the threat from Serbia, and died in 1916, two years before the fall of the Austro-Hungarian empire.

3

- Britain was unlikely to enter a war on Piedmont's behalf: while the British government was sympathetic to Italian calls for freedom, it was concerned about French territorial expansion.

Therefore, of the leading European powers, France was the most likely to support Piedmont's attempts to end Austrian rule in Italy.

France once again became an empire in December 1851, when Louis Napoleon overthrew the republic, of which he was president, and became Emperor Napoleon III. Napoleon III's youth had been a radical one, and he had been a member of the Carbonari. He had known exile and imprisonment and his uncle had been renowned for supporting nationalism, progress and freedom – and for fighting and defeating the Austrians. Unlike the hereditary emperors, Napoleon III's popularity depended on his charismatic personality and his effective use of propaganda. He was ambitious for success, and Cavour had something to offer to France: the border areas of Nice and Savoy. The acquisition of Savoy would extend France's southern border to a natural frontier.

At home, Cavour's power depended on winning sufficient support from a parliamentary coalition and from King Vittore Emanuele II (see 3.2, Cavour and politics), who was boorish and uncultivated and had little sense of vision or mission. The losses and humiliation Piedmont suffered in 1848–49 made many in Piedmont's government cautious about change.

3.3 What was the role of foreign influences in bringing about Italian unification?

Although Charles Albert had said '*Italia fara da se*' (Italy will make itself), it was apparent from events of 1848–49 that this was not possible; Italy or Piedmont was simply not strong enough to drive out Austria. Cavour had really recognised this in his diplomatic efforts to build up support for Piedmont and events in Europe from 1853 onwards would help his cause and ultimately lead to Napoleon III asking 'What can I do for Italy?' Ultimately, foreign developments and influences in the period from 1853 to 1869 would play a crucial role.

The Crimean War and Italian unification

Events played into Cavour's hands when the unofficial agreement among the great powers to keep the peace – the so-called 'Concert of Europe' – was broken by war. In 1853, Russian troops invaded the Ottoman empire, starting war between Russia and Turkey. Although the immediate issues were settled diplomatically, the invasion led to a wider conflict between Russia and the Ottoman empire, France and Great Britain. France and Britain sent an expeditionary force to the Crimean peninsula in southern Russia, and advanced on the Sebastopol naval base. Russia failed to prevent the siege and fall of the naval base, and peace was signed in Paris in 1856. The Crimean War lasted for three years.

Cavour and the Crimean War

The Crimean War gave Cavour an opportunity to move closer to France and to raise Piedmont's status and profile in international affairs. Indeed, some historical accounts – including a major biography of Cavour by William Roscoe Thayer (see Source 3.1) – portray Cavour as enthusiastically using the war.

SOURCE 3.1

The first step, the indisputable step towards Italy's redemption was to strengthen the ties between Piedmont and the great powers that stood for progress; the Crimean War seemed to offer an occasion to do this. While politicians and statesmen were plotting, the one man who was to profit most from the Crimean War was sleeplessly watching events. During the first stages of the quarrel he knew that Piedmont must remain neutral, but afterwards he saw the need for action.

Thayer, W. R. 1911. **Life and Times of Cavour.** *London. Constable.*

In a parliamentary debate of January 1855 on whether Piedmont should enter the war, Cavour argued that, 'The laurels our soldiers will win in Russia will help the future destiny of Italy more than declarations and writings'. Certainly, committing troops to war would do much for Piedmont's international reputation.

More recent historians, such as Christopher Duggan, argue that Cavour initially opposed Piedmont's involvement in the Crimean War. They argue that Russian wheat exports were vital to Piedmont's economy, and so Cavour feared a pro-war alliance between the king and conservative elements. Yet Britain and France wanted Piedmont's professional army on their side. In the end, Piedmont received little from the 1856 Paris peace conference, which ignored minor territorial demands and referred to 'the Italian question' only in passing.

SOURCE 3.2

Piedmont had little to gain from the Crimean War, especially when Austria agreed to refrain from going to the aid of Russia in return for a guarantee from France to preserve the *status quo* in Italy. The King of Piedmont secretly negotiated with the French behind Cavour's back to enter the war. Cavour had no expectation of any clear gain, but the hope that the 18000 Piedmont's troops would distinguish themselves in battle sufficiently to provide him with a strong bargaining counter in a future peace conference. Unfortunately General Lamamora's soldiers were sidelined in Russia. Two thousand died from cholera.

Duggan, C. 2007. **The Force of Destiny**. *London. Penguin. p. 192.*

QUESTION

How do Sources 3.1 and 3.2 give a conflicting picture of Cavour's control and expectations of the Crimean War? Which view do you find more convincing and why?

When 'the Italian question' was raised at the peace conference, the British expressed their disapproval of political repression in Naples and the Papal States. However, there was no foreign commitment to helping Piedmont expand, and Cavour gained no lands from the treaty. Expanding Piedmont's territories would have risked upsetting Austria, which neither Britain nor France wished to do; they were more concerned to keep Austria as an ally against Russia.

Post-Crimean developments

On the positive side, the Crimean War raised the profile and prestige of Piedmont, and it became more important in Europe. European countries began to take a greater interest in Italian affairs. For instance, the king of Piedmont made a state visit to London in 1855, although it is reported that his crude conversation and manners did not impress Queen Victoria.

Britain and France were concerned about the oppressive rule of Ferdinand II, king of Naples, and urged him to introduce reforms. Britain had been increasingly aware of Naples' political prisoners, after the British minister **William Gladstone** visited Naples in 1850. As Russia and Naples were close, the Crimean War discredited Naples in the eyes of France and Britain, which broke off diplomatic relations with Naples in 1856.

William Gladstone (1809–98):

Gladstone began his political career as a Conservative (Tory), but after the fall of his idol, Robert Peel, in 1846, he changed his views. He became a Liberal partly because of his sympathy with the Italian cause. Gladstone was a reforming prime minister. In a career that lasted over 60 years, he was prime minister on four separate occasions – in 1868–74, 1880–85, February to July 1886 and 1892–94. He was also Britain's oldest prime minister, resigning in 1894 when he was 84 years old.

In Piedmont, Cavour encouraged the nationalist group known as the National Society (see 3.2, The reform of Piedmont in the 1850s). This was different from other Italian revolutionary groups in that it regarded Piedmont as the guiding element in any 'rebirth' of Italy.

Unrest continued in Sicily, where there was a failed rising in 1856. The following year, **Carlo Piscane** led Italian patriots in a revolt in Naples, but this was defeated. This nationalist enterprise had the secret backing of Piedmont's government.

Carlo Piscane (1818–57):

Piscane was a Neapolitan duke who was inspired by Mazzini and took part in the revolution in Rome in 1848. He led an expedition to start a revolution in Naples in 1857, but was killed by local people at Sanza, where a statue to him can now be found.

It is possible that Cavour now wanted to bring attention to Italy's revolts so that he could appear a moderate influence. This would help him to take advantage of the weak relations that Austria had with other powers after the Crimean War.

Indeed, the post–Crimean world favoured Piedmont to become the main power in Italy and dominate the north. Russia was busy reforming under a new tsar, Alexander II. Britain had problems in India, namely the First War of Independence of 1857, and was fearful that Russia would extend its influence in Afghanistan.

The greater interest Napoleon III now showed in Italy was to be critical to Piedmont's success. The French emperor seriously thought about reviving a pro-French kingdom of Naples. Furthermore, by 1858 he was contemplating going to war against Austria in support of Italian independence.

Napoleon III and the cause of Italian independence

The attempted assassination of Napoleon III

In 1858, there was an assassination attempt on the French emperor. A group of conspirators that objected to the French occupation of Rome tried to blow up Napoleon III while he was driving in Paris. The plot failed, but the heroic idealism of its leader, **Felice Orsini**, placed Italy once again on the centre stage in Europe. Although Orsini was executed, Napoleon III was moved by his nobility and sacrifice in fighting for the cause of a united Italy.

> **Felice Orsini (1819–58):**
>
> Orsini was born in Meldola in Romagna, which was then part of the Papal States. He gave up training for the priesthood to join Mazzini. He was arrested for plots against the Pope in 1844 and fought in Rome in 1848. He was arrested as a spy in Hungary in 1854, but managed to escape the Austrians. Orsini was convinced that Napoleon III was opposed to Italian unification, and led a plot to assassinate him in Paris in 1858. He wrote a letter pleading for support for Italy before his execution in March 1858, and this was influential in getting Napoleon III to promote Piedmont's cause.

By 1858, Napoleon III viewed Piedmont's cause more favourably: he informed Piedmont's government that he was prepared to discuss the possibility of an alliance and joint military action against Austria. The meeting between Cavour and Napoleon at Plombières on 23 July 1858 can be seen as a major turning point on the path to Italian unification.

The pact of Plombières

The agreement signed at Plombières was in the tradition of the state making of Napoleon I. In it, Napoleon III and Cavour pledged that:

- Austrian power in Lombardy and Venetia would end
- Italy would be a federation under the Pope, which France would protect
- there would be an enlarged Kingdom of Savoy-Piedmont that would include Parma and Modena and part of the Papal States
- Ferdinand of Naples would be replaced by a French ruler – the son of Joachim Murat (one of Napoleon I's generals who had been king of Naples)
- there would be a new and enlarged state of Tuscany
- the French would replace Austria as the key foreign influence in Italy
- France would gain Savoy and Nice (in a secret agreement)
- a marriage alliance would be formed between Princess Clothilde, the daughter of Vittore Emanuele II, and Prince Jérôme Bonaparte, Napoleon III's cousin
- war with Austria would start with a revolt in Lombardy, which Piedmont would not officially support; when Austria retaliated to the revolt with military force, Piedmont would condemn the Austrian response and declare war on Austria, with France as its ally.

Given French support for the Pope, and the fact that France had worked hard to protect Austria from Piedmont's troops in 1854 and 1855, the alliance between Piedmont and France was a remarkable turnaround. An agreement was signed in January 1859, and King Vittore Emanuele II made a provocative speech against Austria. However, there was not a massive upsurge in patriotic and nationalist enthusiasm in Italy as a whole. Other European powers were concerned about the self-seeking nature of the pact between Cavour and the French and by the apparent revival of French expansionist ambitions in Italy. Prussia offered Austria support; Britain was concerned about French power in the Mediterranean; Russia was hostile to revolutionary change and expressed disapproval of French support for Italian nationalism.

By March 1859, however, Napoleon III was beginning to have doubts about the French alliance with Piedmont. Britain and Russia offered to hold a conference with France and Austria to avoid war, but this never took place. Britain now saw Cavour as a dangerous warmonger. By April 1859, the Plombières agreement seemed to have been nothing more than a bizarre incident. Cavour, humiliated, was in despair.

Certainly Cavour's plan to take on Austria was improbable: it depended on Austria allowing an incident to provoke it into a declaration of war. This would have resulted in the loss of international support that was building up for Austria. The plan for French domination of Naples would provoke a massive reaction in Sicily and unrest in Europe. Britain in particular could hardly allow such a shift in the balance of power in an area where its trade routes were so important. Russia could use the war as an opportunity to revenge its defeat at the hands of France and its Piedmont ally in 1856. The conservative Prussian monarchy would support Austria rather than see a re-emergence of revolutionary nationalism.

War also risked igniting the extremism that Cavour so hated, and this threatened to destabilise Piedmont's domestic reforms. Furthermore, the outcome of such a war was by no means assured, since Austria was one of Europe's great military powers. The French had not won impressive victories in Russia in the Crimean War, and British sea power might not be sufficient to defeat Austria. While Cavour was not interested in Italian nationalism, he recognised that the loss of Nice and Savoy to France would be unpopular. As a result of Austrian pressure and the absence of French support, Cavour had no choice but to agree to disarm his forces on 19 April 1859. By then, a Piedmontese alliance with France to secure a united Italy seemed unlikely.

Austria provokes a war

The Plombières agreement stood every chance of becoming a footnote in history. However, Austria's poor judgement became a decisive factor when Emperor Franz Josef decided to take preventative action. Austria was aware of the military build-up in Piedmont and of Cavour's ambitions to gain French support. Franz Josef therefore decided to take the initiative and end the threat to Lombardy and Venetia. On 23 April 1859, the Austrian government issued an ultimatum to Piedmont to further reduce its forces. Just as Franz Josef's actions triggered the First World War in 1914 when Austria decided to invade Serbia, so the emperor's ultimatum of 1859 gave Piedmont the excuse it needed to go to war.

The Austrian action was a totally unforeseen stroke of luck. Cavour was now the head of a state under threat. This provided him with the opportunity to call on the French for help, not as conspirator but as victim. This revived Cavour's popularity in Britain, where he was now seen as a progressive liberal responding to a constitutional threat from an Austrian bully. Austria was already out of favour with Britain because of the weak support it had provided against Russia during the Crimean War. Austrian action also prevented Prussia and Russia from legitimately defending a fellow monarch from revolution and French aggression.

The consequences

The war of 1859 resulted in the expansion of Piedmont and ended Austrian control of Lombardy. Piedmont now became the dominant north Italian power. The war also led to a chain of events that brought southern and central Italy under Piedmont's control in a new Kingdom of Italy.

But how far was Cavour the architect of this transformation, and how much did this greater Italian unity owe to changes in Europe and to sheer chance?

KEY CONCEPTS ACTIVITY

Significance: Look back and remind yourself of Cavour's attempts to increase Piedmont's power and bring about greater Italian unity. Create two charts, like those shown below, to record your findings. An example has been added to each chart, to start you off.

Cavour's policy	How it led to the events of 1859 and the creation of a new Italy	Importance on a scale of 0–6 (explain why)
Cavour's entry into the Crimean War in 1855		

Factors beyond Cavour's control	How it led to the events of 1859 and the creation of a new Italy	Importance on a scale of 0–6 (explain why)
The Orsini plot against Napoleon III		

The war of 1859

On 29 April, 15 000 Austrian troops under Field Marshal **Ferenc Gyulai** moved into Piedmont and advanced on Turin. The French sent an army to defend their ally, making extensive use of trains to transport men and equipment to the battlefront.

> **Ferenc Gyulai (1798–1868):**
>
> Field Marshal Gyulai was a Hungarian general in command of Austria's Italian forces. He served as Austrian minister of defence between 1849 and 1850, and was made Austrian governor of Lombardy–Venetia in 1857. His defeat at Magenta led to him losing his command.

Piedmont's troops fought from prepared defence lines. Neither the Austrian nor the French soldiers acted efficiently, and were unable to move quickly due to poor rail communications. The French army depended on supplies coming into Genoa, and the first operations were near Marengo, on the site of Napoleon I's battles. The Austrians failed to take advantage of Napoleon's error in leaving his rail link exposed and, feeling threatened by France, they withdrew. A Franco-Piedmont force assembled near Magenta, ready to advance on Milan.

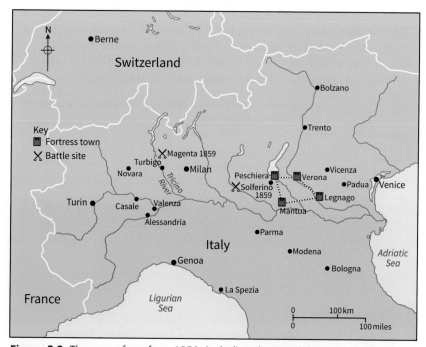

Figure 3.3: The area of warfare, 1859, including the Quadrilateral – the four fortress towns of Peschiera, Verona, Mantua and Legnago

The battle of Magenta

Austria had an army of 60 000 to defend the Tricino River but it
deployed in a weak manner, leaving a crossing open at Turbigo.
Napoleon III planned a joint attack on 4 June, at the bridge at
Turbigo and a railway crossing further north. The Austrians
concentrated their resistance at Turbigo. Their incompetence
prevented a massacre of the French, who crossed the railway bridge
onto an open plain where they were exposed to Austrian artillery.
The French managed to storm a defended canal and link the two
wings of their troops, forcing the Austrians to withdraw from Milan.
Napoleon III and Vittore Emanuele II rode into Milan in triumph on
8 June 1859.

The Battle of Solferino

Austria repeated its tactics of 1848, and its 120 000-strong army fell back
towards the River Mincio. Austrian military power in Italy depended
on four key fortified towns – Mantua, Peschiera, Verona and Legnago,
which controlled the Mincio and Adige Rivers. The four fortresses
were collectively known as the Quadrilateral (see Figure 3.3). There was
a supply route from Austria to Verona, and Mantua was the strongest
defensive point.

The Austrian emperor, Franz Josef, now arrived to take command;
this meant that there were three kings commanding armies. Franz
Josef supported a plan to attack the French troops while they were
advancing; however, neither side really knew the whereabouts of
the opposing forces. Observers in balloons above the battlefield
spotted some Austrian activity, but the French did not realise the
strength of the attack. In the confusing circumstances, there was
a bloody battle at Solferino on 24 June, as the French attacked
what they thought was a limited Austrian force but which turned
out to be the main Austrian army. The battle was remarkable for
poor command on both sides. Austria lost 22 000 men, perhaps
8000 of whom deserted. The Franco–Piedmont army lost 18 000.
The French depended on a rapid frontal attack and their effective
muzzle-loaded rifled artillery, which had a longer range and greater
accuracy than the Austrian guns.

Figure 3.4: Vittore Emanuele II, shown on horseback urging on his troops, during the Battle of Solferino, 1859

Napoleon III's reaction to the war

The unexpected concentration of large forces, the improved rifle and artillery fire and the blundering commanders resulted in a bloody encounter that shocked Napoleon III. There were many casualties and a high proportion of deaths. While the Austrians did not achieve victory, they were not entirely defeated. Napoleon I would not have been concerned about such high casualty figures, but Napoleon III was new to war and had hoped for a quick victory based on heroic and decisive attacks. The grand plans he had made at Plombières for Italian domination and state-making did not come to fruition. Further losses would be to the advantage of Piedmont, not France, and Napoleon III grew concerned about international reactions and internal unpopularity.

Piedmont deserted

To ensure his popularity at home following the war, Napoleon III highlighted the French territorial gains and portrayed the result as a heroic victory inspired by his own brilliant leadership in the tradition of his uncle. The French signed a truce with the Austrians at Villafranca on 11 August 1859, and this was confirmed in the subsequent Treaty of Zurich on 10 November 1859. By the terms of this treaty, Austria gave Lombardy – excluding the fortress towns of Mantua and Peschiera – to France. In a proposed Italian confederation under the Pope, Austria would continue to be a member. During the war, the dukes of Parma, Modena and Tuscany were overthrown by revolts, and these rulers were now restored. France gave Lombardy to Piedmont in exchange for Piedmont meeting the costs of the war.

The Austrians were not too upset by the loss of Lombardy – ruling this region had become problematic due to the increasing unrest that Piedmont encouraged. A Mazzini-inspired revolt there in 1854 had caused bloodshed and increased the unpopularity of Austrian rule. The Austrians had not performed well on the battlefield and needed to focus on other parts of their empire. Little would be gained from continuing the war; although the Austrians had lost Lombardy, they still had Venetia, and indeed retained some Italian lands right up to the fall of the Austro-Hungarian empire in 1918.

French forces made up the majority of the army of the alliance, so there was little that Piedmont's government could do but accept the terms of the settlement. Cavour had to admit that there had been no national uprising. A Piedmont-inspired demonstration, organised by the National Society, had driven out the grand duke of Tuscany, and the duchies of Parma and Modena had been occupied; but even in Lombardy there was limited enthusiasm for Piedmont's troops. If anything, the French were more popular than their fellow Italians.

Napoleon III made the Peace of Villafranca with Austria without consulting Cavour. Vittore Emanuele II accepted the terms of the truce, which still left Austria with territory in northern Italy, but Cavour was so incensed by them that, after much protest, he resigned from office.

The situation by the end of 1859

Piedmont's troops fought bravely and there were many casualties in the war against Austria. The events also generated enthusiasm for Italian unification. During the war, Piedmont encouraged the setting up of new governments in Parma, Tuscany, Modena and the Romagna. These Italian states now sought to join an enlarged Piedmont, and a new British government was sympathetic to these demands. Thus, together with the end of Austrian rule in Lombardy and Piedmont's expansion, the greatest changes in Italy since 1815 occurred in 1859.

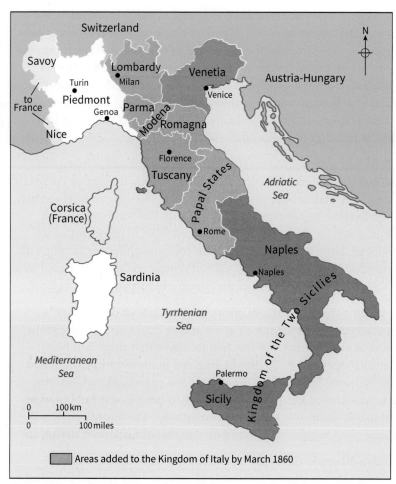

Figure 3.5: The land lost to France and the annexation of Parma, Modena, Tuscany and the Romagna in March 1860

Cavour returned to office in January 1860 and now aimed for a better deal with France. By the terms of the Treaty of Turin of March 1860, Nice and Savoy were annexed to France. In return, Napoleon III agreed to give the duchies of Parma and Modena to Piedmont. Tuscany was also annexed to Piedmont, following a plebiscite (public vote) on 11–12 March 1860. In all these cases, there was considerable dishonesty – Cavour and his agents made false promises of regional autonomy (self-government) for central Italy and there was little chance for opponents in any area to vote 'no'.

The situation by March 1860

The territorial gains were a considerable victory for Piedmont and the moderate and conservative elements. Although Nice and Savoy had been lost to France, the gains in central Italy were considerable. Most significant was the acquisition of Lombardy: for a modern capitalist state such as Piedmont, this area provided fertile agricultural lands, the chance to extend railway networks and to capitalise on the markets of north and central Italy. It can thus be argued that Cavour's diplomacy and Piedmont's modernization achieved more than the revolutionaries' conspiracies and manifestos. Piedmont had also enjoyed its share of heroism and could claim to be part of the 'moral rebirth' of Italian patriotism. Furthermore, Piedmont's position as the leading Italian power was achieved without having to take responsibility for the less-developed parts of Italy – the remainder of the Papal States, Naples and Sicily. The Pope had not emerged as leader of a confederation and had to accept the loss of the Romagna. There was also a new legitimate ruler in Naples: Francis II inherited the throne in 1859 from 'Bomba' Ferdinand II. Francis was not, as Napoleon III had wanted, a French king.

Piedmont could now focus its attention on economic development, as its position with regard to the great powers was secure:

- Austria accepted Piedmont's expansion and there was little support for any attempts to recover Lombardy.
- France had secured its key border areas and did not really dominate the peninsula, as once proposed.
- Britain was happier now that a balance had been achieved in Italy and no single power was dominant.
- Russia was unlikely to support any restoration of Austrian power.

Mazzinian romantic revolutionary radicalism (see section 2.4) now seemed to have little chance of success. The National Society combined nationalist ideas of greater unity and resurgence with Piedmont's liberal and progressive approach. These solid and modest achievements were not what radical nationalists had in mind.

Events in 1860 led to a very different Italy. The radical alternative played a prominent role in this transformation, which saw the re-emergence of the heroes of 1848–49, especially Giuseppe Garibaldi.

3.4 What was the importance of Garibaldi in moving Italy towards greater unification?

Garibaldi's life

Giuseppe Garibaldi (1807–82):

Giuseppe Garibaldi was born on 4 July 1807 in Nice, which was then part of Napoleonic France. His family were Italian, from Chiavari, and were sailors. This was Garibaldi's chosen profession (unusually for the time, he was a strong swimmer). He was uninterested in formal schooling so he worked on his father's ship, trading in the Mediterranean and Black Seas.

At Marseilles he met Mazzini, who was already an influence on some of his fellow sailors. Garibaldi was influenced by the ideals of 'Young Italy', to the point of actually taking part in a seaborne raid on Genoa. The revolutionary attempt failed and Garibaldi found himself an exile in Marseilles. He left Europe for South America in 1836, sailing first to Rio de Janeiro.

Garibaldi then worked as a soldier for the Republic of Rio Grande, which was in revolt against the Brazilian empire. He was wounded in the fighting, imprisoned and tortured by his enemies. Accompanied by his Brazilian wife Anita and his newborn son, Garibaldi was forced into a retreat. Thereafter, he adopted a more peaceful career, first as a cattle driver then as a dealer and teacher in Montevideo. Garibaldi later returned to war in the service of Uruguay, in a conflict with Buenos Aires (Argentina). Here, he led a small naval force, but was at risk from rivals in Uruguay who plotted his death. He later formed an Italian legion of exiles that fought for the Republic of Rio Grande.

Garibaldi won a considerable reputation as a republican soldier, but by 1847 his thoughts had turned once more to Italy. He believed that Pope Pius IX might lead a war against Austria, and offered the services of himself and his legion. In 1848, he raised enough money to travel to Genoa with 85 men to serve with the forces of Carlo Alberto in

Lombardy. When the king made peace, he led his men to the cause of Mazzini, proclaiming, 'The royal war is at an end; the war of the people is now to begin'. However, there was little that Garibaldi could do – his men deserted him, and after some clashes with Austrian forces he withdrew into Switzerland.

When Mazzini became one of the three leaders in the government of the new Roman Republic, Garibaldi joined him in April 1849, and was crucial in defending the republic against the French and Neapolitans. When the republic's defences were outnumbered and further defence became impossible, Garibaldi escaped and set off by sea for Venice, whose republic was being besieged by Austria. He was chased by Austrian warships and landed at Ravenna; Anita died and his closest friends were captured and shot by the Austrians. Garibaldi made his way back to Chiavari, was arrested by the Piedmonts and sent to Tunis.

Garibaldi then went to the island of La Maddalena off Sardinia. Distressed by the failures of 1849 and his personal loss, he sailed for the United States and settled as a candle-maker in New York, until returning to Italy in 1855.

By this time, Garibaldi had abandoned Mazzinian republicanism and, like many other exiles, settled in Piedmont. He lived at Caprera, an island off the coast of Sardinia. In 1859, when war began, he swore allegiance to Vittore Emanuele II and led a paramilitary group called the Chasseurs des Alpes, taking part in campaigns in the mountains above Lake Como. After Villafranca, he went to Genoa to rest and ease his arthritis. It was at Genoa that news came of a revolt in Sicily.

The revolt in Sicily

In Sicily, revolutionary groups, excited by war, were rioting. Yet the revolts that began in April 1860 were more to do with land, taxation and resentment of Neapolitan rule. The riots began in the poorer areas of Palermo and gradually spread to other areas of Sicily. **Francesco Crispi** and **Rosalino Pilo**, both Mazzinians who hoped that Sicily would start a nationalist rising, urged Garibaldi to lead the revolt. Garibaldi was deeply resentful of Cavour giving his home town of Nice to France, but he was uncertain about events in Sicily and wary of rushing in. However, Garibaldi had already gathered 'the Thousand' for a revolt in Nice, so they sailed towards Sicily in two small steamers. By the time they arrived, the revolution was virtually over.

Francesco Crispi (1819–1901):

Crispi was a radical Sicilian journalist who was influenced by Mazzini. He played a key role in the Revolutions of 1848 in Sicily, and was involved in a rising in Milan in 1853 before going into exile. He helped to lead Garibaldi's expedition of 1860. He later became prime minister of Italy, from 1887 to 1891 and then again in from 1893 to 1896.

Rosalino Pilo (1820–60):

Pilo was an aristocrat from Bologna who was hugely influenced by Mazzini. He took part in the Revolutions of 1848, the rising of 1853 in Milan and the expedition of 1857. He also sailed with Garibaldi. He was killed at Palermo in 1860.

Garibaldi's followers were mostly young men from Italy's northern cities, but they were by no means united. Sixty-four of them objected to serving the cause of Vittore Emanuele II, and landed in Tuscany to start a revolt in the neighbouring Papal States; most of them were promptly arrested. Garibaldi then marched on towards a Neapolitan army of 25 000 with 1000 poorly-armed and ill-trained enthusiasts. Dressed in red shirts, the revolutionaries' bayonets and old-fashioned muskets were likely to be useless against professional, well-equipped troops on an island with a history of failed revolts.

Cavour deeply opposed any more revolutions and had little interest in rousing the south. He therefore discouraged the expedition and considered arresting Garibaldi. He even secretly negotiated with the king of Naples, to encourage him to resist Garibaldi. However, Garibaldi's colourful career made him an object of public interest, and the revolt was now so well publicised that it was hard for Cavour to stop it. The National Society supported Garibaldi and the king of Naples was not against him. In any case, it was likely that there would be another heroic failure and Cavour might well be able to benefit from the situation.

Figure 3.6: Giuseppe Garibaldi with the flag of a united Italy and the ships of his expedition of 1860

The events in Sicily

Garibaldi landed at Marsala on the west coast of Sicily. With some local support, and against expectations, he defeated a royal force at Calatafimi on 15 May 1860. This action changed the situation: the Sicilian revolt began again, and volunteers came to support Garibaldi. He was able to take Palermo on 27 May. With his flowing hair and beard, Garibaldi seemed a Christ-like figure and the expedition began to take a crusade-like aspect. Fearing social revolution, Cavour sent his minister, Giuseppe La Farina, to urge the annexation of Sicily by Piedmont. Garibaldi rejected this and pressed on with plans to cross into Naples.

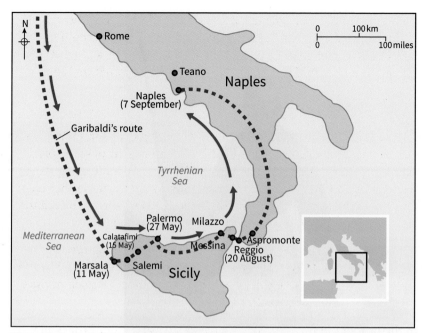

Figure 3.7: Garibaldi and the revolt in Sicily in 1860

The invasion of Naples

Cavour tried to encourage a revolt in Naples that would lead to demands for Piedmont to annex the country. Piedmont's troops were ready for invasion, but the revolt did not happen, and it would have been impossible to invade without a pretext for fear of foreign intervention.

By this time, Britain was offering tacit support for the Sicilian revolt. The British admiral Sir George Mundy helped to negotiate the surrender of Palermo, and British naval forces offered discreet protection for Garibaldi's crossing to Naples. While the British government sympathised with the plans to overthrow the king of Naples, it also wanted to prevent French intervention. This meant the initiative remained with Garibaldi, who entered Naples in triumph on 7 September 1860.

In a rapid and unexpected way, the dreams of the radical Mazzinians were now coming true: the Bourbon rule of Naples and Sicily had collapsed. Mazzini and his associates rushed to Naples. Garibaldi needed little persuading to revive his republican past and march on French-defended Rome and Austrian-held Venice, resulting in further war and revolution. Whatever happened, it was clear that a new Italy would be established, and even Cavour was now thinking in these terms. This raised questions of what form the new Italy would take, and what would happen to the south. The radicals were ready for an attack on Rome.

Cavour's reaction

Cavour now regained command of events. His ambassador in Paris was sure that France would accept a Piedmont-led invasion of the Papal States, to prevent Garibaldi marching on Rome and confronting the French forces there. On 11 September, with no justification other than Piedmont's desire to control the revolution, Cavour's forces entered the Papal States and papal opposition troops were defeated.

In September, Garibaldi's forces were occupied in fighting the Neapolitan army on the Volturno River. The king of Naples still had an army of 50 000, but Garibaldi's flexible tactics were once again decisive and he continued northwards.

In the heat of momentous events, a plebiscite was held in Naples and Sicily: were people in favour of a united Italy led by Vittore Emanuele II? The overwhelming response was 'yes'. Garibaldi met Vittore Emanuele at Teano on 26 October 1860 (Figure 3.8).

Figure 3.8: The legend – Garibaldi salutes Vittore Emanuele II at Teano

This emotional and momentous meeting effectively ended Garibaldi's control of events, and his forces were placed under the control of Piedmont's troops. Piedmont defeated the rest of the Neapolitan forces and confirmed the end of the rule of Ferdinand II. Garibaldi was refused permission to rule southern Italy as temporary dictator. On 9 November 1860, he returned to his home on Caprera.

The new kingdom

Plebiscites in the Papal States confirmed support for Italian unity, and Britain lent its diplomatic support. Elections were held for an Italian parliament in January 1861, and on 17 March 1861, parliament invited Vittore Emanuele II to become king of Italy. Rome remained outside the new Italy, as did Venice.

The new parliament and Cavour's ministers refused to accept Garibaldi's red-shirted leaders as officers in the new army. This provoked a furious intervention, when Garibaldi entered parliament and attacked Cavour. Bitterly resentful, Garibaldi returned home. Cavour was distressed by this turn of events, and also concerned about the continuing French presence in Rome. However, he died on 6 June 1861, before he could either establish a new Italian state or pursue diplomacy to ensure complete unification.

The new Italy owed much to the various contributions of Garibaldi and Cavour, but many patriots were also inspired by Mazzini.

Mazzini and the radicals: an alternative vision

The way in which events in Italy unfolded did not reflect the radical dreams of a republican Italy. Mazzini had remained a shadowy threat to some and an inspiration to others throughout this period. He continued with his conspiracies and propaganda, and this provided an alternative to Cavour's moderate monarchical vision. The events of 1848 elevated the conspirator and writer to a position of authority as one of the three leaders of the Roman Republic, living in the Pope's palace. The heroic defence of the Republic – though owing little to Mazzini himself – made his radicalism famous. Rome under his rule offered a model for democracy and participation by ordinary citizens that was not to be achieved in Italy before the 20th century. In this respect, Mazzini offered hope for a new republican and united Italy. However, the failures of 1849 found him once more in exile.

Mazzini founded the Friends of Italy Society in England and hoped for change, so Cavour's dominance in Piedmont was a blow to him. Mazzini had previously offered a clear choice – republican idealism as opposed to the old absolute rulers of Italy. However, Cavour offered a third way – moderate constitutional monarchy and modern economic reform. Cavour's solution presented the possibility of greater Italian unity without revolution and conspiracy, and this option was preferred by many of Mazzini's middle-class supporters. In exile and with limited hope of success, Mazzini's movement splintered. Former revolutionaries such as Daniele Manin (see 2.6, 1848: the main events of the revolutions), who had led the Venetian Republic, turned against violence and were welcomed by Cavour as exiles in Piedmont, leaving Mazzini isolated.

Mazzini remained committed to conspiracy behind the façade of respectable organisations, and he tried to stir up mutinies among Hungarian troops in Italy. He encouraged a secret workers' movement in Milan, but this was uncovered by the Austrians and the leader of the movement was executed. He also supported a rising in Milan, but it was firmly repressed. Although moderate support for Mazzini fell away, he persisted, founding a Party of Action in 1853, with more risings planned for 1853 and 1854.

Mazzini's role, 1859–60

When Garibaldi – Mazzini's former faithful supporter – returned to Europe, he did not revive his links with Mazzini, although there was some communication between them in 1859. Yet, Mazzini supported the plan for Garibaldi to march south to liberate Naples and Sicily; so Mazzini played a role in Garibaldi's expedition, if only indirectly.

Mazzini maintained contact with Garibaldi through a supporter among 'the Thousand' and went to Naples on 17 September 1860. Garibaldi kept his distance, but Mazzini encouraged revolution. However, there was no future cooperation between them. The way that Italy had been united went directly against Mazzini's anti-monarchist ideals, and he was angry and frustrated by the continuing French and Austrian control of key cities.

Mazzini did not die until 1872, but he played little role in the political life of Italy after 1861.

KEY CONCEPTS ACTIVITY

Significance: As a class, divide into three groups: the Cavourians, the Garibaldians and the Mazzinians. In your group:

- Look back through this chapter and any sources available to you, and think of ten reasons why Cavour/Garibaldi/Mazzini should be considered important in achieving Italian unity.

- Share your findings and make a poster incorporating your points and the evidence for them.

- Display the posters. Next to each one, put a blank sheet for members of the other groups to add comments – for example, to disagree with one of your points or the evidence for it.

- When peer comments have been made, consider how you will respond to the points raised.

- Present your poster, the objections to it and your counter-objections.

Finally, write an essay in response to this question: Who played the greatest part in the unification of Italy by 1861 – Cavour, Garibaldi or Mazzini?

Theory of Knowledge

History and the national myths:

The unification of Italy has led to myths, especially about Garibaldi. The term *Risorgimento* itself may indicate myth rather than reality. Should historians have ethical concerns about undermining unifying national myths, or should they put academic judgement above any other value?

The situation by March 1861

Events had moved so rapidly and dramatically between April 1860 and March 1861 that both Europe and the people of the Italian peninsula were unable to keep up. Twenty-two million people were now in a new Kingdom of Italy, but few had actually campaigned for it. This new Italy was the result of an unlikely series of events that were little understood by many Italians:

- The Austrians were removed from Lombardy by French troops.
- Discontented peasants and workers in Sicily, with little interest in a united Italy, allowed Garibaldi to embark on a revolt that had little chance of success.
- Weak Neapolitan opposition allowed the revolt to succeed.

- Tacit (implied) British support helped the invasion of Naples.
- French consent allowed Piedmont's troops to take over the process of unification.
- Approval was given in a series of hurried plebiscites in a time of excitement and war.
- There was no real development of national consciousness – it was said that most of Sicily thought that '*l'Italia*' (Italy) was '*La Talia*' (the wife of the king).
- The elections to the new parliament only involved a small minority of voters, and it was clear that Piedmont's government was to dominate the new Italian state.

Analysis: what were the prospects for the future?

In truth, these momentous changes in Italy were not popular with the key players:

- Garibaldi was deeply distrustful of Piedmont's rule and Cavour. He also resented the loss of Nice to France and the continued exclusion of Rome and Venice – Italy's two major cities – from the new Italian state. Furthermore, the new kingdom did not seem to appreciate his followers' heroism.
- The south did not gain freedom from 'foreign domination' – and Piedmont's rule was experienced by the people as more alien than rule by the Bourbon monarchs.
- Cavour was depressed about the prospects of parliamentary rule. He thought that the bulk of Italians would probably support dictatorship under a charismatic, Garibaldi-like figure.
- The Pope regarded himself as imprisoned by a godless people.
- Napoleon III failed to control Italy in the way he had planned in 1858, in alliance with Piedmont as a sort of junior partner.
- Russia and Austria were hostile to the new kingdom. Unification had come about by violation of international law and by armed revolt.
- The Mazzinian idealists saw only domination by a state with a reactionary, military and monarchist tradition.

KEY CONCEPTS QUESTIONS

Causation: Would you agree that Austrian weakness was the main reason for the success in unifying Italy in the period 1859–60?

Change/Continuity: Do you think that French attitudes towards Italian unification changed or stayed the same in this period?

Paper 3 exam practice

Question

Did Garibaldi or Cavour make the more important contribution to achieving Italian unification? **[15 marks]**

Skill

Planning an essay

Examiner's tips

As discussed in Chapter 1, the first stage of planning an answer to a question is to think carefully about the wording of the question so that you know what is required and what you need to focus on. Once you have done this, you can move on to the other important considerations:

- Decide your **main argument/theme/approach** *before* you start to write. This will help you identify the key points you want to make. For example, this question clearly invites you to make a judgement about which factor was the more important. Deciding on an approach will help you produce an argument that is clear, coherent and logical.

- Plan **the structure of your argument** – i.e. the introduction, the main body of the essay (in which you present precise evidence to support your arguments) and your concluding paragraph.

For this question, whatever overall view you have about the relative importance of Cavour and Garibaldi, you should try to make a balanced argument by considering the counter view. For instance, was Cavour merely interested in the expansion of Piedmont; did he actually try and ensure the failure of Garibaldi's expedition *or* was Garibaldi actually endangering the achievement of unity and making hostile foreign intervention likely?

A good starting point is why it is possible to think that Cavour was more important than Garibaldi and why it is possible to think that Garibaldi was more important than Cavour. This is better than merely thinking about what happened, as the focus will be on the arguments. Whatever the question, try to **link** the points you make in your paragraphs, so there is a clear thread that follows through to your conclusion. This will help ensure that your essay is not just a series of unconnected paragraphs. You may well find that drawing up a spider diagram or mind map helps you with your essay planning.

You have to be careful not to write two mini-essays, though. So after this groundwork, expand the plan to focus on arguments and don't just describe what happened.

When writing your essay, include linking phrases to ensure that each 'factor' paragraph is linked to the question. For example:

- Cavour's diplomatic policies made a greater contribution than Garibaldi's expedition *because*…

- *However*, without Garibaldi's heroism, Italy would not have been united to the extent that it was.

- *In this respect*, Mazzini offered hope for a new republican and united Italy. *However*, the failures of 1849 found him once more in exile.

- Mazzini's contribution was different, but equally important *because*…

- The development of Piedmont into a modern, economically successful state by Cavour was important for unification *and indeed* was a major contribution to its success…

- This was a long-term development. *By contrast*, in the short term, it was Garibaldi who made the greater contribution…

There are clearly many factors to consider, which will be difficult under the time constraints of the exam. Producing a plan with brief details (for example, dates, main events/features) under each heading will help you cover the main issues in the time available. It will also give you something to use if you run out of time and can only jot down the main points of your last paragraph(s). The examiner will be able to give you some credit for this.

Common mistakes

Once the exam time has started, one common mistake is for candidates to begin writing **straight away**, without being sure whether they know enough about the questions they have selected. Once they have written several paragraphs, they run out of things to say – and then panic because of the time they have wasted.

3 Italy (1815–1871) and Germany (1815–1890)

Producing plans for **each of the three questions** you have to write in Paper 3 at the **start** of the exam, **before** you start to write your first essay, will help you decide whether you know enough about the questions to tackle them successfully. If you don't, then you need to choose different questions!

Remember to refer to the simplified Paper 3 mark scheme in Chapter 9.

Activity

In this chapter, the focus is on planning answers. So, using the information from this chapter and any other sources of information available to you, produce essay plans – using spider diagrams or mind maps – with all the necessary headings (and brief details) for well-focused and clearly structured responses to **at least two** of the following Paper 3 practice questions.

Paper 3 practice questions

1 Examine the reasons why the attempts to unify Italy were more successful in 1859–60 than they had been in 1848–49?

2 Evaluate the importance of the intervention of foreign powers in Italy in 1815–61?

3 To what extent was Italian unification brought about by nationalist ideas?

4 Evaluate the reasons for the growth of Italian nationalism in the 19th century.

5 Discuss the ways in which the obstacles to Italian nationalism were overcome by 1861.

6 Compare and contrast the roles of France and Austria in the Unification of Italy in the period from 1849 to 1861.

Italy, 1861–71

4

Introduction

This chapter deals with the problems Italy faced in trying to build a new united country from the disparate states that existed before 1861. The excitement of the events of 1860 quickly diminished, to be replaced by the harsh realities of rule by Piedmont. There was unrest in the south leading to a virtual civil war. Garibaldi returned from exile and tried to seize Rome by armed uprising – to the embarrassment of Italy's new rulers. In the period after 1871 the Italian state still had to try and unify the country and create Italians. This development was hindered as the economic gap between the developing economy of the north and the poverty-stricken south widened. In order to try and create a sense of pride in the new nation Italy attempted to gain great power status – a new generation of politicians sought to increase Italy's standing abroad by alliance with Austria and Germany. However, Italy's military failures continued and attempts to use foreign policy to engender a sense of national pride were not successful. Further unification came only through Prussia's war with Austria.

TIMELINE

1861	**March:** Kingdom of Italy proclaimed
	Jun: Death of Cavour
	Aug: Pontelandolfo incident
1861–65	Brigands war in southern Italy
1862	**Jul:** Revolt in the south led by Garibaldi
	Aug: Garibaldi defeated and wounded at Aspromante
1864	The *Syllabus of Errors* published
1865	Italian Civil Code enacted
1866	**Apr:** Italy signs treaty with Prussia; war with Austria
	Jun: Italy defeated at Custoza and Lissa
	Jul: Battle of Sadowa (Koniggratz)
	Aug: Treaty of Prague; Italy gains Venetia
1867	Garibaldi leads attack on Papal States
	Nov: Garibaldi defeated at Mantana
1870	**Jul:** Franco–Prussian War; Vittore Emanuele II enters Rome
	The Doctrine of Papal Infallibility defined
	Oct: Rome was added to Italy and became its capital

1872	**Mar:** Mazzini dies
1875	Reformers win elections; *trasformismo* begins
1878	**Jan:** Death of Vittore Emanuele II
	Nov: Assassination attempt on Umberto I
1882	New electoral law increases electorate to 2 million
	May: Italy signs Triple Alliance with Austria and Germany

KEY QUESTIONS

- What were the problems facing Italy in the 1860s?
- State building in the 1860s: a new Italy or an expanded Piedmont?
- How united was the new Italian state?

Overview

- Since Italy was unified by fast-moving events in 1859 and 1860, there was not time to establish clear agreement among its people and discuss a new constitution. This meant that Piedmont's government was imposed on Italy. This caused resentment and a virtual civil war in the 1860s.
- Garibaldi continued to lead armed risings to complete the unification of Italy.
- There were territorial gains including Venice (1866) and Rome (1870) because of Prussia's wars with Austria and France.
- The new Italy remained a divided country and faced difficult political, social and economic problems. The gap between the north and south was considerable.
- Italy became a significant European power and was involved in the alliance system that developed after 1879, joining with Germany and Austria in 1882. Italy also gained colonies during this period.
- By 1890 the new Italian state had made progress towards greater unity, although there were still problems.

4.1 What were the problems facing Italy in the 1860s?

A major problem facing Cavour just before he died was the 'Roman Question'. The Pope had lost the Papal States to the new Italy, and papal lands were now restricted to Rome, which was protected by French troops. Yet the fact that the new Italian state could not call its most famous city its own, implied a rift with the Catholic Church. This was serious, because the majority of Italians were Catholics and Italy's neighbours, France and Austria, were Catholic countries. Hostility between the new state and the Catholic Church could mean loss of support at home and the risk of conflict abroad. Italy's problematic relationship with the Church continued well into the 20th century.

The way that Italy was created caused significant problems. There had been little spontaneous national feeling, even in Sicily – indeed, Sicilians had hoped for a different outcome than rule by Piedmont. The diversity of cultures, languages, histories and economic development in the new kingdom – and particularly the gap between north and south – put a considerable strain on policy-makers.

Furthermore, there was the problem of developing a constitutional and parliamentary state when the bulk of the kingdom had little experience of such government. Piedmont imposed its model of constitutional government – this was not a parliamentary liberal state emerging by consent.

Many of the requirements for a successful liberal state – an educated population, a large middle class, a supportive élite with a tradition of selfless public service, a willingness to settle issues by negotiation and consensus – simply did not exist in Italy as a whole in 1860. What emerged in 1861 was a political system based on the British and French model, but without the social, political and educational development that had evolved in those countries. Much of Italy had to make a sudden switch from absolutism to liberalism. As Italy in 1861 was still largely agricultural, with mass illiteracy, Italy's ruling class faced considerable difficulties in trying to make the new parliamentary system work.

Economic integration and development was closely linked to the other problems of regional differences and political development. There was a considerable gap between the emerging capitalism and developed agriculture of Piedmont and Lombardy, and much of the rest of Italy. The danger was that a sort of colonial economic system would develop, in which the north prospered on the back of southern cheap labour and agricultural produce, in this way further cementing the north–south divide.

There were also significant unresolved issues about the hardships of farming. These were made worse by increasing population pressure, with Italy's population growing faster than its food production and job opportunities. Again, such issues were a considerable challenge for the governing élite of the new Italy.

Finally, there was the problem of Italy's position in the world. The new Italy was not what the French emperor Napoleon III had planned. Austria remained a potentially hostile power that continued to hold Italian territory. Italy needed to uphold its defences and maintain a navy – its long coastline left the new kingdom vulnerable to attack. This put a strain on its internal finances and economy. It also meant that the Italian government needed the friendship of other European powers.

Italy's unification was incomplete, and this caused discontent among nationalists; thus the republican conspiracies and uprisings continued. In addition, Italy became susceptible to radical ideas of socialism and demands for agrarian change that were developing in Europe. More and more of Europe's working class were drawn to ideas based on those of Karl Marx (see 7.2, German socialism). Marx argued that greater democracy would occur when the lower classes staged a revolution and took control of the state. Marx also envisioned the break-up of large estates and more equal share of the land for the peasants.

The problem of the south

The new subjects of the king of Piedmont faced the immediate problem of taxation: Italy was heavily in debt. Piedmont had been forced to take on the debts of the states it annexed and also to deal with the financial burden resulting from the war; Napoleon III insisted that French loans were repaid. The creation of a united Italian state resulted in heavy spending on public buildings, a navy, a unified army and an education system.

Further south, Italy was a poor country. Outside Piedmont there were limited railways, and roads in some areas were badly in need of repair. Agricultural productivity in many areas was low and farming methods backward. The new government raised taxes on salt and tobacco and applied the Piedmontese tax on milling grain – the *macinto* – to the whole of Italy. Mules were taxed while the horses of the rich were left untaxed; this caused resentment among the poor, who relied on mules for transport.

There was anger in the south as a result of these new taxes. In areas of central Italy, attacks on tax collectors were accompanied by shouts of 'Long live the Pope!' Another response to the increase in taxes was emigration to North and South America. In 1850, less than 4000 Italians were reportedly in the USA; after mass emigration began in 1876, the Italian population of the USA grew to 44 000 by 1880 and 484 027 by 1900. While this emigration relieved economic pressures on Italians for land, food and jobs, it also deprived Italy of workers and taxpayers. Older Italians were distressed to see their sons and daughters move so far away, and they worried about the break-up of the extended family, on which so many Italians relied.

The resentment against taxation was heightened by language barriers. The census of 1871 showed that only 2.5% of the total population of 26.8 million actually spoke the Florentine-Tuscan Italian that, as the language of Piedmont, was the official language of the new state. The south struggled to understand the new officials and their demands. As there was a 70% illiteracy rate in the south, Piedmont's new tax forms and bureaucracy caused distress and bewilderment.

Overcoming illiteracy, the product of generations of neglect by both Church and state in the south, was a major undertaking.

Case study: Pontelandolfo

The start of the new kingdom caused considerable unrest in many areas of the south of Italy. After the old authority of the rulers of Naples broke down, there were more bandit groups in the countryside. Some young men joined these groups to escape being called up to the army.

On 14 August 1861, a band of outlaws entered the small town of Pontelandolfo in the Campania (in the region of Benevento) and started rioting against conscription. They burned the Italian flag and murdered a tax collector. Piedmontese troops entered the town. One of them left an account of what happened:

SOURCE 4.1

We entered the town and immediately began shooting the priests and any men we came across. Then the soldiers started sacking, and finally we set fire to the town…What a terrible scene it was, and the heat was so great that you could not stand it there. And what a noise those poor devils made whose fate it was to die roasted under the ruins of their houses. But while the fire raged, we had everything we wanted – chickens, bread, wine and capons.

Contemporary account of rioting in the town of Pontelandolfo, 1861.

Another massacre took place at the neighbouring town of Casalduni. The outlaws escaped, but 573 local people were tried for rebellion and collaboration with bandits.

The events in Pontelandolfo of 1861 are of considerable interest to present-day inhabitants of the Campania region, and there is still resentment of the violence and the imposition of what seemed to be alien rule by a foreign power.

The Italian state failed to acknowledge the civil war in the south, regarding it as merely a campaign against 'bandits'. However, the truth was that large numbers of the annexed inhabitants of the south resisted rule by Piedmont. Italy's new government used the results of the hasty plebiscites of 1860 to justify the view that any opposition it faced in the south was unrepresentative and undemocratic. Yet, by 1864, 100 000 troops were being deployed in the south.

Local communities were afraid to inform on rebellious gangs and so were punished by unsympathetic occupying forces. A cycle of violence began, and atrocities on both sides increased. The south saw itself, and indeed was seen by the Italian state, as occupied territory. Cultural differences now erupted – the south's reliance on personal networks of family and patronage seemed, to the northern mind, merely corrupt or 'medieval'. It was easy for Piedmont's government to summon up images of a healthy north allied with a diseased south that was infecting Italy with a sort of moral gangrene.

There developed a prolonged, secret conflict between irregular freedom fighters and Piedmont's well-trained army. Official figures stated that 5200 were killed in the ongoing conflict, but the figure may have been as high as 150 000. The introduction of the unpopular milling tax in 1869 also provoked large-scale unrest among the peasants of north and central Italy. Here, too, troops had to be used.

The new Italy suffered from both regional and social discontent. As the historian Giulano Procacci (1970) comments, 'Mass protest thus became a constant social and political feature of the new Italy'.

Historians and the new Italy

The nature of the new Italy is the subject of much debate among Italian historians. Liberal historians such as Benedetto Croce, writing *A History of Italy* (Clarendon Press, 1929), developed a view of sincere and high-minded liberal leaders – a kind of 'spiritual aristocracy' – establishing and maintaining a new and better Italy. In this view, unification was associated with improvement. The British historian G. M. Trevelyan, in his biography of Garibaldi, *Garibaldi and the Thousand* (Longmans, Green & Co., 1909), shared this assumption that the nationalists worked towards and achieved a better Italy.

Yet, when the 'better Italy' led to the Fascist state of Benito Mussolini and disaster for Italy in the Second World War, there was reappraisal. For Marxist historians such as Antonio Gramsci, writing in *The Prison Notebooks* (International Publishers, 1971), the liberal Italian state was created to fulfil the selfish and conservative interests of the middle classes, who suppressed the lower classes and succeeded in creating only political instability and social discontent. In this view, the *Risorgimento* is seen as a myth. Denis Mack Smith, writing in *Cavour and Garibaldi, 1860: A Study in Political Conflict* (Cambridge University Press, 1954), became unpopular in Italy for suggesting that Cavour's aims were to restrain unification rather than to promote it.

There has been discussion about the various strengths and weaknesses of the Italian states before 1859, the role of the Catholic Church, and the nature of opposition to the new state in the 1860s.

Marxists such as Eric Hobsbawm (see Source 4.3) saw the 'peasants' war' as primitive social protest. More recent studies acknowledge a greater civil war between two different cultures, perhaps comparable to the conflict between the north and south of the USA in the 1860s.

The historiography has been reviewed by Lucy Riall in *Risorgimento: The History of Italy from Napoleon to Nation State* (Palgrave Macmillan, 2009). The debate about European unity in the wake of the various economic crises after 2008, Italy's debt crisis in 2011, and Brexit and the Italian referendum in 2016, may lead to reappraisal of the benefits of Italian unification and the extent of popular nationalism.

SOURCE 4.2

A savage brutality characterised the struggle on both sides. There were reports of men being crucified or burnt…Apart from the large numbers of people killed in the fighting, very large numbers became helpless refugees; agricultural land was abandoned; shops and businesses closed; unemployment spread. In short, civilization receded. The 'brigands' war' continued through the 1860s and is believed to have killed more people than all the wars of independence between 1848 and 1861.

Hearder, H. 1983. **Italy in the Age of the Risorgimento.** *London. Longman. p. 241.*

SOURCE 4.3

In their primitive way the Southern Italian brigands of the 1860s saw themselves as the people's champion against the gentry and the foreigner. Perhaps Southern Italy provides the nearest thing to a mass rebellion and war of liberation led by social bandits (i.e. rebels rather than criminals). Among the Southern Italian peasants the 'years of the brigands' became, unlike the kings and the wars, among the few parts of history which remained alive and well. If their way was a blind alley, let us at least not deny them the longing for liberty and justice which moved them.

Hobsbawm, E. J. 1959. **Primitive Rebels: Studies in Archaic Forms of Social Movement in the 19th and 20th centuries.** *Manchester. Manchester University Press. p. 24.*

QUESTION

Read Sources 4.2 and 4.3. What is the difference in the way the two historians write about the 'brigands' war' of the 1860s?

4.2 State building in the 1860s: a new Italy or an expanded Piedmont?

The chain of events that rapidly unfolded in 1859 and 1860 resulted in some decisions that Italians lived to regret. During the first crucial years of state building (until 1864), the capital of Italy was Piedmont's capital city, Turin. Italy's centre of government, court and parliament therefore remained in a northern city that many Italians found difficult to reach, especially given Italy's limited railways. A second oddity was the decision of the new king of Italy to continue to use the title Vittore Emanuele II. This made a distinction between his status in Piedmont and his status as the first king of a united Italy. To some, this suggested that Piedmont was more important to him than Italy.

New nations with varied regions – such as the USA, Germany and the Soviet Union – usually reserve some powers for the central government and some for the regions or states in a federation. When Italian unification was considered before 1861, the most common model was a confederation under a neutral president. Some in Piedmont contemplated this idea and drew up plans, but events occurred too quickly to put such plans into action. Garibaldi's idea of a dictatorship over the south for a temporary transition period was rejected, and the idea of autonomous administration in the regions – drawn up by **Luigi Carlo Farini** and **Marco Minghetti**, two of Piedmont's ministers – was abandoned. The quickest solution was to impose a uniform administration – that of Piedmont – on the whole of Italy, and to introduce a system of prefects on the former states. These officials were appointed in Turin and answerable to the government there. The model was closer to the system Napoleon had adopted after 1804. However, what was acceptable and enforceable before 1814 was more difficult to enforce in the 1860s.

> **Luigi Carlo Farini (1812–66):**
> Farini was a moderate nationalist and historian from Ravenna. He served Pope Pius IX as a minister in 1848 and was minister of education in Piedmont from 1851 to 1852. He supported Cavour and was administrator of Modena in 1860.

Marco Minghetti (1818–86):

Minghetti was another moderate administrator. Born in Bologna, he hoped for a papal-led unification. He was an economist and diplomat who also supported Cavour. He became minister of the interior in 1862. Both Farini and Minghetti were typical of middle-class moderate nationalists who worked for Cavour and had no time for Mazzinian revolution.

The new constitution of the Kingdom of Italy

The constitution of Piedmont became, more or less, the constitution of Italy. It was remarkable for being the only constitution in Italy but it was not very democratic, even by the standards of the time. The German constitution, which was written in 1871, gave all adult males the right to vote. Britain extended the vote to more working-class men in 1867; the USA had extended voting in the 1830s. Russia had no national parliament, but there was peasant participation in local assemblies called *Zemstva*. By contrast, in Piedmont there was a very small electorate – only men who owned quite a large amount of property could vote. As Piedmont was the most prosperous area, if this system were applied to the rest of Italy then voting would be even more restricted. In fact, in the elections of 1861 there were 167 000 voters in the extended Piedmont (including Lombardy and the lands annexed in 1860), 55 000 in central Italy and 125 000 in southern Italy, with another 66 000 in Sicily and Sardinia. In terms of size of regions and population, this amounted to considerable disparity.

As there was little real opportunity to express discontent through the ballot box, it is not surprising that so many Italians turned to direct protest and even violence. However, Cavour had no desire to increase the popular vote, as republican ideas were common and there were a number of radical leaders, including Mazzini. Furthermore, widespread illiteracy made 'normal' politics difficult.

Instability in the 1860s

The alliance of the centre groups in the Italian assembly became known as 'the right' after 1861. Thus, no one political party was able to emerge as a strong unifying force. Also, no single outstanding personality emerged as prime minister. With the exception of the king, Italy's new national leaders were more like administrators – cool and conservative. They also had to win the support of a bad-tempered king and a new and inexperienced assembly.

Initially, ministries were short-lived and this led to instability. Between 1861 and 1864, there was a series of prime ministers – **Bettino Ricasoli** gave way to **Urbano Rattazzi**, who gave way in turn to Farini and then Minghetti. These men were typical of the well-educated, moderate conservatives that ruled Italy in the 1860s: lacking in charisma, they failed to achieve a popular following. As well as creating new institutions, they faced a civil war in the south and resentment about the continuing exclusion of Venice and Rome from Italy. They also had the immediate problems of debt. Their difficulties increased when Garibaldi's attempts to free Rome proved a major embarrassment, and with the military disaster of 1866 when Italy went to war to gain Venice.

Bettino Ricasoli (1809–80):

Ricasoli was a Florentine liberal minister. He brought about the union of Florence with Piedmont in 1860 and became prime minister in 1861–62 and 1866–67. He worked to reconcile the Pope with the Italian state, and helped to integrate Garibaldi's followers into the Italian army. Severe and with high principles, Ricasoli was known as 'the Iron Baron'.

Urbano Rattazzi (1808–73):

Rattazzi was a lawyer from Piedmont. He was a moderate liberal who had been prime minister in 1848. He founded a left-centre party and allied himself with Cavour. A respected minister of justice, Rattazzi was prime minister in 1862 and 1867. He repressed Garibaldi's revolts, which only increased his unpopularity.

In 1867, the king appointed a conservative prime minister – the general **Federico Luigi, Count Menabrea**. From this point until 1876, the politicians of the right dominated Italy's parliament. They favoured conservative policies, kept the number of voters low and did little to pass reforms to help peasants or workers.

Federico Luigi, Count Menabrea (1809–96):

Count Menabrea was part of Piedmont's élite. He commanded a corps of engineers in 1859 and represented Italy at the Treaty of Prague in 1866. He wanted to re-establish links with the papacy and was hostile to Garibaldi. He served as prime minister from 1867 to 1869, and was succeeded by General Lanza. Menabrea's appointment as prime minister represents a move to conservatism in the 1860s. He had no popular support, but he was a respected expert.

The case for achievement

Voting rights

In Italy, the franchise (right to vote) was determined by literacy and the payment of a minimum amount of tax. The universal suffrage of Napoleon I of France, and later Bismarck's Germany (see Chapter 5), failed to produce very liberal or democratic regimes. In a developing country, it could be argued that stability had to come before universal voting. Enfranchising large numbers of illiterate peasants who voted without secret ballots (not usual at the time and not introduced in Britain until 1872) would leave voters open to landlord intimidation, and this could undermine the democratic process. Though not a popular view in the 21st century, this was a common liberal and progressive view of the period, when political participation was seen as a major duty that depended on voters being literate and capable of independent decision-making.

A uniform system of government

Italy's system of centrally-imposed government was not completely new; it had also been used by the Popes and the kings of Naples, and it had been the Italian system of government during the Napoleonic era. The big change was that the new system aimed to be uniform and fair: to apply the same laws equally throughout Italy with just and efficient administration. The hope was that the type of modernisation that had transformed Piedmont would modernise and transform Italy as a whole, which was in desperate need of economic, social and political progress. This may suggest a sort of colonial attitude, but it also reflected a strong element of idealism and desire for improvement.

4 Italy (1815–1871) and Germany (1815–1890)

Freedom of speech and political freedom

An important element of this new system was a commitment to free speech and unrestricted political activity. This liberal attitude was mostly absent outside of Piedmont before 1861, making Piedmont a haven for political exiles in the 1850s. It was now transferred to the rest of Italy. Liberal parliamentary government continued up to the dictatorship of Mussolini from 1922. Given the problems of poverty, illiteracy, diversity and a lack of liberal traditions in the new kingdom, this could be seen as a significant achievement (for example, when compared with the survival of democracy in India after 1947).

A new legal and penal code

Italy's conservative government also succeeded in establishing a common legal and penal system for the whole of Italy after 1861. The system showed considerable flexibility; for instance, the government allowed Tuscany to operate a more liberal penal code and did not enforce the harsher Piedmontese system of punishments.

Civil law

The government also took its time in creating a common civil law for Italy, the result of prolonged and complex discussions. The Italian Civil Code of 1865 was influenced by the Napoleonic law codes in Italy between 1804 and 1814, and was a major achievement that lasted well into the 20th century. For the first time in Italian history, complex local codes were brought together in one national body of law. The civil code made clear important principles necessary in a modern state:

- All male citizens were equal before the law.
- The special rights of hereditary nobility and class privileges were ended.
- Church courts could no longer have jurisdiction over non-churchmen (the laity).
- Freedom of person, freedom of contract and rights of private property were confirmed for the whole of Italy.

In modern terms, though, the civil code was limited – the rights of women were seriously neglected and the rights of male heads of families were excessive. However, it did allow civil marriage and probably reflected contemporary beliefs and practices.

Defending the new kingdom

Given ongoing disputes with France and Austria, and Italy's exposed geographical position, defence was a key issue of the new regime. The Italian government needed to integrate its armed forces, which were made up of Piedmont's army, the large army of the former king of Naples, the remnants of the smaller states' armies, and the volunteers of 1859 and 1860. By 1870, a national army was created, but Italy's armed forces were mainly used for internal repression and suffered defeat against Austria in 1866. From 1870, Italian military training and organisation was strengthened along the lines of the highly successful Prussian model (see Chapter 5). However, Piedmont's generals and officer class dominated the armed forces at the expense of soldiers from other regions, although one of the leading military reformers was from Naples. Furthermore, the navy did not develop in line with the importance it merited given Italy's long coastline.

Education

There was also some progress made in education. Italy's illiteracy rate in 1860 was a staggering 75%. From the point of view of Piedmont's progressive administrators, the previous Italian states had simply allowed their people to remain in ignorance – a major argument against continuing regional self-government.

Francesco de Sanctis, a major literary figure, was appointed as minister of education in 1861. He believed in a unified state system and introduced free elementary education for children aged 6–13 years. However, the poverty in the south meant that any progress in education occurred mostly in the north: as in many poor countries, poverty requires child labour, so families have little incentive to spare their children for school. In turn, lack of education means that people cannot escape poverty. Breaking this cycle is difficult or impossible for many modern governments, and it was certainly beyond the power of Italy's new government in the 19th century. Yet at least the problem was acknowledged and some modern administrative solutions attempted.

The broader debate

Historians can be quick to spot the limitations of government; to highlight the gap between aspirations and realities, and to point to the neglect of local rights and authoritarianism.

SOURCE 4.4

Italy was not, in 1870, ready for political unification. Some of her best friends thought that Italy had been made too fast. Cavour, if his hand had not been forced by Garibaldi, would have gone slower; and Cavour was the wisest statesman Italy has produced. A period of apprenticeship to federalism might ultimately have served the cause of unity, and in the meantime avoided much embarrassment and disappointment. A crushing burden of taxation, grinding poverty, social unrest, and more than one military disaster – this was the price paid by Italy for the impatience of Mazzinian and Garibaldian enthusiasts. The price of unity has proved to be unexpectedly heavy.

Marriott, J. A. R. 1945. A History of Europe from 1815 to 1939. *London. Methuen. p. 247.*

ACTIVITY

Look at Source 4.4. Marriott offers a number of judgements here – try to identify and explain them. What evidence supports Marriott's view? What evidence would you use to argue that Marriott's judgement is too harsh?

Theory of Knowledge

Counter-factual history:

In Source 4.4, Marriott suggests that a period of federalism – a looser union of semi-independent states – would have been better for Italy than the system of unification it adopted in 1860. Is it the responsibility of a historian to think in terms of what *might* have been? Or should a historian simply look at what happened – not what *could* have happened?

The expansion of Italy after 1861

'Unredeemed Italy'

In 1861, Italy's two most famous cities – Venice and Rome – remained under foreign control, and the frontiers of the new Italy did not include all Italians. This gave rise to the concept of *Italia irridenta* ('unredeemed Italy'). This was the idea that Italy could not be 'whole' while some of its lands remained under foreign rule. The territories in question included Nice and Savoy, but it was not possible to recover these without a major war against France, for which Italy was not equipped. There were hints that the French occupation of Rome would be open to future negotiations, but Napoleon III was mindful that French Catholics wanted to ensure the Pope's 'protection', and the Pope himself was extremely hostile to the new Italian state.

The areas of '*Italia irridenta*' were of different significance:

- The largest collection of so-called 'unredeemed' lands was in the northeast. It included the city of Venice, the province of Venetia, the south Tyrol (Trentino) and the areas on the Adriatic coast that were once the possessions of Venice – Istria, Dalmatia and the city of Trieste.
- There was also Ticino, the Italian-speaking canton of Switzerland, but few regarded this as an essential part of Italy.
- Italian nationalists regarded the incorporation of Rome as a priority, and there was restlessness among Garibaldians to achieve this.

History repeated

The 1860s saw events already familiar in Italian history. In July 1862, Garibaldi was once again in Sicily. He was frustrated at his restricted role in the new kingdom and obsessed with liberating Rome. He gathered together a group of volunteers, crossed the mainland and advanced up Calabria towards Rome. The new government could not afford a war with France, and given the conflict in the south it also did not want to see Garibaldi stirring up unrest there.

Garibaldi fought the Italian army at Aspromante on 29 August 1862. He was wounded and held as prisoner. Luckily for the government he was not killed, or the embarrassment of Italian forces fighting the hero of a united Italy would have been even greater. Garibaldi was pardoned and enjoyed a rapturous welcome on a visit to Britain, to the displeasure of France.

A period of diplomacy followed Garibaldi's revolt. In 1864, after negotiations in Paris, Napoleon III agreed that French forces would withdraw from Rome in due course, and it was accepted that the Italian capital would move to Florence – a move that took place in 1865.

However, progress towards Italian unity again depended on external factors, and the key issue now was the threat of a war between Austria and Prussia. Since the appointment of Otto von Bismarck as minister-president of Prussia (see Chapter 5), there had been an increase in tensions between Prussia and Austria. It seemed only a matter of time before war broke out, and Bismarck needed an ally. The new Italy was an obvious choice: if war broke out between Austria and Prussia, then Austria could be distracted by Italian intervention. If this happened, Italy would be well placed to gain control of Venetia.

Italy first offered help to Austria for this reward. When Austria refused, Italy's prime minister, General La Marmora, signed an alliance with Prussia in April 1866. Bismarck was contemptuous of Italy's motives:

SOURCE 4.5

Insatiable Italy, with furtive glance, moves hither and thither, instinctively drawn on by the odour of corruption and calamity – always ready to attack anyone from the rear and make off with a bit of plunder.

Otto von Bismarck, speaking in 1870.

DISCUSSION POINT

Read Source 4.5. What do you think led Bismarck to write so scornfully? Was he right to do so, or was this an unfair judgement?

The Austro-Prussian War 1866

When war broke out between Austria and Prussia in 1866, Italian forces moved against Austria. Their aim was to complete the work of 1859 that had been interrupted by the Peace of Villafranca, and to gain territory that still remained in Austrian hands – especially Venice. So, once again, unification progressed because Piedmont went to war in alliance with an ambitious foreign power. Prussian forces moved quickly and the

Austrian army was unable to resist them. The war lasted only a matter of weeks before Prussia won a decisive victory at Sadowa. Prussia had hardly needed Italian help – although this could not have been foreseen before the war.

Military disaster

There was an enthusiasm for Italy to go to war in 1866. Garibaldi returned to head a force of volunteers, and Italian forces outnumbered the Austrian forces in the Veneto. However, there was little attempt to coordinate the Italian commands or to liaise with Prussia. The Italian armies advanced with no real plan or sense of purpose, and were defeated at Customary. To make matters worse, Italy's fleet was destroyed by a less well-equipped Austrian naval force while attacking the Austrian naval base on the island of Lissa, with the loss of more than 700 men.

Figure 4.1: The destruction of the Italian fleet at Lissa, July 1866

Austria ceded Venetia to Napoleon III, who gave it to Italy. It could hardly be said that Italy had won Venetia. Real gains were limited: the 370 000 inhabitants of Trentino remained under Austria, as did Istria and the Dalmatian coast. Prussia did not insist on these areas being transferred in its peace negotiations with Austria – 'Venetia' was interpreted in the narrowest possible sense. Italy's international reputation fell, while Prussia's status grew. Rome remained under French control.

Conspiracy and victory

In 1867, Garibaldi's son **Menotti Garibaldi** led a force into the Papal States. Garibaldi joined him and they defeated a papal army at Monte Rotundo. The victory was short-lived, however – French troops arrived from their base in Rome to disperse the volunteers, and Garibaldi returned to Caprera.

Menotti Garibaldi (1840–1903):

Menotti was born when his father was in exile in Brazil. He fought with his father in 1860, for Italy in 1866 and for volunteers against Prussia in 1870. He later was a deputy for Velletri and became a farmer.

Figure 4.2: The unification of Italy up to 1870

Once again, change came with developments outside Italy. In 1870, Napoleon III went to war with the enlarged state of Prussia that had emerged after the victory of 1866. The war required all French forces, so troops were withdrawn from Rome in 1870.

There was now no barrier to Italian forces taking Rome, and they entered the city on 20 September 1870. A plebiscite was held, and the city became the new capital of Italy, with the Pope a sovereign prince of the Vatican City. King Vittore Emanuele II made a formal entry into the city on 2 June. The Pope regarded himself as a prisoner, but the formal unification of Italy was now complete.

4.3 How united was the new Italian state?

Although Italy was now united geographically, with only the Vatican City outside the state, it did not mean that a nation of Italians had been created. This was particularly true given the strong regional identities that were present in the period leading up to Unification and the speed at which the country was unified. The limitations to this unity become even more apparent by looking at developments in the period from 1871 to 1890.

Economic problems

Up to 1890, Italy remained primarily an agrarian economy. From 1860 to the mid 1870s, there was a general rise in demand for Italian agricultural produce, and prices increased. However, from the mid 1870s there was a fall in demand and the price of Italy's agricultural produce dropped creating further poverty that only added to a sense of disillusionment with the new state.

There was a fall in prices of almost 30%, which made much domestic grain-growing unprofitable and also affected fruit and vegetables and dairy farming. Although grape growing was cushioned by an outbreak of disease in the French vineyards, generally the income from agriculture fell by almost 10% in the 1880s. The crisis hit a peasantry that was already on the margins of survival and gave them little reason to view the new Italian state as a success. A report of 1877 revealed that diseases associated with malnutrition were rife and millions of people were sick and undernourished. Even in the richer north, pellagra – a disease associated with a limited diet of maize – was common. The poorer peasants and workers could not even afford bread, while the new government seemed unable or unwilling to deal with the problem.

Many Italians emigrated either to other parts of Europe or to North and Latin America, the figures reaching 220 000 a year in the late 1880s. However, although there was a population outflow by 1900 of around 2 million, the population of Italy continued to rise and only added to the problem of poverty.

Social unrest

The new governments also faced the problem of social unrest with agricultural strikes and land occupations from the 1880s. These continued beyond the end of the First World War in 1918, and proved central in the rise of Mussolini's dictatorship. Unlike the 'brigands' war', this unrest began in the north, in the richer areas of the Po Valley around Mantua. It was encouraged by the new ideas of socialism, as well as the ongoing resentments towards larger landowners over low wages and poor living conditions, which served only to create another division in Italian society. Fundamental land reform and redistribution was needed to solve the problem, but it went against popular liberal beliefs, and Piedmont had thrived in the 1850s on free trade policies. In other countries, the free trade era was giving way to a more active role for the state in promoting and protecting key areas of the economy. The Italian governments responded to this pressure far more than in the agrarian sector, and moved away from the Cavour-type free trade policies for the first time in 1878.

DISCUSSION POINT

Imagine that you are an advisor to a bank that is considering investing money in Italy in the 1880s. You have been asked for a report on Italy's recent growth and potential. How would you describe the country and what advice would you give? Sum up in no more than 300 words. You will need to re-read the section above and read the information below carefully.

Industrial growth

By the 1880s there were some signs of economic improvement, as Italy was starting to enter a period of economic growth. Investment banking firms were set up. They made funds available for urban development; for instance, there was slum clearance and rebuilding in Rome, Naples and Florence. There was also capital available for industrial growth in cotton textiles, chemicals, engineering and power.

Italian industrial growth between 1881 and 1887 had an annual rate of 4.6%. This did not happen in accordance with Piedmont's free trade model of the 1850s, but rather on the model of Prussian and Russian economic growth, with a measure of state support. For instance, the navy was the major customer of the big Terni steelworks, and the state subsidised key industrial concerns in ship building. Some famous names emerged in this period, such as the rubber manufacturer Pirelli.

In 1887, the state applied new tariffs to protect Italy's industries; these included tariffs on some agricultural products – sugar, hemp and rice as well as corn. Raising duties on imported goods from abroad helped the more specialised northern farms and the big estates in the south.

On one hand, the Italian state promoted key areas of the economy and Italy experienced high levels of economic growth that continued into the 20th century. On the other hand, little was done to address regional inequality which only added to the sense of a lack of unity. The north had a semi-colonial relationship with the south, which provided its food and took its products. As factories grew in the north, the south had little industrial growth – so the wages of the southern work force remained low and their living conditions poor, adding to the divide between the North and the South. Thus the key element in Italy was the gap between the economies of the north and south – and Italy's government failed to introduce effective measures to resolve it.

Economic development and political life

The dominant force in politics since 1861 were groups loosely termed 'the right'. These were made up of conservative moderates who favoured Cavour's modernising approach rather than the republican radicalism of Garibaldi, who died in 1882, and Mazzini, who died in 1872. However, there was a strong element of resistance from 'the left' which only added to a lack of unity:

- In the north, opposition came from the some of the middle class and upper working class, who criticised the restrictions on voting rights and the conservative policy of centralisation, and called for greater democracy.
- In the south, there was opposition to taxation and calls for more money to develop the region; backwardness, crime and unrest were blamed on Piedmont's administration.

Reforms were introduced after 1875 to improve the democratic process. For example: free compulsory education for two years was introduced in Piedmont in 1859; after 1875, it was extended to the whole of Italy for children between six and nine years. However, the most famous development was *trasformismo*.

Trasformismo

Trasformismo ('transformation') describes a change in how Italian politics worked. It was a flexible approach that united the centre of politics and isolated more extreme groups. Parliamentary majorities were maintained by negotiations with opposition individuals or the groups that could give them a seat in government. However, this meant that the system was open to corruption: parliamentary representatives (deputies) or the areas they represented were often influenced by bribes or favours and did little to create a sense of confidence or trust in the new state. The system alienated many from parliamentary politics, thus sowing the seeds for the later rise of Benito Mussolini and Fascism.

In an attempt to involve more people in the electoral process a new electoral law in 1882 increased the electorate from 500 000 to 2 million – from 2% to 7% of the population – by lowering qualifications of age, literacy and wealth. Again, this widened the gap between north and south Italy. However, there was a greater interest in national unity and reform. There was also considerable economic growth, and Italy was becoming a major power. However, few of these developments benefitted the very poorest in society. A sign of growing political discontent was the election of the first socialist, Andrea Costa (1851– 1910), who founded the Italian Socialist Party in 1892. At the same time, the period also saw the rise of a new political class when the northern middle class established an alliance with the landowners and traditional gentry of the south.

However, there were some signs that Italy was developing a greater national identity. In 1878, Vittore Emanuele II died. His successor did not take the title Umberto IV – his Piedmontese inheritance – but was crowned Umberto I of Italy. The new monarch was promoted as a unifying symbol – though later in 1878 a young anarchist tried to kill him as part of a campaign of terrorist bombing in Italy's major cities. Umberto was eventually assassinated in 1900.

Figure 4.3: A sketch by an eyewitness of the assassination of King Umberto I of Italy, at Monza, in June 1900

There was an aspiration among some political leaders for unity. In 1882, the future prime minister, Francesco Crispi, spoke for the nationalist cause:

SOURCE 4.6

I want to nationalise the Chamber…that those who in future enter this hall (of the national parliament) should forget where they were born, their parish pump, their local ties, and the wishes, the needs and demands of the region of their birth, and should instead be inspired by a single concept, that of the good of the nation.

Francesco Crispi, speaking in 1882.

ACTIVITY

Look at Source 4.6. How realistic were Francesco Crispi's hopes for greater Italian unity in 1882? In charts based on those shown below:

- list the developments that encouraged greater Italian unity and nationalism after 1861
- list the developments that divided Italy.

For each development, explain its significance and assess the extent to which it did or did not support greater unity. The first row has been completed in each chart below, to start you off.

Positive developments since 1861	Explanation	Assessment
Development of a single parliament for whole of Italy – more voted after 1882	With little previous parliamentary tradition in most of Italy, it was an achievement to establish a parliamentary state in which the chamber rather than the monarch had power.	Limitations in terms of *trasformismo* corruption, weak coalitions, and poor image of politicians as corrupt. However, key unifying measures passed in 1860s and possibility of reforms later.

Negative developments since 1861	Explanation	Assessment
Hostile attitude of pope and Roman Catholic Church	Pope had lost lands; he condemned nationalism and the new Italian state. Hostility between the Church and government challenged Catholic loyalties – would they support the new Italy and betray their religion?	The new Italian state lacked important support from a major spiritual leader. However, this did not stop progress in practice.

Use your completed charts to come to a decision in response to these questions: Was Crispi right to have hopes of greater Italian unity in 1882? Was Italy more united by 1882 than it had been in 1871?

Foreign affairs, 1870–90

It was possible for foreign policy to act as a unifying factor: if Italy became internationally respected, the status of the new kingdom would rise at home. A sound foreign policy could therefore encourage a sense of national pride. There was also the long-term aim of recovering those areas of Italy that remained under foreign rule.

Though Italy's military reputation was poor after the disasters of 1866, Europe was at this time becoming divided into two power blocs, and so Italy's position as a potential ally was an advantage. Italy also wanted to have its share in the colonial expansion that was taking place after 1879 by the European powers, known as 'the Scramble for Africa'.

The Triple Alliance, 1882

Germany and Austria signed a Dual Alliance in 1879. On 20 May 1882, a five-year alliance was signed to make the Dual Alliance a Triple Alliance, with both Germany and Austria pledging to defend Italy if attacked by France. The alliance brought Italy into the orbit of major powers and increased its prestige in Europe.

Italy also joined the so-called Mediterranean Agreements with Britain and Austria in 1887, to help maintain the existing state of affairs in the Mediterranean.

Italy and colonisation

After 1870, the great powers showed more interest in having formal control of areas they had previously merely traded with, or where they had small settlements. This was called 'the Scramble for Africa'. Italy joined in, as such involvement was seen as part of being a great power and increased the status of a country:

- An Italian shipping company obtained a coaling station on the Red Sea in 1870.
- In 1882 the government took over the Eritrean area of the Bab-el-Mandeb strait as a formal colony.
- In 1885, government forces occupied Massowah on the Ethiopian coast and pushed inland, only to be attacked and defeated by Emperor Negus of Ethiopia. Italian troops established defensive lines in Eritrea, which was made a protectorate as Italian Somaliland.
- On 24 May 1890, Italy reorganised its Red Sea territories into the single colony of Eritrea.

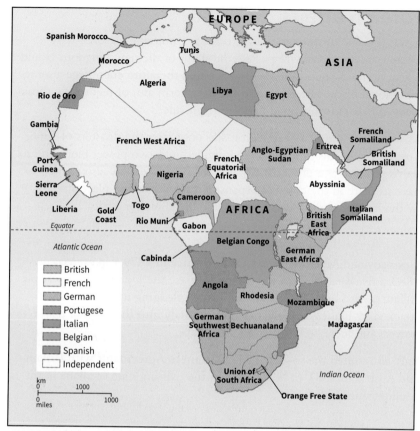

Figure 4.4: Africa after 1890, showing colonisation by European powers

This great power imperialism needed more resources and experience than Italy possessed. In 1893, with British encouragement, Italy attempted larger-scale colonisation, but it led to the disastrous defeat at Adowa in Ethiopia in March 1896.

Risorgimento did not transform Italy into a great military power, but it did give the appearance of Italy being a great power, which brought some pride to the new nation, even if defeat at Adowa was a national humiliation.

Assessment

Italy had become one of the great powers – it had acquired colonies; it had important allies; it was deeply involved in the diplomatic life of Europe. The statesmen of the post-*Risorgimento* era sought to unite the nation and show that Italy should be seen and treated as a major power. Yet the new Italy was not as influential or as wealthy as the older European powers.

KEY CONCEPTS ACTIVITY

It will be valuable for you to think about how far Italy was united in the period after 1871 as this will help you to understand the extent of unification by 1871. Continue the discussion thread 'Italy by 1890'. Make sure that you address as many of the points here as possible, by stating whether you agree or disagree with them and why.

Silvio writes: *Italy was deeply divided by 1890. Its cultural and linguistic differences had not been resolved, and there was a gulf between north and south. Its politics were a by-word for corruption and its attempts to make itself a great power had failed. It had, in the words of R.J. Bosworth, more in common 'with a small Balkan state or a colony than a great power'.*

Harry writes: *The problems of the Italian south in the 1860s were a result of war and unemployed and disaffected ex-soldiers. This should not obscure the successes of the new Italian state. A British-style parliamentary state was established when parliamentary tradition was weak, and French-style modern administration – a new legal code and uniform weights, measures and currency – was introduced with remarkably little disturbance. Outside the south, Italy was ready for unity. Internationally, Italy made itself sought-after by great powers and began to acquire colonies – not the signs that it was a sort of Balkan power or that it was a colony.*

Priti writes: *Too much can be made of linguistic divisions – successful states exist with linguistic diversity, for example Belgium or Canada or more spectacularly India with hundreds of languages. Even if influential people preferred French or local dialects, they often wrote important works in Italian.*

Chimamanda writes: *If Italy was so divided and unsuccessful, then how did it achieve such high economic growth rates in the 1880s?*

KEY CONCEPTS QUESTIONS

Significance: What do you think was Garibaldi's most significant contribution towards Italian Unification?

Causation: Why do think that Piedmont was the dominant force in the new Italian kingdom?

Paper 3 exam practice

Question

To what extent was Italy united by 1871? **[15 marks]**

Skill

Writing an introductory paragraph

Examiner's tips

Once you have planned your answer to a question (as described in Chapters 1 and 2), you should be able to begin writing a clear introductory paragraph. This needs to set out your main line of argument and to outline **briefly** the key points you intend to make (and support with relevant and precise own knowledge) in the main body of your essay. *'To what extent…?'* and *'How far…?'* questions clearly require you to analyse opposing arguments and reach a judgement. If, after doing your plan, you think you will be able to make a clear final judgement, it's a good idea to state in your introductory paragraph the overall line of argument/judgement you intend to make.

Depending on the wording of the question, you may also find it useful to define in your introductory paragraph what you understand by any 'key terms'. For example, 'united' can mean different things:

- There was territorial unity – were all Italians actually in the new Italy?

- There is the unity of institutions – laws, government, constitution, administration.

- There is unity in national feeling – were Italians emotionally committed to their new state by 1871?

For this question, you should:

- define the terms of the question

- consider arguments for and against unity

- write a concluding paragraph that sets out your judgement.

You need to cover the following aspects of Italian unity:

- territorial additions, especially Venetia and Rome, and the lands (*Italia irridenta*) that remained outside Italian control until 1919

- the religious disunity and the problem of the Pope being hostile to the new Italian state

- regional divisions, especially the problems of the south

- the development of a distinctly Italian state, institutions, laws and parliament, and how successfully this unified Italy

- the social divisions that were developing (which became more apparent in 1871–90).

Setting out this approach in your introductory paragraph will help you keep the demands of the question in mind. Remember to refer back to your introduction after every couple of paragraphs in your main answer.

Common mistakes

A common mistake (which might suggest to an examiner that a candidate hasn't thought deeply about what's required) is to fail to write an introductory paragraph at all. This is often done by candidates who rush into writing *before* analysing the question and doing a plan. The result may be that they focus entirely on the word 'unity' and give a long introductory account of unification. This approach may result in a narrative of events in the 1860s. Even if the answer is full of detailed and accurate own knowledge, this will *not* answer the question, and so will not score highly.

Remember to refer to the simplified Paper 3 mark scheme in Chapter 9.

Sample student introductory paragraph

'We have made Italy, now we must make Italians.' Cavour recognised that there was a difference between establishing a common monarchy, government, parliament and government and bringing about a real sense of unity among the people of Italy. There was long-standing loyalty to different regions and many linguistic, historical and cultural barriers to true unity. Given these problems, it could be argued that Cavour's successors had made some progress towards unity by 1871. In terms of adding territory, establishing new institutions, increasing the international standing and therefore national pride of Italy, there was

some progress. However, there were limitations to this, and in some areas – the integration of north and south, relations with the Church and preventing growing social and economic division – the new state did less well.

EXAMINER COMMENT

This is a good introduction, as it shows a clear grasp of the topic, and sets out a logical plan that is clearly focused on the demands of the question.

It demonstrates a sound appreciation of the fact that, to assess success, it is first necessary to identify aims. It also explicitly states to the examiner what aspects the candidate intends to address. This indicates that the answer – if it remains analytical, and is well-supported – is likely to be a high-scoring one.

Activity

In this chapter, the focus is on writing a useful introductory paragraph. Using the information from this chapter and any other sources of information available to you, write introductory paragraphs for **at least two** of the following Paper 3 practice questions.

Paper 3 practice questions

1 'Piedmont did not unite Italy, it merely conquered it.' To what extent do you agree with this statement of developments in the period 1861–71?

2 Discuss the strengths and weaknesses of Italy in 1871.

3 To what extent was Italy still only a geographical expression in 1871?

4 Evaluate the problems facing Italian governments in 1871.

5 'Unification in Italy created more problems than it solved.' To what extent do you agree with this statement?

6 Compare and contrast the strengths and weaknesses of the Italian and German states in 1871.

Germany
1815–49

5

Introduction

This chapter deals with the position of Germany in 1815, following the French Revolution and the Napoleonic Wars. It looks at the creation of a new association of German nations at the Treaty of Vienna, and considers how some Germans resented the Austrian control that the treaty established. The chapter explores why there were major revolts in Germany in 1848 as well as attempts to establish a united Germany with an elected parliament, and why they failed. It also examines the growth of Prussia, which by 1862 was becoming the major German power.

TIMELINE

1815 Congress of Vienna; creation of the German Bund (Confederation)

1817 **Oct:** Festival of Wartburg reveals extent of German nationalism

1818 **May:** Prussian Customs Union; foundation of the Zollverein

1819 **Sep:** Karlsbad Decrees

1821 Metternich appointed chancellor of Austria; he seeks to end south German constitutions at Congress of Troppau

1823 Provincial assemblies established by royal decree in Prussia

1830 Disturbances in many parts of Europe; unrest in Hesse, Brunswick and Saxony

1832 **May:** Hambach festival – liberal and nationalistic meeting

1834 **Jan:** Zollverein formed

Jun: Metternich's Six Articles

1840 Frederick Wilhelm IV crowned king of Prussia

1848 **Feb:** Revolution in Paris sparks off revolutions in Europe

Mar: Unrest in Berlin

May: First session of Frankfurt parliament; restoration of royal authority through Europe

Overview

- Before the French Revolution Germany did not exist as a country and the term 'Germany' had little political significance. However, Napoleon's conquest provided the initial push towards German Unification as French alienated many Germans.
- The defeat of the great powers of Austria and Prussia by France in the Napoleonic Wars brought new unity to Germany, and swept away the old order of the Holy Roman Empire. Prussia modernised rapidly after 1806. However, Austria was dominant, controlling the new Bund (a loose confederation of states).
- A growing number of German intellectuals began to stress the importance of a common language and cultural tradition.
- While there was a desire for change, attempts at political reform in the period from 1815 to 1848 (usually known as the Vormärz or pre-March) were mostly unsuccessful. In particular, the Austrian chief minister, Prince Metternich repressed any form of either liberalism or nationalism.
- The July Revolution in France in 1830 led to demonstrations and riots in some south German states. As a result, some states issued constitutions or reformed existing constitutions so that they were more liberal.
- There was a new economic union – the Zollverein – in 1834, which helped to increase Prussian influence and economic power at the expense of Austria, who was excluded from it.

- In 1848, as in much of Europe, revolts broke out in the German Confederation and the Habsburg lands, including Austria and Hungary. Despite being serious and gaining initial success, loyal armies restored the old order.

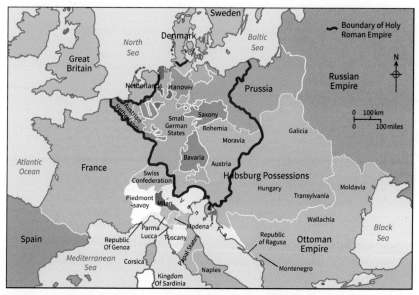

Figure 5.1: Central Europe at the end of the 18th century

5.1 What was Germany like before 1815?

As with Italy, there was no modern equivalent of 'Germany' at the end of the 18th century. The area in which the German language – or versions of it – was spoken did not correspond to any specific country. Most of the German-speaking parts of central Europe were part of the Holy Roman Empire. This empire dated from the Middle Ages, and by the late 18th century it was ruled by the Habsburg dynasty of Europe.

The Holy Roman Empire

The Holy Roman Empire was not a country or a real empire. It was a collection of lands whose rulers in theory owed allegiance to the Holy Roman Emperors; however, in practice the emperors had little effect on how they ruled. The Holy Roman Emperors were also emperors of the Austrian empire. Austria was the greatest German power, but it also contained many non-German lands.

Within the Holy Roman Empire, there was a bewildering variety of tiny states presided over by lesser rulers with titles such as margraves, dukes, princes, electors, prince-bishops or archbishops. There were also a number of bigger states. The most significant of these was Brandenburg-Prussia in the northeast. The ruling family here, the Hohenzollerns, were kings of Prussia (the most easterly part of the empire). The neighbouring kingdom of Saxony was also one of the larger German states. In the south was the kingdom of Bavaria, again an electorate, and the duchies of Baden and Württemberg.

It was a complex picture:

- 'Germany' as such did not exist – in 1792 there were more than 250 small states linked by language, which were all part of the wider Holy Roman Empire.
- The empire did not rule Germany in any meaningful sense.
- The key figures in the empire were the rulers. The people of 'Germany' owed personal allegiance to the rulers of their particular state, and there was little sense of nationalism.
- Some rulers of German states sometimes presided over non-Germans – for example, Prussia ruled Polish speakers and Austria ruled many different nationalities.
- 'Germany' was not united by religion. Since the Reformation of the 16th century, it was divided between Catholics and Protestants. The south and west were predominantly Catholic, and the north and east were mainly Protestant. The most important of the Protestant Churches was the Lutheran Church.
- Germanic life in the 18th century was largely organised around agriculture and small towns. There were few big cities, except for Vienna. There were also important ports such as Hamburg, but most Germans lived in villages or small towns.
- Most people in these Germanic lands saw themselves as members of their particular area – their margravate, electorate, kingdom, archbishopric, duchy, county, landgravate or city.
- There were many different dialects and languages. In eastern Prussia there were Slav languages, and in the western borders there were dialects closer to Dutch. However, the linguistic differences were not as great as those in Italy.

ACTIVITY

Test yourself:

- The ruler of which country was always also head of the Holy Roman Empire?
- Which important German state was ruled by the Hohenzollerns?
- Roughly how many independent states made up 'Germany' by 1789?
- Did all the people in 'Germany' speak German?
- Was all of 'Germany' within the Holy Roman Empire?

DISCUSSION POINT

Imagine that you are a German student in 1789, with your future ahead of you. Do you want to change the 'Germany' in which you live? Why?

In practice, the larger powers in the Holy Roman Empire acted independently in the 18th century, forming alliances with each other or with foreign powers against their internal enemies. For example, at various times Prussia fought extensive wars against Austria, supported by England, while Austria fought Prussia in alliance with France and Russia. Prussia, Austria and Russia joined together to divide up Poland. Saxony and Bavaria also allied with different countries.

It is important to note that when 'Austria' or 'Prussia' fought or made an alliance, we are referring to the rulers of those countries. These were not national wars but rather dynastic conflicts for territory, influence or glory. The conflicts and diplomacy of the 18th century were not about who should control 'Germany'.

ACTIVITY

Make a poster showing the main problems in creating a more united Germany in 1815.

The leading powers by the end of the 18th century

The leading powers in Germany by the end of the 18th century were Austria and Prussia.

Prussia

As the map of central Europe in 1815 shows (see Figure 5.4), Prussia had acquired different lands in Germany from the 15th to the late 18th centuries. These lands were separated from each other and some of them were very small. However, there was a substantial homeland in Brandenburg – the home of the Hohenzollerns, who had risen to be electors and kings of Prussia. These rulers were supported by the upper classes, which were known as *Junkers* (the name derives from 'Jung' and 'Herr', which translates as 'young lord'). Junkers ruled over their lands and peasants, but gave service to the state.

Junkers were the landed gentry of eastern Prussia. They often ruled directly over their peasants, holding their own courts. They were influential in the Prussian army and civil service. The sign of Junker status was the use of 'von' (meaning 'of') in their names – as in the case of Otto von Bismarck-Schönhausen.

Prussia's rulers had effective administration and a large, powerful army that reached its height under **Frederick II**. However, Prussia's great military reputation suffered when it was defeated by Napoleon's army in 1806. Prussian reformers then introduced a series of military and administrative modernising reforms.

Frederick II (1712–86):

Frederick, or Frederick the Great, also known as Der Alter Fritz (Old Fritz), was a militarist who spent most of his long reign (1740–86) at war. His palace at Potsdam – Sans Souci – reflects his interest in art and architecture. His military tactics were adopted by Napoleon, ironically to defeat the armies of Frederick's successor.

Figure 5.2: The palace of Frederick the Great at Potsdam, just outside Berlin

While Prussia was a great military power, its eastern provinces were not economically strong. The sandy soils of Brandenburg did not produce rich crops, and the great estates of the more remote eastern provinces were farmed in a relatively backward way when compared to the great estates of southern Italy. Prussia's lands were not as fertile as Austria's, and its resources were not as plentiful. However, unlike Austria, Prussia did not have the concern of ruling a large non-German empire.

By the 18th century, there emerged a strong Prussian tradition – of service to the state, hard work and religious devotion, as well as respect for the army and monarch. Although there was artistic development and an interest in economic growth, Prussia's military ensured its reputation as 'the parade ground of Europe'.

Austria

The Austrian rulers had to deal with a mass of different nationalities – 1.5 million Czechs, 3.3 million Magyars (Hungarians), Slovaks, Croats, Italians, Poles, Romanians, Ruthenes, Serbs, Slovenes and Belgians. The Austrian empire's official language and culture was German, but only two provinces – Lower and Upper Austria – had a solid German-speaking majority. The Austrian rulers were, theoretically, kings of

Germany, although this meant little in practice. However, Austria was the most powerful nation of the Holy Roman Empire.

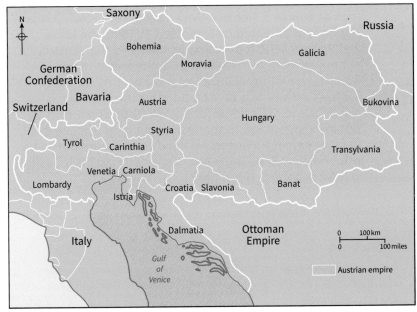

Figure 5.3: The Austrian Empire in 1830

KEY CONCEPTS ACTIVITY

Perspectives: Look at the map of the Austrian empire in the 19th century and read the information on Austria above. Complete a SWOT analysis (Strengths, Weakness, Opportunities, Threats) that a modern analyst might draw up for an incoming ruler. You will need to think about the size, diversity and geographical position of the Austrian empire, and whether this resulted in more weaknesses than strengths.

Strengths	Weaknesses	Opportunities	Threats

Theory of Knowledge

History and hindsight:

Look at Source 5.1 below. We know that the Holy Roman Empire was defeated by Napoleon in 1806. We know that Prussia defeated Austria in 1866 and that Austria lost power with the creation of the new 'Germany'. We also know that Austria lost most of Italy, and that Austria's empire was broken up after the First World War. However, should historians ever use words such as 'doomed' or assume that any development is inevitable? To what extent do historians need to take care not to be influenced by knowing what happened next? Is it possible to have too much hindsight?

SOURCE 5.1

The century towards which the Habsburgs were moving was to see the gradual triumphs of two concepts: democracy and nationalism. Each was in itself a threat to the survival of the dynasty. When the two joined hands, any hope of stability...was doomed.

Brook Shepherd, G. 1997. **The Austrians**. *London. HarperCollins. p. 30.*

The impact of Napoleon Bonaparte

In April 1792, France declared war on Austria because the Austrian emperor was supporting aristocratic exiles and this threatened France's revolution. Prussia was concerned about the risk of the revolution in France to its monarchy, so joined Austria's war against France. The left bank of the Rhine was ceded to Napoleon in 1801, and 25 000 people and 25 000 square miles of the Holy Roman Empire passed to France.

Between 1805 and 1807, France was at war with Austria and Prussia in the War of the Third Coalition. After initial victories, the Austrians and Prussians were defeated by Napoleon's troops. The defeat led to the French conquest of much of German-speaking central Europe. This resulted in major changes, although Prussia and Austria remained independent.

- In 1806, the Holy Roman Empire was abolished and a new Confederation of the Rhine was established.
- In return for supplying taxes and soldiers to Napoleon, the larger states were allowed to take over smaller, independent territories.
- In the northwest of the confederation, Napoleon's brother Jerome was given a new kingdom – Westphalia, which later included Hanover.

Napoleon's domination of the Germanic lands lasted until he decided to take a huge army into Russia in 1812, where the French armies were defeated. With the defeat of the French armies, Austria and Prussia seized the opportunity to capitalise on French weakness, renewing the wars with France. The subsequent battles resulted in heavy casualties on all sides. However, by 1814, Austria, Prussia and Russia – in alliance with England – had defeated Napoleon and were in a position to remake Europe.

As with Italy, French rule of Germanic lands produced major changes. The ending of the old Holy Roman Empire, the introduction of small church states and free cities, and the general consolidation of smaller states, reduced the complexity of 18th-century Germany.

In response to French rule, a patriotic resistance also emerged. The extent and importance of this growth in nationalism and anti-French feeling is a matter of debate (see Section 5.3).

Prussian reforms

The wars with France led to major reforms in Prussia. These were introduced by a group of modernising nobles led by Baron **Heinrich von Stein** and Karl August von Hardenburg.

Heinrich von Stein (1757–1831):

Stein took over the Prussian government after the disastrous defeat of Prussia in 1806. He introduced vital modernisation: ending serfdom, loosening the rigid class system and rebuilding the army. Many see this stern and humourless figure as the true father of modern Germany.

The reforms included:

- Serfdom (the control of peasants by nobles and the king) was abolished in 1807, and this reduced class restrictions. For example, nobles were allowed to trade and rich non-nobles could acquire land.
- Army reforms under Gerhard von Scharnhorst and August Neidhardt von Gneisenau meant that non-nobles could now become officers, thus beginning the system of promotion by merit. The reforms also put an end to severe corporal punishment. A citizen army called the Landwehr was created, and universal military service was introduced in 1814.
- There was limited parliamentary government through the creation of an assembly. This was dominated by the nobles.
- There were educational reforms under the famous scholar Wilhelm von Humbold.

Over the long term, these changes in Prussia proved considerable. The wars brought about much greater unity, and this resulted in a different political structure. There were new legal systems and a French style of government. The new Prussian legal codes – based on the famous Code Napoleon of 1804 – introduced equality under the law and offered simplified and more uniform systems of justice. These changes meant that the Prussia of 1815 was very different to that of 1789.

Reforms in Austria

Austria emerged from the French wars as a major victorious power. Its military performance improved significantly during the period of the wars – the Battle of Aspern in 1809, for instance, demonstrated that Austria's military tactics were far better and more successful than they had been in 1805–06. However, the Austrian army was unable to defeat Napoleon until he was seriously weakened by the loss of 500 000 men in Russia in 1812.

KEY CONCEPTS ACTIVITY

Change: Create a chart like the following example to summarise the various changes to the Holy Roman Empire brought about by the Revolutionary and Napoleonic Wars. You may wish to complete the 'Evaluation of importance' column after studying what happened in Germany after 1815. Once you have made a list of the changes, rank them in order of importance.

→

Change	Explanation	Evaluation of importance
End of the Holy Roman Empire	In 1806, after defeat by France, the Austrian emperor had to agree to the formal end of the Holy Roman Empire.	This reduced the power of Austria over Germany. It also ended the historic role of the Habsburgs in Germany.

5.2 What was the impact of the Congress System on Germany?

The Congress of Vienna, 1814–15

The great powers of Europe met in 1814 and again in 1815 to redraw the boundaries after the Napoleonic era. The European monarchs had spent years fighting the French, and they blamed the French Revolution for the instability and conflict since 1792. They hoped for a lasting peace and a return to the old order. The priority at the Congress of Vienna was therefore to protect Europe against France and to maintain the old monarchies.

However, there had been various changes in Germany since 1789, and it was not possible to restore the hundreds of small states. Although nationalists hoped that a united Germany might result from the defeat of Napoleon, they were disappointed by the terms agreed at the Congress of Vienna. One of the most important reasons for the lack of unity was the rivalry between Austria and Prussia, both of whom wanted to control Germany, but were also determined to limit the influence of the other. As a result, the new Germany that replaced the Holy Roman Empire consisted of 39 states in a confederation. Representatives from the governments of these states – princes and kings – now met in an assembly. This organisation was called the Bund (confederation) and was presided over by Austria.

The terms of the settlement

The Congress of Vienna resulted in several key developments:

- Germany was reduced to 39 independent states and free cities organised in a loose confederation (Bund) that was dominated by Austria.
- The Bund had an assembly called a Diet, with 17 members. The Diet met at Frankfurt, and its permanent president was the Austrian member. In theory, the Bund could make war, conduct diplomacy and raise armies. In practice, there was no effective Bund government; the representatives spoke on behalf of their independent states and there was rarely unanimous agreement.
- Austria was strengthened by the Vienna settlement, gaining land in Italy, eastern Galicia (Polish territory), Salzburg and the Tyrol, the Voralberg, Lombardy, Venetia and the Adriatic coast (Dalmatia) (see Figure 5.4, a map of central Europe after the Congress of Vienna).
- Prussia was also strengthened by the treaty, gaining land in the west of Germany on both sides of the Rhine – Westphalia, Cleves, Cologne, Aachen, Bonn, Koblenz and Trier. Prussia was deliberately given lands in western Germany as a barrier to French expansion.
- France was allowed to keep Alsace and Lorraine, even though Prussia wanted control of these areas.

The territorial arrangements at the Congress of Vienna were complex, but the main changes can be summarised as follows:

- Austria emerged as the dominant power in central Europe, and gained valuable lands in Italy.
- Prussia increased its lands and gained valuable economic resources that provided the basis of its later growth. The new lands in the west were rich in coal and iron ore. At the time, though, Prussia resented losing Polish land and not gaining all of Saxony. Austria's dominant position in central Europe also left Prussia's rulers feeling somewhat inferior.
- The new Bund had little power and was controlled by Austria. The Austrians opposed any signs of German nationalism that might create a strong German state.
- Fewer smaller states meant there was much greater unity than during the 18th century, but it is doubtful whether there was much German nationalism by 1815.

Although Prussia was the big winner from Vienna, this was not obvious at the time as Austria's influence at the Congress was greater. This was aided by the importance of Prince Metternich, who was determined to retain Austria's authority over the German states and was resolved that Germany would not become a political entity, but would remain a lose confederation under Austrian control.

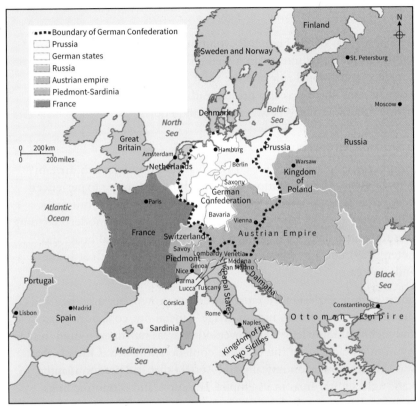

Figure 5.4: The division of central Europe after the Congress of Vienna in 1815

What were the forces for change after 1815?

The rulers, particularly of Austria, at the Congress of Vienna hoped for a return to the old principles of monarchy – a respect for religion, privilege and order. However, the spread of French revolutionary ideals had given rise to new ideas of representative government, democracy, opposition to the control of the Church, free trade and greater national feeling. Broadly speaking, there were two forces at work – liberalism and nationalism – and both challenged the settlement of 1814–15.

Liberalism

The new ideas of the French Revolution meant that, after 1815, there was increased interest in liberal change – that is, people sought constitutional rule and the right of subjects to participate in government. There was also greater enthusiasm for a new German nation and more unity between German peoples.

Economic growth

Another important force for change was economic growth. Britain was the first industrial nation, but the whole of Europe experienced economic expansion after 1815. Cities and their populations grew. There were new production techniques and factories, modern farming methods, and new methods of transport including canal boats and (after 1829) railways. There was also increased trade, both at home and overseas.

Some regions experienced rapid economic growth because they had the best resources for an industrial age – metal ore, coal, power, markets and technical knowledge. However, other areas remained rooted in old economic practices. In the German confederation, it was Prussia that was able to grow economically and Austria that had predominantly static agricultural areas in its empire. Transport and economic links improved ties between Germany's various states, while economic growth shifted the balance of power from Prussia to Austria.

So, was Germany open to new ideas of liberalism and nationalism in 1815? It had a rising population with more people living in cities. Its growing middle class was sufficiently well educated to be influenced by new ideas. Economic growth was transforming Germanic central Europe as a whole and Prussia in particular. All these developments indicate that future changes to the Vienna settlement were likely.

Forces opposing change in 1815

On the other hand, there were various factors that were likely to prevent the move towards greater unity or liberalism:

- The German confederation was established in 1815 by a meeting of the great powers, so any changes would require their agreement. The rulers of Austria and Russia were absolute emperors with large armies that they used to suppress change. The kings and princes of Germany were more interested in preventing revolution than in national unity, and had similar interests to Austria and Russia. They saw nationalism as a revolutionary movement and believed that a united Germany would weaken their independence.
- As with Italy, the 'Congress System' was to be used to maintain the status quo and suppress any liberal or revolutionary activity. Metternich saw the 'system' as a way to ensure that the Great Powers crushed unrest and supported any government that was overthrown by revolution. However, the conservative nature of much of German society and the desire of rulers to maintain their independence helped ensure that there were only limited challenges to the status quo, at least in the early period after Vienna.
- Metternich used the meetings of the Great Powers of Austria, Prussia, Russia, Britain and France to settle disagreements and keep peace, but most importantly to stifle revolution. This was seen clearly at the Congress of Troppau in 1820 which followed the outbreak of revolutions in Spain, Portugal and Piedmont. Metternich put forward a proposal that Russia, Austria and Prussia would act together to restore any government overthrown by force. This proposal was accepted and became known as the Protocol of Troppau. This was completely against liberal and nationalist views that were developing in some German states, but was a clear indication that both Austria and Prussia were opposed to such developments.
- The German confederation was still predominantly agricultural and made up of small towns. The new ideas that so excited Paris in the revolutionary period did not win the same enthusiasm from a conservative, traditional peasantry or small-town merchants.

- Like Italy, the German confederation was used to local traditions, and these often acted as a force for conservatism:
  - In Prussia and Brandenburg, there were strong military traditions and respect for authority. The heroic figures of the past were militaristic kings, such as the Great Elector and Frederick the Great. The Prussian Junkers (nobles) had considerable influence in the east, and they were conservative monarchists.
  - In the smaller states such as Hanover, there was distrust of Prussia and a tradition of links with other countries.
  - The south and west of Germany were divided from the north by religious differences. For example, Roman Catholic Bavaria was much closer in culture to Austria; the Rhineland had more cultural links with Catholic France than with Protestant Prussia.
  - Centuries of division had entrenched loyalties to local rulers. The four free cities of northern Germany guarded their municipal independence fiercely, having little wish to be ruled by kings and princes.
  - There were also linguistic differences and a distinct gap between the outlook and culture of north Germany and that of the south.
- National unity was associated with French rule, which had been more unpopular and resented in Germany than in Italy. Napoleon Bonaparte was of Italian origin, so he may have been more palatable to the Italians; many in Germany saw him as merely a foreign tyrant. Some Germans appreciated the end of feudalism, the introduction of a fairer legal and administrative system and greater trading opportunities; but most resented conscription, the loss of German troops in Russia, higher taxation and the restrictions on trade with Britain.
- There was no consensus about what a German nation would entail. Two models emerged: a Grossdeutschland ('big Germany') would include Austria and the south, while a Kleindeutschland ('small Germany') would consist of an enlarged north Germany. Within these models there was no agreement on the form that unity would take:
  - What would be the status and position of non-Germans – for example, Austria's multinational empire to the east or Prussia's Polish subjects?
  - Would either model be liberal, democratic or monarchical?
  - Would Germany have a federal structure with real power held by an overall government, or would its internal organisation be looser?
  - What would be the role of Prussia, which amounted to two-thirds of the German confederation (excluding Austria)?

Without agreement on these fundamentals, any plans for future German unity were problematic. These difficulties strengthened reactionary elements in the Bund that wanted to avoid major change. As a result, the major powers were not faced with challenges to the status quo in the period immediately after 1815.

KEY CONCEPTS ACTIVITY

Perspectives: What were the advantages and disadvantages for Germans in 1815 of a Grossdeutschland and a Kleindeutschland? Copy and complete a table like the one below.

Grossdeutschland		Kleindeutschland	
For	Against	For	Against

5.3 How strong was nationalism in the Vormärz period in Germany?

The key question is whether the forces of nationalism in the German confederation were significant enough to overcome these obstacles to change in the period between 1815 and 1848. Some have described this entire period as the Vormärz years – that is, pre–March 1848, when the 1848 Revolutions began. However, others have argued that the term should be used only to describe the period after the revolution in France in 1830. However, whichever date is used the term describes a period of repression led by Metternich, but despite this liberal and nationalist views did survive.

During the period German nationalism took different forms in the period after both the Congress of Vienna and the 1830 Revolution in France:

- the official organisations and supporters of greater unity
- cultural elements that brought Germany closer together
- economic factors that encouraged unification.

5

Nationalism in the Napoleonic era

There had already been some growth in nationalist feeling during the Napoleonic period, with the emergence of some leading figures:

- Friedrich Jahn, a teacher and writer, hoped for a youthful nationalist renaissance. He founded a so-called Gymnastics Club in 1811. This was in fact a paramilitary nationalist organisation that raised forces against Napoleon.
- Johann Fichte was a Berlin academic who published *Addresses to the German Nation* in 1807–08. He sought the creation of a German nation.
- Ernst Moritz Arndt was a popular nationalist writer. He urged opposition to France, reform of serfdom and the creation of a united Germany. His book, *The Spirit of the Age* (1806), was influential, as were his patriotic songs.

These literary nationalists often expressed anti-Semitic views and opposed revolutionary ideas from France. When Jahn tried to raise troops in his Free Corps in 1813, about 30 000 people volunteered. However, many of the volunteers were simply loyal to the Prussian crown and there were relatively small numbers of idealistic nationalists.

Student nationalism and Austrian repression in the period before 1830

The most enthusiastic national feeling was found among students. Burschenschaften student movements were inspired by liberal and nationalist ideas. The first one was founded in 1815, and they were based in leading university towns during the first half of the 19th century.

In October 1817, the Burschenschaften student movement assembled at Wartburg Castle near Eisenach – a town associated with the Protestant reformer Martin Luther – to urge German unity. Eisenach was in the lands of the duke of Saxe-Weimar, one of the few rulers to have kept his word and introduced a constitution. Although only 450 students attended the Wartburg festival, where reactionary books were burned, this marked the start of a nationalist reform movement.

In 1819 a nationalist student, Karl Sand, went one step further when he killed the conservative playwright **August von Kotzebue**. The foreign minister, Klemens von Metternich, used this as an excuse to repress students in Germany.

August von Kotzebue (1761–1819):

Kotzebue was a somewhat controversial playwright from Weimar. He wrote 200 plays and received the patronage of the Russian tsar, who gave him an estate. He satirised Napoleon but also the German nationalists, whom he disliked. His magazine attacked nationalist demands for a free Germany, which Kotzebue thought narrow minded and anti-European. His books were burned by students at Wartburg in 1817, and he was murdered in 1819.

There was little suggestion of a widespread nationalist movement, but the Austrians were alarmed by this student activism and the efforts of Bavaria, Baden and Württemberg to introduce constitutions.

The Austrians persuaded the Bund to pass the Carlsbad Decrees in 1820, controlling universities and tightening censorship. Metternich gloated, 'A word spoken by Austria is an unbreakable law for Germany'.

The repression had the desired effect. Friedrich Jahn was arrested and imprisoned, and nationalist or liberal professors were hounded. The Burschenschaften split up, and nationalist publications were censored and banned. The Prussians were especially active in opening mail and searching homes.

Nationalism after the 1830 Revolution in France

The period from the 1830 Revolution in France to March 1848 when further revolutions broke out in much of Europe is referred to as the Vormärz or before March years.

In 1830, revolution in France and unrest in Italy and Poland triggered disturbances in Germany, particularly in some south German states, when a mixture of constitutional demands, peasant unrest and worker discontent swept the country. There was some nationalist feeling mixed in with the disorder:

- The Duke of Brunswick was driven out and his successor was forced to grant a more liberal constitution.
- A constitution was granted in Hanover in 1832.
- More liberal constitutions were gained in Saxony and Hesse-Cassel.

- Liberals gained parliamentary seats in Bavaria, Baden and Württemberg.
- In some states greater freedom of the press was gained and this led to criticisms of the governments.

On 22 May 1832, 25 000 nationalists marched to the Hambach Castle in the Palatinate. Three-quarters of the demonstrators were students, academics or middle-class professionals. The king of Bavaria sent troops, and ringleaders were arrested. Frightened by the demonstration, the princes agreed to pass the repressive Six Articles demanded by Austria. This was swiftly followed by the Ten Acts. These laws prevented any parliamentary assemblies reducing princely power and banned all political clubs, 'subversive' literature and the national flag (the flag with the so-called 'national colours' of black, red and gold that student and national groups had adopted). The 39 states were expected to cooperate in repressing any national unrest. Despite this, armed students attacked the main gatehouse of the Bundestag in 1833 in the hope of starting a general revolt, but this failed. Student protestors and trouble makers were soon rounded up and membership of student associations was seen as treasonous. As a result much activity was driven underground, while some radicals fled abroad.

'Subterranean' nationalism

After 1833, nationalist activity took place either in private meetings between enthusiasts in homes or universities, or was disguised by gymnastic clubs and musical societies. By 1847, there were 85 000 members of gymnastic clubs, including many apprentices, trainee journeymen or small masters. The singing clubs attracted up to 100 000 members; they spent their time singing patriotic songs and attending musical festivals. Historical ceremonies attracted large numbers; for example, a ceremony in Detmold in 1838 commemorated Arminius, the mythical leader of the German tribes who triumphed over the Romans. German nationalism was becoming more widespread, even though it could not be openly expressed as Metternich intensified press censorship and placed further controls on universities, which were seen as the centres of subversive activity. Despite these actions, it was this national sentiment that surfaced in the Revolutions of 1848.

However, it was not until 1859 that a Nationalist Association (*Nationalverein*) was formed. The singing and hiking clubs lacked a clear national programme and leaders. There was no leading German figure to inspire nationalist feeling equivalent to Giuseppe Mazzini (see Chapter 2). So nationalism took the form of generalised patriotic sentiment, rather than an effective movement, at this time.

Cultural nationalism

Cultural nationalism was probably more important than the conscious nationalism described in the preceding pages. It took the form of greater awareness of German culture among the broad middle classes – from independent craftsmen to academics and businessmen. The peasant masses, however, did not flock to opera, nor did they go on nationalist walking tours.

Figure 5.5: Jacob and Wilhelm Grimm; their first collection of German folklore, *Children's and Household Tales*, was published in 1812

5 — Italy (1815–1871) and Germany (1815–1890)

There were several aspects to this cultural renaissance:

- There was the rediscovery of German folklore in the books of the Brothers Grimm, and a literary flowering in the works of Johann Wolfgang von Goethe and Friedrich Schiller. Goethe's dramatic poem *Faust* and Schiller's plays, such as *The Robbers* and *Mary Stuart*, are seen as being among the finest German literary works.
- German music developed a distinct style, in contrast to the Italian influences of the previous century. Carl Maria von Weber wrote operas with German texts using national folk stories and history. Ludwig van Beethoven and Franz Peter Schubert were German composers with an international reputation. The great opera composer Richard Wagner used Germanic legends, such as Tannhäuser and Lohengrin, in his early operas.
- German historians were renowned for their scholarship – for example, Barthold Niebuhr's celebrated *Roman History* and Leopold von Ranke's *History of Germany* (1824).
- Schinkel's architecture transformed Berlin by introducing a distinctive classical style.
- German songwriters such as Robert Schumann based their music on settings from German poets and poems.
- Caspar David Friedrich's paintings (see Figure 5.6) celebrated romantic 'German' forests, landscapes and seascapes.

Germany ceased to be an artistic backwater in which its creative artists were expected to use foreign models, and became a major cultural centre. However, this creative upsurge coincided with a period of economic and social change, and it is often argued that this encouraged nationalism more than anything else.

KEY CONCEPTS ACTIVITY

Select a piece of music, painting, text or poem from Germany in the period 1815 to 1848 and give a short presentation on it. Comment on how your chosen work illustrates the growth of a specifically German national art and encouraged German national feeling.

Figure 5.6: *Wanderer Above the Sea of Fog*, a German romantic painting of 1818 by Caspar David Friedrich

Although there were some signs of nationalist activity in this period, it was largely powerless against Metternich's policies. He, and Austria, remained in control of the Bundestag, while Prussia was just as reactionary which meant there was little chance of bringing about change.

5.4 What was the significance of the Zollverein?

Given the repressive nature of Prussia in this period it is perhaps surprising that it would eventually be the state that brought about unification. Yet, it was the development of the customs union or

5 Italy (1815–1871) and Germany (1815–1890)

Zollverein in this period that laid the foundations for unification. In 1818, Prussia introduced a tariff reform law – all raw materials were to be free of duties and, within the Prussian territories, all internal customs duties were abolished. This established free trade within the largest state in north Germany. As a result, other neighbouring states sought to sign up to an agreement that would allow them to trade freely with Prussia. This union of states – called the Zollverein (*zoll* meaning customs and *verein* meaning association or union) – was formalised in 1834. It incorporated 17 states and 26 million people, though Austria was never a member.

In the Zollverein:

- there was an assembly of members called the Zoll parliament
- any changes were made by unanimous consent
- the tariff was uniform on all imported goods
- the proceeds were divided between the states according to size of population
- raw materials and semi-manufactured goods entered the union for free to help industry.

The Zollverein also made economic treaties, for example with Holland in 1831, Great Britain in 1844 and Belgium in 1844.

Contemporaries saw a link between the Zollverein and the development of a separate German nation. A report on the Zollverein drawn up for the British government in 1840 commented that, 'The general feeling in Germany is that it is the first step towards the Germanisation of the people'. What was remarkable was that:

- Nearly all the German states, with the exception of Austria, joined the Zollverein, accepted a common tariff policy and worked together in an annual assembly.
- The initiative came from Prussia, which suggested that Prussia was the natural leader of a more united Germany.
- The Zollverein almost acted as a nation, making commercial treaties with other nations.

Historical debate

Helmut Böhme, in *Foundation of the German Empire* (Oxford University Press, 1971), agrees with the view of contemporary writers such as Friedrich Engels that the Zollverein was the major step towards a politically united Germany. It is also suggested that somehow the tariff policies allowed the economic expansion that made Prussia stronger than Austria and put it on the way to becoming the dominant power.

Historians such as James Sheehan have questioned this. It was in the economic interests of other states to have internal free trade, but that was not the same as accepting Prussia's leadership. As the history of the post-1945 European Community shows, economic cooperation does not mean political unity. When Prussia went to war with Austria in 1866, most of its Zollverein partners sided with Austria, even though it was not a member of the customs union. Also, there is a weak link between economic development as such and the customs union. The union was primarily a revenue-raising scheme for its governments and a way of protecting German small industries from foreign competition. It was not really seen as a political forerunner of unification – to which there were still formidable obstacles.

Theory of Knowledge

Economic and political development:
When studying the history of economic development, should we assume an automatic connection with political development? Research other economic unions to see if they contributed to political developments. For instance, you could look at the European Union or the USA.

5.5 What accounts for the rise of Prussian economic and military power?

The acquisition of the Rhineland in 1815 gave Prussia – previously not a strong economic power – important resources of coal and ore. The increase in territory, together with the rise in population and the opening up of the free trade area of the Zollverein, meant Prussia had a large and growing internal market for its produce.

5 Italy (1815–1871) and Germany (1815–1890)

Railway building was planned in the Prussian Rhineland as early as 1832. Wider railway projects finally got official backing in 1838, supported by the Crown Prince, and between 1841 and 1847 the railway network grew from 375 km (233 miles) to 2325 km (1444 miles). Prussia owned 56% of all railways in Germany by 1847. Railway building was a major stimulus for coal and iron production.

Investment in metals and fuels doubled in the 1840s. Deep shaft mining developed from shallow surface mining. Charcoal-smelted iron gave way to the use of coke, and hand-operated machines were replaced by industrial tools. There were advances in Prussian technology and technical knowledge, and there was the money and official backing to support these developments. There were ample markets for produce, and the population rise provided labour and markets. In this way, between 1815 and 1852, the foundations were laid for substantial economic growth later in the century.

This economic growth also provided the basis for increased military power. However, until the military reforms of the 1860s, the Prussian army had little opportunity to show its skills. A key military development of the period was the invention of the needle gun and, later, the Krupps breech-loaded artillery:

- The needle gun was invented by Dreyse, a blacksmith, and issued to Prussian forces in 1848. It set off the cartridge with a long needle driven into it when the trigger was pulled. It could fire five times faster than conventional rifles and had a longer range. It was first used against German radical forces in 1849, and was a major weapon in Prussia's wars against Denmark (1864), Austria (1866) and France (1870–71) (see Chapter 6).
- By 1870, the weapons manufacturing firm of Krupps, based at Essen in the Rhineland, was making significant advances in artillery. Here, the breech-loading big guns were developed that made Prussian artillery such a devastating force in the war against France (1870–71).

Figure 5.7: Wood engraving of the German inventor Johann Nikolaus von Dreyse with his needle gun

There were also improvements in Prussian military planning, and the setting up of a general staff (a body of highly-trained senior officers to oversee the planning and organisation of the army). The military used Prussia's industrial power to produce superior artillery, and it used an efficient railway system to transport troops. These developments reflected the economic changes, but also a strong military tradition and the thoughtful, flexible approach of the military leaders of the Junker class. The army also had the widespread support of its citizens, who were linked to it by the reserve army – the Landwehr. This growth in Prussian strength will be examined further in the next chapter.

5.6 Why did revolution break out in the German confederation in 1848?

The spread of liberal and national ideas inspired hopes for a more united, constitutional Germany. Austria's repressive measures became more difficult to enforce with changes in German society and the economy. Growing trade and industry meant Germans were confident in their own strengths and reluctant to be ruled by Austria; improved communications raised Germans' awareness of nationalist ideas. By 1848, national discontent and ambitions took various forms. Unrest was gathering in many parts of Europe and, as in 1830, there was a knock-on effect as revolution broke out, first in France before spreading to Italy, Germany and the Austrian empire.

In February 1848, news came of the overthrow of the French monarchy after street demonstrations in Paris, and there were peasant disturbances in southwest Germany. A poor harvest and the failure of the regimes to enforce the promised abolition of serfdom led to large-scale peasant unrest, which had not been seen since the 1520s. The peasant disturbances spread through Saxony and Thuringia and into Prussian and Austrian rural areas.

Alongside the peasant unrest, middle-class reformers demanded freedom of the press, responsible governments and constitutions. The authorities gave way and abolished the Carlsbad Decrees of 1820, which had restricted universities and tightened censorship.

One result of the period of economic growth was that a greater number of workers faced unemployment and poor conditions during the economic turndown of 1847–48. In Vienna in March 1848, workers and students clashed with troops. Many cities experienced similar disturbances. Faced with large-scale crowds, the rulers showed reluctance to enforce control – since this could turn bloody – and either made concessions or fled. When Metternich fled from Vienna, the dissatisfied urban workers, nationalist students and local Brandenburg farm hands began to demonstrate in Berlin. In response to the demonstrations, on 18 March 1848, **Frederick Wilhelm IV** announced a new constitution for Prussia.

Frederick Wilhelm IV (1795–1861):

Frederick Wilhelm ruled Prussia between 1840 and 1857, when brain disease left him unfit to rule. He resented Prussia's defeats in 1806 and disliked revolution. Nevertheless, he agreed to call a parliament in 1848. He refused the throne of Germany in 1849 and used force to restore his power, though he kept the constitution. He sought a new union, but was forced to back down by Austria in 1852.

Figure 5.8: Frederick Wilhelm IV

The rapid collapse of authority in March 1848 can be explained by social factors:

- There was a rise in population without sufficient economic development to provide for it, leading to poverty.
- Though some areas had seen reforms in agriculture, feudalism continued in other areas and this caused resentment among the peasantry.

- Traditional production methods were under threat from early industrialisation, and this created anxiety in some areas.
- The new factories led to harsh working conditions, urban overcrowding in some areas and problems with periods of falling trade, as in the economic downturn of 1847–48.
- There was an increase in nationalism, though this national feeling was not shared by all German classes or regions. However, a growing middle class was increasingly unhappy with Metternich's repressive system, and was prepared to take advantage of the current unrest by insisting on reform.
- The ruling class may have lost confidence in the 'old system' re-established in 1815, yet they lacked the courage to embrace nationalism and reform.

Weakness in Austria

Austria had gained considerable lands in 1815, and had taken on the role of defending Europe from the forces of change. These responsibilities proved increasingly difficult, with revolutions and unrest undermining Austria's control, an issue that will be developed further in the next chapter.

The Austrian empire had become hard to manage and coordinate:

- Austria suffered from poor harvests in the 1840s and its economy did not modernise. The financial burden of maintaining a large military force was considerable.
- There was unrest in key areas, especially in Hungary and Italy. In Vienna, the Austrian capital, there was an underground student movement that campaigned against Metternich's oppressive measures.
- Vienna experienced an influx of people that caused rapid population growth in poor districts.
- The news of revolution in France in 1848 led to panic and a run on the Austrian banks.
- The Austrian system of government had grown inefficient, and there were divisions in the imperial ruling council.
- Emperor Ferdinand in 1835 did not provide Austria with a sound monarch – he was seen as mentally deficient and did not command the respect that might have prevented unrest.

When faced with rebellion in Vienna and unrest throughout the empire, the Austrian leaders showed a fatal lack of self-confidence and the 'strong man', Metternich, fled.

The main events of 1848–49

In March 1848, with the sudden and unexpected collapse of Austrian authority, the Confederation's princes and cities brought opposition leaders into government. These new leaders were often intellectually respected but they lacked political experience. Nevertheless, they tried to end rural unrest by introducing agrarian reforms that finally ended serfdom.

The aim of these new liberal governments was the creation of a united Germany. In April 1848, eminent Germans who saw themselves as 'trusted men of the people' met in Frankfurt to discuss a new German nation. This group was known as the 'Pre-parliament' and it faced considerable divisions of opinion about what should happen next. For instance, some German states wanted a republic while others sought a union of princes.

The radical leaders, **Friedrich Hecker** and **Gustav von Struve**, tried to rally support for a popular republic. They led a revolt in Baden, but their hastily gathered army was suppressed by the Duke of Baden's soldiers on 20 April 1848. Following on from this, a group of radical émigrés led by Georg Herweg was defeated by soldiers from the new constitutional regime in Württemberg.

Friedrich Hecker (1811–81):

Hecker was a radical lawyer from Baden. He took part in the 1848 revolutions, and raised an armed force in 1849 that was defeated by Prussian troops. He later fought in the American Civil War on the Union side.

Gustav von Struve (1805–70):

Struve was the son of a Russian diplomat. He was a liberal and revolutionary agitator who led revolution in Baden in 1848 and was provisional head of government there in 1849. He demanded a republic for Germany. When his forces were defeated by Prussia at Rastatt, Struve fled abroad.

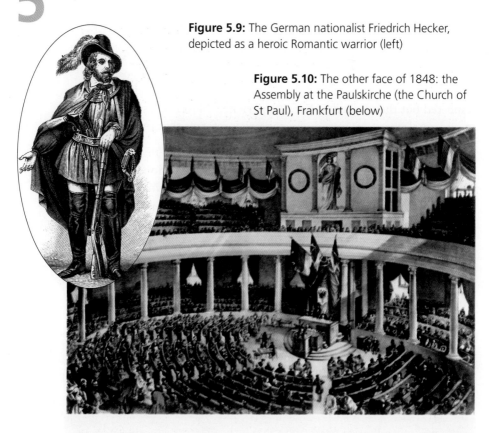

Figure 5.9: The German nationalist Friedrich Hecker, depicted as a heroic Romantic warrior (left)

Figure 5.10: The other face of 1848: the Assembly at the Paulskirche (the Church of St Paul), Frankfurt (below)

ACTIVITY

Compare the image of Friedrich Hecker with that of the politicians at the Frankfurt Assembly. What does a comparison of these images of the revolutionaries of 1848 show? How useful are they in showing the divisions between those who worked for change in Germany?

In May 1848, elections were held for the new national assembly, which met in Frankfurt on 18 May. Each German state chose its own method of election and restricted voting to the propertied classes. The result was a middle-class assembly of lawyers, professors, doctors, writers and other professionals. The 800 representatives who came to the Paulskirche (St Paul's church) in Frankfurt could not reach consensus, so formed different political sub-groups, from conservatives to republicans. No one decisive leader emerged.

By the summer of 1848, it was clear that not much had changed – the new German parliament and government had little power, and the old princes kept control of their armies. A dispute over Schleswig and Holstein showed the weakness of the new Germany. The Danish king annexed Schleswig in March and sought control of neighbouring Holstein. Holstein asked the new regime for help. The only armed forces were those of Prussia, who fought the Danes but then decided to make peace with Denmark on 26 August without consulting the German parliament, out of fear of Russian and British retaliation. The parliament condemned the peace, which stirred up nationalist feeling and mob violence in Frankfurt, and two conservative representatives were killed.

Many feared that events in the new Germany were getting out of control, and there was a subsequent loss of support for the new nation. In the German countryside, influential landlords urged action to restore royal authority. In other parts of Europe, rulers were re-asserting their authority and gradually the 'old' system was regaining control. For instance, Austrian forces suppressed revolution in Prague in June 1848 and, after divisions in the Austrian assembly, Habsburg troops restored order to Vienna in October.

In Berlin, the Prussian king was fearful of the increasing street violence. When the new Prussian Diet (or parliament) created in March 1848, called for an end to the king's power of veto, Frederick Wilhelm IV of Prussia sent for his army. In November, 13 000 troops marched from Potsdam to Berlin to disperse the Diet and end the unrest.

In an attempt to protect the gains of the revolution, a new Association for the Preservation of the Victories of March was formed by more radical representatives; it had 500 000 members and 900 branches. Now opinion was divided – between radical democrats, monarchists who wanted to create a new German kingdom, supporters of the Kleindeutschland or Grossdeutschland solutions, and Protestants and Catholics. By March 1849, there was an agreement to offer the throne of a Kleindeutschland to Frederick Wilhelm IV, but he refused to accept a crown that was not offered to him by his fellow princes.

By April 1849, 29 German states had accepted the Frankfurt constitution and the regency of Archduke Johann. However, Bavaria, Saxony and Hanover held back from the union. Then Austria and Prussia refused and ordered the delegates to return home. Troops forced the remains of the Frankfurt parliament to leave the city. Prussian troops crushed the parliament of Saxony in Dresden and moved westwards into Baden. There was a brave but futile resistance by a hastily raised rebel army at Waghausel on 21 June, by which time the revolutions and hopes of a new German state had been crushed.

The collapse of authority in March 1848 was not exploited quickly enough by those who sought change. There was insufficient agreement on the form of a new united Germany. It was quickly clear that a new German nation could not raise its own army but would be dependent on Prussia's army. Within the states, there was no real confidence in the new constitutional regimes and fears of continuing working-class unrest grew among the propertied middle and upper classes. The peasantry, who had begun the revolts, were settled by agrarian reform and they had little interest in complex constitutions or national unity. The old rulers remained even if their ministers, such as Metternich, were driven out. They waited for the revolutionary impetus to die down and called on traditional supporters, especially the army, to restore order. The revolutions did not produce effective leaders, either at state or national level. The Austrian and Prussian armies were led by effective loyalists. Had Frederick Wilhelm IV taken the lead, the results might have been different; but it was virtually impossible for him to endanger his position by leading a revolution – he would probably have shared the fate of Carlo Alberto of Piedmont (see 2.4, The Revolutions of 1820–21). Foreign powers were also unlikely to have accepted Prussian rule of Germany in 1848.

KEY CONCEPTS ACTIVITY

Causation and significance: On cards, write down reasons for the failure of the Revolutions of 1848. Compare your reasons with other members of the group. Then discuss which order to put the cards in – this will help you decide on the most important factors.

KEY CONCEPTS QUESTIONS

Continuity: Would you agree that German nationalism in this period was largely confined to the middle classes?

Significance/Consequence: What was the significance of the 1848 Revolutions for the development of nationalism in Germany?

Paper 3 exam practice

Question

Examine the main events of the Revolutions of 1848–49, and their immediate consequences for Germany. **[15 marks]**

Skill

Avoiding irrelevance

Examiner's tips

Do not waste valuable writing time on irrelevant material. If it's irrelevant, it won't gain you any marks. This problem can arise because:

- the candidate does not look carefully enough at the wording of the question (see Chapter 2, End of chapter activities)

- the candidate ignores the fact that the questions require selection of facts, an analytical approach and a final judgement; instead, the candidate just writes down all they know about a topic (relevant or not) and hopes the examiner will do the analysis and make the judgement

- the candidate has unwisely restricted their revision (for example, if a question crops up on the consequences of the events of 1848–49 in Germany, the candidate may write about the causes of the events, because that was the topic he or she wanted to write about!); whatever the reason, such responses rarely address any of the demands of the question asked.

For this question, you will need to look at:

- the short-term consequences of the Frankfurt parliament and its failure

- the role of King Frederick William of Prussia and the Prussian ministry

- the attitude of individual states and ruling princes

- the Prussian constitution

- Prussian and Austrian action in 1849.

You also need to discuss views about the extent of failure and disappointment.

Common mistakes

One common error with this type of question is for candidates to write about material they know well, rather than material directly related to the question.

Another mistake is to present too much general information, instead of material that is specific to the person, period and command terms.

Finally, candidates often elaborate too much on events outside the dates given in the question (see the guidance in Chapter 2).

Remember to refer to the simplified Paper 3 mark scheme in Chapter 9.

Sample paragraphs of irrelevant focus/material

Before examining the main events and consequences of the 1848–49 Revolutions, it is important to see what led to the revolts and what the aspirations of the revolutionaries were. Those who hoped for democracy in Germany – with an end to the reactionary domination of Austria, and a new German parliament that would allow Germany to develop its economy and to modernise and unite its society – were disappointed.

The demand for German unification went back to the days of Napoleon. Then Germany had been changed from an area with thousands of small states to a much more unified area with the Confederation of the Rhine and then the Kingdom of Westphalia. Napoleon brought in many changes in law and administration, and this led many Germans to hope that after his defeat these changes would remain and grow into a united Germany. After 1815, one group who wanted more unity were the students. In 1817, there was a big festival at Wartburg which celebrated German culture and burned books of those who seemed to oppose German nationalism. Thus there were long-term causes of the unrest that broke out in 1848.

EXAMINER COMMENT

This extract from a student's essay shows an example of a **weak answer**. Although a brief comment on the causes of 1848 would be relevant and helpful, there is certainly no need to go into detail about the period before 1848 and especially about the Napoleonic era. Thus, virtually all of the underlined material is irrelevant and will not score any marks. Instead, the candidate should have used their time to provide relevant points and supporting knowledge.

Activity

In this chapter, the focus is on avoiding writing answers which contain irrelevant material. Using the information from this chapter, and any other sources of information available to you, write an answer to one of the following Paper 3 questions, keeping your answer fully focused on the question asked. Remember: writing a plan *first* can help you maintain this focus.

Paper 3 practice questions

1 Evaluate the reasons for the Revolutions of 1848–49 in Germany.

2 To what extent were divisions among the revolutionary groups, or the strength of the princes, the main reason for the failure of the 1848–49 revolutions?

3 Discuss the reasons for the growth of German nationalism in 1848.

4 Compare and contrast the reasons for the outbreak of revolutions in Germany and Italy in 1848.

5 'The Revolutions of 1848–49 achieved more for the cause of German unification than for Italian unification.' To what extent do you agree with this statement?

6 Examine the reasons why Austrian power in Germany was weakened in the period from 1815 to 1848.

6 | Germany and unification, 1849–71

Introduction

This chapter looks at the dramatic and complex series of events that resulted in German unification in 1871. It shows how Bismarck used Prussian economic and military power to start a war with Austria in 1866. This war, the result of disagreements about provinces taken from Denmark in a joint Austro–Prussian War in 1864, established a Prussian-dominated Confederation in North Germany. There is debate about whether this made conflict with France inevitable, as it changed the whole balance of power in central Europe. There are also questions as to how far Bismarck planned for or even wanted to add the Catholic states of south Germany to a new German state. The conflict was triggered by the proposal that a German prince be made king of Spain in 1869. Prussian victory in a third war against France in 1870 resulted in the proclamation of a new German empire in 1871.

TIMELINE

1848 First issue of Dreyse needle gun to Prussian troops

1850 **Mar:** Erfurt Union

Nov: Declaration of Olmütz

1858 Wilhelm II becomes regent of Prussia

1860 Prussian army reforms under Minister of War, Roon

1861 Death of Frederick Wilhelm IV of Prussia; he is succeeded by his brother

1862 **Sep:** Bismarck made Minister-President of Prussia

1863 **Jan:** Polish revolt

Feb: Alvensleben Convention; Christian IX claims duchies

1864 **Jan:** Alliance between Prussia and Austria; war between Denmark, Austria and Prussia

Oct: Peace with Denmark in Vienna

1865 **Aug:** Gastein Convention

Oct: Meeting at Biarritz between Bismarck and Napoleon III

Dec: Renewed Zollverein (excludes Austria)

1866 **Jun:** War between Austria and Prussia

Jul: Battle of Sadowa

Aug: Peace of Prague; Prussia annexes Hanover, Hesse-Cassel, Schleswig-Holstein, Nassau and Frankfurt

6 Italy (1815–1871) and Germany (1815–1890)

1867 North German Confederation; Luxembourg crisis

May: London conference confirms independence

1868 Sep: Isabella of Spain is overthrown

1870 Jul: Hohenzollern candidature crisis; Franco-Prussian War

Sep: French defeat at Sedan

1871 Jan: Proclamation of German empire at Versailles

KEY QUESTIONS

- What were the consequences of the 1848 Revolutions in Germany?
- How strong were Austria and Prussia after 1848?
- How did Bismarck rise to power?
- What led to the creation of the North German Confederation?
- Why was there war between Prussia and France in 1870–71?
- What was the nature of the German empire of 1871?
- 'How did Bismarck do it?'

Overview

- After 1848, Austria was weakened diplomatically by the Crimean War and its armies suffered defeats in Italy in 1859 (see Chapter 2).
- The period after the 1848 Revolutions saw Austria lose influence in the Prussian dominated economic coalition of German states, while Prussian economic power continued to grow.
- Prussia was able to take advantage of Austria's weakness after 1848–49. The reform of the Prussian army after 1858 and the emergence of Otto von Bismarck in the Prussian leadership heralded a new age of 'blood and iron', which transformed Germany.
- Bismarck's rise to be chancellor in 1862 marked the start of some remarkable diplomacy that resulted in the isolation of Austria and France from other European powers, their defeat and the creation of a new German empire.
- Bismarck defied parliament by raising money for a new army. He undermined the Austrian-led Bund by bringing about a joint war between Austria and Prussia against Denmark.

- He then used a dispute about lands gained in the war with Denmark to go to war with Austria, ensuring that Austria was isolated in Europe. As a result of that war, Austrian power over Germany ended.
- Unification was completed by another war in which the southern German states joined Prussia's North German Confederation against France. The German empire was proclaimed at Versailles in 1871 by the princes of Germany.

6.1 What were the consequences of the 1848 Revolutions in Germany?

Despite the failure of the 1848 Revolutions there was no return to how things had been in 1815. Even hardline conservatives saw the need to keep the constitution and the Diet (parliament), which controlled the Prussian budget. Prussia had been the choice to lead a new Germany, so its prestige was not lost. The Zollverein remained as a source of Prussian influence.

German national feeling continued to develop. The years between 1848 and 1862 saw a growth in creative work by musicians, artists and writers. It also saw the beginnings of the best-organised nationalist group – the National Association (*Nationalverein*). This was founded in Frankfurt in September 1859 by businessmen and professionals, and its membership reached 25 000. The centenary of the playwright Schiller's birth in 1859 also prompted large nationalist rallies. There was an increase in the number of all-German associations, such as gymnastic and choral groups, whose festivals attracted very large crowds in the early 1860s.

Austria had successfully quashed internal revolution and was not prepared to abandon any of its power and influence in the Bund. A proposal for a new union to be led by Prussia in 1850 – the so-called Erfurt Union – was rejected on Austria's insistence. Elections on a very restricted voting system were held in January 1850, and representatives came to the city of Erfurt to discuss a constitution for a new German union run by the princes. Under Austrian pressure, supported by Russia, 14 out of 26 states in the Union rejected the proposed constitution. Frederick Wilhelm IV considered fighting Austria over this, but Prussian conservatives would not agree to go to war. In November 1850, at the Declaration of Olmütz, the proposed new union was abandoned and Austria again took control of the Bund.

Prussia dared not oppose Austrian rule. For the moment, it seemed that Austrian power over the German confederation, as well as over its other possessions in Italy and Hungary, had been strengthened. Some Prussian patriots experienced this as an intense humiliation. One such patriot was a Junker who had represented Prussia at the Frankfurt parliament in 1848 and was seen as a strong opponent of liberalism and change – Otto von Bismarck. However, as a loyal Prussian he became increasingly anti-Austrian.

The revolutions in Germany in some ways revealed the weaknesses of nationalism, liberalism and democracy. The quarrels in the Frankfurt parliament and the very limited resistance offered to the restoration of princely authority throughout Germany indicated that revolution would not occur easily. It also suggested that unification could not be brought about by parliamentary means. The Prussian nobleman and statesman Otto von Bismarck put this strongly in a speech of 1862: 'The great questions of the day were not settled by speeches and parliamentary majorities – that was the mistake of 1848 – but by blood and iron' (that is, by military force and economic power).

This also showed the influence that outside powers had, even indirectly, on German affairs. Prussia's war with Denmark on behalf of the new German government was stopped due to fears of Russian and British hostility. Austria's defeats of revolutions outside Germany were effective, and Austria had the support of Russia and its large armies.

In addition, the weaknesses of leaders were revealed. Archduke Johann, the parliamentary leaders and Frederick Wilhelm IV were not able to harness national feeling or lead the movement for change. There was no inspirational figure, such as Count Cavour, Giuseppe Garibaldi or Carlo Alberto. Despite the cultural developments, trade agreements and advances in railways and industry, Germans were not united enough to bring about a new state. However, the events of 1848–49 showed that the existing situation was not secure either.

There was too much excitement and discussion about change for Germany to simply go back to how it had been in 1815. In this sense, the constitutional gains were not all lost. When the unification of German did come about, the mistakes of 1848–49 were not repeated, although the divisions did not simply disappear.

Consequence: Which of these statements is closest to the truth?

- Little that was positive came of the Revolutions of 1848.
- The 1848 Revolutions had important consequences and were not a complete failure.

SOURCE 6.1

Historical narratives of the 1848 Revolutions commonly end with an elegiac [mournful] reflection on the failure of revolution, the triumph of reaction, the execution, imprisonment, persecution or exile of radical activists. It is a commonplace that the restoration of order in 1848–49 ushered in an era of reaction in Prussia.

Yet there was no return to the conditions of the pre-March era. Nor should we think of the revolutions as a failure. The Prussian upheavals of 1848 were not, to borrow A.J.P. Taylor's phrase, 'a turning point where Prussia 'failed to turn'. They were a watershed between an old world and a new.

Clarke, C. 2006. **The Iron Kingdom.** *London. Allen Lane. p. 501.*

SOURCE 6.2

Parliamentary assemblies had gained no credit in the events of 1848–50, whereas it was the armies that had won in the end. When the gatherings of enthusiastic middle-class representatives had finished talking, it was the professional armies of Russia, Austria and Prussia, under their professional generals that settled the fate of Europe. Governments would in future rely much more on organised military power to achieve their ends.

Thompson, D. 1957. **Europe Since Napoleon.** *London. Longman. p. 234.*

Compare the views expressed in Sources 6.1 and 6.2.

6.2 How strong were Austria and Prussia after 1848?

Austria's problems in the 1850s

The revolution in Austria in 1848 was followed by a counter-revolution: the constitution granted in 1849 was revoked in 1851, and Franz Joseph ruled as an absolute monarch. However, not only did the government enforce its authority within Austria, it looked to do the same in Germany.

At first, with the defeat of the Prussian Union Plan at Olmutz, it appeared as if Austria was able to regain its position and that Prussia had suffered a major humiliation. However, Austria, despite its efforts, was unable to create an 'Austrian Middle Europe' that included all the German states and the Habsburg Empire, and instead the German Confederation was re-established. Austria also introduced a number of policies that alienated many. Firstly, they insisted that all civil servants, judges and army officers had to speak German, which alienated non-Germans in the Austrian Empire. Secondly, the 1855 Concordat with the Catholic church, which made Catholicism the state religion in the Austrian Empire, angered German Protestants and anti-clerical liberals. However, perhaps Austria's greatest problem was its economy. It attempted, but failed to create a customs union between Austria and the Zollverein in 1849. This was followed in 1851 by an attempt to establish an alternative customs union between Austria and the German states outside the Zollverein. These failures meant that Austria was excluded from the Prussian dominated economic-coalition in Germany.

Despite this, the Austrian economy grew in the 1850s, but its finances were a major problem and it was unable to reduce its large deficit, which had only been increased by having to suppress the revolutions of 1848. Therefore, despite its 'victory' at Olmutz, it was weakened both economically and financially.

It also lost international prestige with its defeats against the French in the 1850s at Magenta and Solferino, in part because it had been unable to reform its army because of its financial plight, but also because it was poorly led. As a result, its position in Italy was weakened with the loss of Lombardy to Piedmont. Moreover, the cost of these conflicts further weakened Austria's perilous financial position. It also lost the friendship of Russia by not backing it in the Crimean War, leaving it further weakened and largely friendless. This further weakened its position not just in Europe, but particularly in the German Confederation, while Prussia's strength, particularly economic, continued to grow.

Prussian recovery and growth

Although it appeared that Prussia had suffered a political humiliation at Olmutz, its power within Germany grew in the 1850s. This was largely due to its economic success, with industrial production more than doubling. The reasons for this economic growth are much debated by historians, with some arguing it was largely due to the success of the Zollverein, but others have argued that as the Zollverein did not protect Prussian industry it must have been the result of other factors. It has been suggested that the supply of raw materials such as iron and coal were important and their development was further encouraged by the growth in railways, which also meant it had a good communications network. At the same time, rail development was encouraged by the state, who subsidised its building. This economic growth gave it a considerable advantage over Austria.

Prussian liberalism also continued to grow, despite repressive policies after the 1848 Revolutions. There was a growing middle-class, which joined liberal associations and became influential across Germany, not just in Prussia. They won seats in elected assemblies and both left and right wing liberals argued for national unity.

Reform also took place in Prussia, despite the conservative views of the Minister-President (1850–58) Otto Theodor von Manteuffel. He believed that the best way to prevent further revolution was to improve the living and working conditions of the people. As a result, there was reform in both the countryside and towns. The peasants were freed from their feudal obligations to landlords and loans were made available for them to buy land. In the towns, economic growth helped improve conditions and the government also encouraged a minimum wage and appointed inspectors to improve factory conditions.

Political change was further encouraged with the accession to the Prussian throne in 1861 of William I. Not only did he dismiss Manteuffel, but his reign ushered in an era of greater freedom in comparison with the earlier period. However, it was his belief that if Prussia was to achieve greatness it needed a modern and reformed army that transformed the situation and ultimately brought Bismarck to power.

6.3 How did Bismarck rise to power?

In September 1862, Otto von Bismarck became the chancellor of Prussia. Under his leadership, the dreams of the nationalists for a united nation were fulfilled in a way that seemed impossible after the failures of 1848–49. The new Germany grew into a military and economic power of great strength. The creation of this new power in central Europe was profoundly significant for world history. It was fundamental to two massive world wars in the 20th century, and to the Cold War that lasted from 1945 to 1989.

Early life

Otto Eduard Leopold von Bismarck-Schönhausen was born on 1 April 1815. His father was a landowning Prussian gentleman, of a class known as the Junker (see 5.1, The leading powers by the end of the 18th century). On his estate in eastern Prussia, Otto's father spent his time farming, hunting, fishing and drinking. His mother was from a more aristocratic background. After a wild time at university, Bismarck did not seek a military career. Instead, he took a minor post in the Prussian civil service at Aachen in 1836. Here, he neglected his duties. As a result, he was sent to Potsdam in disgrace as a lower court official, a position that bored him. Attempts to evade a year of military training failed and in 1839 he returned home to run the family estates. Drunkenness, reckless rides and use of pistols earned Bismarck the nickname 'the Mad Junker', and this large, restless man seemed to have ambitions far beyond being a rural squire. Bismarck entered the circle of

Otto von Bismarck (1815-1898):

Bismarck was born into a moderately wealthy Prussian Junker or landowning noble family. However, his mother was from a middle-class merchant family from Hamburg. He was brought up in a deeply conservative household and did not get on well with his mother. He entered the civil service and then did a year's military service. He returned to help run the family estates after the death of his mother. He married in 1847 and became involved in Prussian politics, entering the Prussian diet and serving as the Prussian delegate to the Bundestag.

influential Christian nobles who had connections with the Prussian king. He became the friend and protégé of Ernst von Gerlach, an influential conservative politician and judge, and threw himself into local politics. He became one of the most extreme conservatives, defending the crown and opposing reforms such as full civil rights for Jews.

Figure 6.1: Otto von Bismarck

The revolution of 1848: the ultra-conservative Bismarck

In March 1848, revolutions took place in Berlin. Street demonstrations forced King Frederick Wilhelm IV to agree to a new constitution. Bismarck, appalled, was prepared to raise a peasant army against the revolution, but this was too much even for the royal family. Bismarck was deeply opposed to revolution and wrote extreme monarchist articles for the ultra-conservative newspaper *The New Prussian Daily*. In 1848, the king rejected a suggestion that Bismarck serve in a new government in Prussia on the grounds that Bismarck was bloodthirsty – a 'red reactionary, only to be used when the bayonet rules'. In 1849, Bismarck was elected to the new Prussian Landtag (Assembly). He supported the king's decision not to accept the German crown offered by the Frankfurt parliament. Bismarck had no interest in Frederick being anything more than the King of Prussia. In no sense did he believe in German nationalism. However, he did believe in greater Prussian power.

Austria forced Prussia to renounce the Erfurt Union at the Declaration of Olmütz in November 1850. Bismarck disliked the king's humiliation but he was not troubled by the failure of a more united Germany. He was more concerned for Prussian interests.

Bismarck's conservatism and loyalty to the crown gained him the post of Prussian ambassador to the Bund, the old Austrian-dominated organisation for Germany based in Frankfurt, in 1851. He made a point in offending the Austrian envoys and in trying to undermine Austrian interests, all the time promoting the views of Prussia.

Changes from 1858: the new era

In 1858, Bismarck suffered a setback: the illness and mental breakdown of King Frederick Wilhelm IV (see Section 5.6) led to a new regime under his brother, the regent Prince **Wilhelm I**. In the so-called 'New Era', the foreign minister and the conservatives who previously supported Bismarck now deserted him, to be replaced by more liberal ministers. Bismarck did not keep his job and was sent to the embassy in Russia instead.

Wilhelm I (1797–1888):

Wilhelm was Wilhelm I of Prussia from 1861–88, and became the first German emperor in 1871. He was the second son of Frederick Wilhelm III. Poorly educated, he was a soldier who had fought in Napoleon's armies and suppressed the 1848–49 rebels. He was known as the 'Prince of Grapeshot' (grapeshot being a type of cannon ammunition). His wife, Augusta of Saxe-Weimar, had come to detest Bismarck as early as 1848. Wilhelm supported Bismarck consistently but their relationship was always volatile. Wilhelm's son, Frederick, and his English wife, Victoria (the eldest daughter of Queen Victoria I of Britain), viewed Bismarck as the enemy.

Bismarck was known as a determined diplomat and strong defender of the Prussian monarchy. He won the admiration of Prussia's military leaders, especially **Albrecht von Roon**, with whom he had been friendly since 1839. Bismarck was frustrated by the growth of liberal opinion in Prussia's parliament and the unwillingness of the government to take a more active stance against Austria.

Albrecht von Roon (1803–79):

Roon was a deeply monarchist and conservative general who had been a friend of Bismarck since the 1830s. His plans for army reforms sparked the crisis that brought Bismarck to power. He was an expert in military geography and had met Bismarck while surveying East Prussia. He was an instructor at the Staff College in Berlin and was later promoted to the General Staff. He was concerned about inefficiency in the army and proposed the first major changes since the time of the Napoleonic Wars. He was made Minister of War by the regent, Wilhelm, in 1859. Supported by like-minded officers, such as Manteuffel and Moltke, he was determined to reform the army and needed the support of Bismarck, a tough-minded civilian diplomat and politician, to do this.

In 1859, Austria went to war against France, but Prussia's army was too weak to take advantage of this situation as Bismarck wanted. Also, there was no political motivation among Prussia's rulers to act against Austria. The weakness of plans for mobilisation in 1859 had worried the king and army leaders, and they appointed Roon as a reforming minister of war in November 1859.

Roon proposed increasing the army by 23 000 more men, creating 49 new regiments and separating the Landwehr (the part-time reserve army) from the professional field army. He also wanted a larger, better-trained, better-led force with a three-year military service period. In February 1860, the Prussian parliament strongly objected to Roon's proposals, fearing the use of a professional army against parliament in the future and defending the 'citizen army' of the Landwehr. The Prussians refused to give Roon the necessary funds, and tensions ran high.

This was a crucial turning point. To overcome Austrian dominance and become a greater power, Prussia needed a larger, stronger army. Yet the liberals feared this would lead to a militaristic state and undermine the constitution. After 1848, Wilhelm feared revolution if he supported the changes to the army. However, he knew that they were essential. The situation required a strong leader – if there was too much provocation, the monarchy might fall.

In the elections of May 1862, the liberals gained a substantial majority and rejected Roon's proposed military budget. Roon urged for Bismarck, who had been sent as ambassador to Paris, to return. Wilhelm reluctantly agreed to install a strongman to end the crisis. On 17 September, while in Paris, Bismarck received the following telegram from Roon: '*Periculum in Mora. Dépêchez-vous.*' ('Danger in delay. Come at once.') On his return to Prussia, Wilhelm appointed Bismarck minister-president on 22 September 1862.

'Blood and iron'

A week into his appointment as minister-president, Bismarck made his views known in his 'blood and iron' speech:

SOURCE 6.3

Prussia must build up and preserve her strength for the advantageous moment which has already come and gone many times. Under the Treaty of Vienna, Prussia's borders were not ensuring the healthy existence of the State. The great questions of the day were not settled by speeches and parliamentary majorities – that was the mistake of 1848 – but by blood and iron.

Bismarck speaking before the Budget Committee of the Prussian Landtag, 29 September 1862.

ACTIVITY

Look carefully at Bismarck's 'blood and iron' speech (Source 6.3) and analyse its meaning and significance. Think about:

- What did Bismarck mean in the first sentence – what moments had Prussia failed to take advantage of?
- Why were the borders of 1815 so unfavourable?
- What did Bismarck mean about 1848?
- What did he mean by 'blood and iron'?
- Why do you think Bismarck made the speech to that particular group in the parliament?
- Why did his speech cause so much uproar?

This speech caused uproar and the king nearly sacked him. Bismarck's memoirs of the 1890s recall a dramatic scene. Wilhelm told him: 'They will cut off your head – and mine a little while afterwards', to which Bismarck replied '*Et après?*' (And afterwards?) We will all die sooner or later and can we perish more honourably – I fighting for my king's cause and your majesty dealing with his blood rights as king by the grace of God.'

Bismarck as prime minister?

Bismarck was not a popular figure and he was not well known to the people of Prussia. What they heard about him was unfavourable – he was described as an extreme, undemocratic Junker. Educated Prussians saw him as a brutal, cynical, provincial amateur politician. The king, and especially the queen, were fearful that Bismarck would bring down the monarchy. On the other hand, Bismarck's devoted allies saw him as a strong outsider who was worth taking a risk for – if he failed, Prussia would never be strong enough to be a great power.

Bismarck's judgement of the strength of the liberal opposition is significant here. The liberals of 1862 were, in his mind, the failed revolutionaries of 1848–49, with neither the conviction nor the popular support to carry out an equivalent of the French Revolution of 1789–93. Bismarck saw their ideology as devoid of passion, and he viewed the liberals themselves as lacking the personal dynamism to resist his realism. The 'blood and iron' speech was a masterly summing up: talk had failed; only action would bring about change. With the backing of the army and the support of the king, Bismarck held a powerful position. Without the support of the urban masses, the middle-class liberals could do little to resist him.

Although it was unlikely that the liberals would effectively oppose him, Bismarck still needed to justify his actions in a state that prided itself on law and order. He therefore came up with the 'gap theory' (*Lücketheorie*) – if parliament failed to grant money to expand the Prussian army, then Bismarck could take advantage of a legal gap (loophole) that allowed the government to collect taxes without parliament's approval. This is exactly what Bismarck did between 1862 and 1865. However, with a nervous king and a hostile queen, little experience in governing and a poor reputation, Bismarck knew he would not be able to retain this dictator-like power for long. He therefore needed success to convince the monarchy, the military and the nation that he was taking Prussia forward. He, too, was conscious that opportunities to take advantage of Austria's weaknesses in 1859 had been missed, so some swift successes were vital.

> **DISCUSSION POINT**
>
> What does the 'gap theory' indicate about Bismarck's attitudes to parliamentary government? Why was there not more resistance to Bismarck?

The debates

The successes that Bismarck sought came quickly:

- Bismarck secured the neutrality of Russia, which made no attempt to intervene in German affairs as it had previously done.
- Austria was drawn into a war against Denmark in 1864. Disagreement about the gains from this war led to a war between Austria and Prussia in 1866.
- The other European powers did not interfere and Prussia was allowed to defeat Austria and its German allies. The victory of 1866 silenced most liberal opposition.
- Bismarck annexed some lands in north Germany and set up a Prussian-dominated North German Confederation in 1867 in alliance with the south German states.
- In 1870, he provoked and then won a war against France, which was seen as a threat to the new Germany. France was unable to ally with any major European power.
- As a result, Bismarck set up a German empire in 1871, transforming central Europe and bringing Germany under Prussian control.

The odds against these developments happening so quickly were enormous. In 1862, Prussia was deeply divided, with the new Minister-President widely feared and disliked. The Prussian armies had not fought a major war independently and successfully since the 18th century. Austria was still a powerful military force and had greater support in other parts of Germany than Prussia, which was widely mistrusted. The other European powers – France, Britain and Russia – had no interest in seeing a strong power emerge in central Europe, and there was every expectation that they would interfere to prevent a massive change in the European hierarchy of power.

Did Bismarck achieve major change against the odds simply by taking advantage of events, or did he have a clear idea of what to do? Would the unification of Germany have come about because of historical trends and pressures even if Bismarck had gone back to being ambassador in Paris or running his country estates in Brandenburg?

DISCUSSION POINT

Historians such as C. Grant Robertson (1919) and Bismarck's biographer, Emil Ludwig (1922–24) assume that Bismarck had a distinct plan, and this remained the common view well into the 1960s. Keep this debate in mind as the events of the 1860s are discussed, so that you can assess these historians' views.

In June 1862, Bismarck attended a gathering at the home of the Russian ambassador in London. It was attended by the future British prime minister **Benjamin Disraeli**. Disraeli recorded what Bismarck said.

SOURCE 6.4

I shall soon be compelled to undertake the conduct of the Prussian government. My first care will be to reorganise the army, with or without the help of the Landtag. As soon as the army has been brought into a condition to inspire respect I shall seize the first pretext to declare war on Austria, dissolve the German Bund, subdue the minor states and give national unity to Germany under Prussian leadership.

British prime minister Benjamin Disraeli's account of Bismarck's views, given during a visit to London in June 1862.

Benjamin Disraeli (1804–81):

Disraeli was a writer and politician who became Conservative prime minister of Britain from 1874 to 1880. He believed in social reform, imperialism and defending Britain's interests in foreign policy. Disraeli worked with Bismarck in 1878, and Bismarck admired him.

In his memoirs, written in the 1890s, Bismarck reinforced the idea that his policies had been planned. Older historians and early biographers accepted this. The English historian Herbert Fisher wrote in 1935:

SOURCE 6.5

Only the most elaborate military and diplomatic preparations could ensure the success of German unification. The titanic figure of Bismarck was Nature's lavish response to these exacting requirements. While infinitely flexible in detail, he envisaged from the first the conditions of the German problem and allowed no scruple of conscience to interfere with the execution of his plans. Bismarck got the wars which from the first he had seen to be essential to his political designs.

Fisher, H. A. L. 1935. **A History of Europe.** *London. Eyre & Spottiswood. p. 376.*

Friedrich Meinecke, in *The German Catastrophe* (Beacon Press, 1946), saw Bismarck's plan leading to wars and dictatorship. However, an influential counter-view came in 1958 with Alan Taylor's biography of Bismarck:

SOURCE 6.6

During Bismarck's first few months of office he had been trying to carry out a preconceived plan – a plan formally advocated by him for more than a decade. Now he discovered that events would not conform to his plan; and he began to live with reality instead of trying to force his will on it. By January 1863 he came to realise that European politics could not be forced into a pattern by a man of ruthless will.

Taylor, A. J. P. 1958. **Bismarck: The Man and the Statesman.** *London. Hamish Hamilton. pp. 64–65.*

Taylor's account portrays Bismarck responding to circumstances, with an end result for which he had not planned.

Historians have moved between these views. Otto Pflanze, writing in *Bismarck and the Development of Germany* (Princeton University Press,

1963), argued for a middle course – the so-called 'strategy of alternatives' – whereby Bismarck had fall-back positions within a broad strategy. In a 2002 biography, Edgar Feuchtwanger wrote:

SOURCE 6.7

Great men like Bismarck can only do their work because they know how to use the circumstances and pressures of their time. Prussia, the Zollverein, the national liberal movement, industrialisation and other historical figures lay to hand, but the way Bismarck used them was not premeditated.

Feuchtwanger, E. 2002. **Bismarck.** *London. Routledge. p. 261.*

Jonathan Steinberg returns to the older idea of a political genius:

SOURCE 6.8

The power he exercised came from him as a person, not from institutions or forces and factors. The power rested on the sovereignty of an extraordinary, gigantic self, he was that rare character, a 'political genius, a manipulator of the political realities of his time'.

Steinberg, J. 2011. **Bismarck: A Life.** *Oxford. Oxford University Press. pp. 4–5.*

DISCUSSION POINT

It is helpful to keep these views of Bismarck in mind through the survey of key elements that follows. What does the evidence show in support of these models?

A manipulator of events	Someone driven by events
Unification deriving from the policies of genius	Unification coming from a variety of complex circumstances
Unification as a triumph	Unification as a tragedy

Theory of Knowledge

Subjective interpretation:

If historians disagree, does this weaken or strengthen history as a discipline? Is it possible to be objective when writing about the past? A postmodernist view would deny that words themselves have any meaning outside the perception and experience of the reader. As Geoffrey Elton stated in *The Practice of History* (Fontana Press, 1967), do the professional skills of historians allow them to avoid subjective 'interpretations', or does simply writing about the past at all mean that historians are bound to be subjective?

6.4 What led to the creation of the North German Confederation?

Bismarck was determined to continue with his policies. He prevented Wilhelm I from attending an Austrian-backed conference to discuss changes to the Bund. To allow such changes would be to acknowledge that the Bund could be reformed and would give Austria the initiative, making Prussia merely one of the German states who followed. Bismarck's aim was to abolish the Bund, not to reform it.

Bismarck also took advantage of every opportunity to win diplomatic support. One opportunity came in 1863 when the Poles revolted against Russian rule. Prussia also had a Polish population, as a result of annexations of Poland by Austria, Prussia and Russia at the end of the 18th century. As an east Prussian, Bismarck had little sympathy with the Poles – either racially or in any cause of freedom. It therefore made good sense to cooperate with Russia. The Alvensleben Convention, named after **Gustav von Alvensleben**, was signed in February 1863 for joint Prussian and Russian action against the Poles. The Convention was a step too far, and the other European powers opposed it. In the end, Bismarck merely agreed to be neutral and to not aid the Poles.

Gustav von Alvensleben (1803–81):

Alvensleben was the Prussian king's adjutant (military officer). He was chosen by Bismarck to agree a plan with Russia to defeat the Polish rebels. However, the agreement was renounced after opposition from the other European powers.

Bismarck's neutrality was welcomed in Russia; it was one of the reasons why Russia did not intervene in the wars of the 1860s and stood by to allow Prussia to expand. Russia even threatened to mobilise against Austria in 1870 if it interfered in the war between France and Prussia, so this Prussian policy of gaining Russia's friendship turned out to be of crucial importance.

Denmark

There were two provinces on the border of the kingdom of Denmark and the German Bund, called Schleswig and Holstein. Holstein was predominantly German-speaking and part of the Confederation; Schleswig had a more mixed Danish and German-speaking population and was not part of the Confederation. The king of Denmark was also the duke of Schleswig, the duke of Holstein and part of the German Bund. When King Frederick of Denmark died in 1863, he left no direct heir so his distant relative **Christian of Augustenberg** inherited the throne. However, there was some disagreement about Christian's claim to be duke of Schleswig and Holstein as well – a German duke of Augustenberg also claimed these duchies, and was enthusiastically supported by many German nationalists.

Christian of Augustenberg (1803–81):

Duke Christian of Augustenberg claimed Schleswig and Holstein, having ruled these duchies in 1850 as the head of a provisional government supported by German nationalists. He was ousted by Denmark, but his claim was supported by Russia and confirmed by international agreement in 1852. He later renounced his claim, although his son Frederick (1829–80) took it up in 1863; though supported by the Bund, Frederick was rejected by Bismarck. Although Frederick was Danish, he was seen as the 'German' claimant and in fact served in the Prussian army in 1870.

The states in the Bund rallied in favour of Augustenberg. However, Bismarck did not want to see the duke inherit – it would add to the power of the Bund, which was dominated by Austria. He had no interest in German nationalism as such, and managed to persuade Austria not to support the Bund or Augustenberg but to join with Prussia and act against Denmark. In retrospect, Austria was highly unwise to do this. Supporting the Bund would have raised Austria's standing in Germany at the expense of Prussia. However, Austria did not want to encourage German nationalism, so was persuaded to go to war to gain territory.

Figure 6.2: Prussian soldiers at Düppel, 18 April 1864, after the storming of Danish defences during the Schleswig–Holstein war

Prussian forces defeated the Danes at the Battle of Düppel on 18 April 1864. Austria then occupied Holstein and Prussia occupied Schleswig. The duke of Augustenberg gained nothing. Prussia now appeared as the champion of German nationalism by taking on and defeating the Danes.

The victory at Düppel was also a demonstration of success for Prussia's new army, and weakened opposition in the Prussian parliament to army reforms. It also showed that the other European powers, such as Britain and Russia, who had objected to German intervention in the region in 1848, were not going to interfere in German affairs.

The Convention of Gastein in 1865 established a short-lived agreement between Austria and Prussia over the duchies. Did Bismarck now deliberately plan a war with Austria by promoting agitation in the two duchies for annexation by Prussia? He demanded control over the military forces in both duchies and announced plans for a military canal – the Kiel Canal. The Austrian administration in Holstein objected to this Prussian intervention, and relations with Austria grew worse.

War with Austria

By the summer of 1865, Bismarck, Wilhelm I and the Prussian military chiefs were discussing a war with Austria. Bismarck's diplomacy focused on determining the extent of French friendship and neutrality, and to this end he met the French emperor Napoleon III in October 1865.

From this meeting, Bismarck understood that Napoleon would be neutral if Prussia went to war with Austria, although Napoleon did not officially agree to this. In April 1865, Prussia signed a military alliance with Italy that was valid for three months. This stated that Italy would have Venetia in the event of a joint war against Austria.

Then, on 9 April 1866, Bismarck made an astonishing proposal – there should be a new Bund parliament elected by all German males over 25 years. The most reactionary noble in Prussia now sought public support for his war with Austria by proposing a democratic voting system for Germany.

Bismarck gambled on many things at this stage, including Russian and French neutrality and British unwillingness to commit forces to support Austria. He speculated that Austria had been weakened by defeats in Italy, and that Prussian military reforms and the leadership of his ally Field Marshal **Helmut von Moltke** would be strong enough to result in a swift Prussian victory. He also gambled that the war would be supported by Prussian nationalists and that any internal opposition to the war would disappear as soon as Prussia defeated Austria. He predicted that an Austrian defeat would allow Prussia to link its territories and establish dominance over north Germany. There is little indication that Bismarck had the wider aim of German unification.

> **Helmut von Moltke (1800–91):**
>
> Moltke was one of the greatest generals since Napoleon I. He believed in planning, getting troops efficiently to the battlefields and then being flexible. He supported Bismarck and the army reforms.

On 9 June 1866, Prussian troops invaded Holstein. Austria got the support of every member of the Bund except one in opposing Prussia, so Bismarck declared the Bund to be dissolved. A long German civil war may have resulted in French and Russian intervention. Few in Europe saw Prussia as the stronger power.

The Prussian military campaign against Austria

The Austrians assembled large forces in Bohemia (the modern-day Czech Republic, then an Austrian province) to invade Prussian Silesia. However, they were faced with opposition from Prussian forces much sooner than expected, as the rapid mobilisation of Prussian troops and the use of railways meant that three Prussian armies invaded Bohemia. Their superior needle gun meant they had an advantage over Austrian's army.

The Prussian and Austrian armies clashed at Sadowa on 3 July 1866. Although Austria had the larger army, it failed to take advantage of this, and the rapid movement of the main Prussian army meant that 100 000 more Prussian troops joined the battle. This gave Prussia 221 000 men against the Austrian and Saxon force of 206 000. The outcome of the battle was a heavy defeat for Austria, with substantial casualties.

The war with Austria continued until 22 July, when a decisive battle ended Austria's control of Germany.

Austria's German allies took little part in the fighting. The Italians launched attacks on Austria, but did less well, losing in most of their encounters – with the exception of Garibaldi's alpine campaign. Nevertheless, Italy benefited from the Prussian victory in gaining Venetia.

The results of Prussian victory

The Peace of Prague signed in August 1866 gave Venetia to Italy as promised. Austria lost no territory, apart from the recently occupied Holstein, but it did lose control of Germany. The Bund was replaced by a North German Confederation that was dominated by Prussia. There were no reparations or victory parades. Russia was pleased to see its main rival in Eastern Europe humiliated. Britain had no real interest in the outcome of the war. France was taken aback by the speed of events, and Napoleon III felt he had been cheated of the chance to mediate or to support Austria and thereby increase his influence in central Europe.

Bismarck now became the hero of German nationalism. The victory against Austria softened parliamentary opposition to him. Bismarck took advantage of this change in attitude by introducing an Indemnity Bill that validated his prior collection of taxes without parliamentary consent (6.3, Bismarck as prime minister?). Bismarck could have argued that the illegality of his actions were justified by military victory, but he knew better – by voting to pass the Bill, parliament retrospectively corrected any suggestion of Bismarck's wrongdoing.

DISCUSSION POINT

The Treaty of Prague was more lenient than the army and King Wilhelm wanted. Was this because Bismarck already had an eye on the next war – with France – and did not want to rule out securing Austrian neutrality? Or were there more practical short-term issues – for example, the need to reduce costs and to end the war quickly before France intervened?

ACTIVITY

Carry out some further research on the Treaty of Prague and its consequences.

The key elements of this victory for Bismarck were the end of Austrian rule and the strengthening of Prussia, which annexed territory and dominated a unified north German state. It was the Kleindeutschland (small Germany) solution to German weakness. Any larger Prussian expansion would have included the Catholic states of south Germany, who were traditionally anti-Prussian, as well as Austria with its large multi-national empire and problems. Instead, Bismarck's north Germany was a predominantly Protestant state that could be controlled by the strong Prussian army and economy. Bismarck did not want a dictatorship or an absolute monarchy, so he simply applied the Prussian parliamentary system to a wider area. This parliamentary system had proved totally incapable of opposing him, so provided the image of a modern parliamentary state without any of the inconvenience of a real liberal democracy. A smaller Germany, too, offered less of a threat to neighbouring states and therefore a greater likelihood of being accepted as a fellow power in Europe.

Analysis: did Bismarck plan the war?

It is doubtful that Bismarck was only interested in the duchies of
Schleswig and Holstein as a way of engineering a war with Austria. The
area was on Prussia's borders. If the duke of Augustenberg had gained
control of the duchies with the help of the Austrian-dominated Bund,
this would have threatened Prussia. To have acted alone by sending
Prussian forces would have risked a war with Austria, opposition from
the Bund, and possible intervention by other European powers to help
Denmark, whose boundaries had been guaranteed by international
treaties. The Austrians, under foreign minister **Johann von Rechberg-
Rothenlöwen**, were willing to support Prussia in war since they feared
French intervention and were unwilling to stir up German nationalism.

> **Johann von Rechberg-Rothenlöwen (1806–99):**
>
> Rechberg was a Bavarian noble who was in Austrian service as
> a diplomat. He was Austrian foreign minister from 1859–64. He
> allowed himself to be manipulated by Otto von Bismarck into the
> joint war against Denmark.

The Prussian attack on Danish fortifications of Düppel resulted in
an easy victory, with only 1000 Prussian casualties. This, together
with the Prussian army's victory at Alsen Island, was used to show
the bravery and determination of the Prussian army, bringing it huge
popularity at home.

Did the joint occupation of Denmark in 1864 mean war between
Austria and Prussia was inevitable? The presence of Austrian forces in
Holstein was not something that Prussia could have tolerated. Austria
saw this and offered to withdraw in return for compensation in Silesia.
An agreement was reached in August 1865 in the Convention of
Gastein for joint sovereignty: occupation of Holstein by Austria and
occupation of Schleswig by Prussia. However, on 28 February 1866,
Bismarck made it clear to the Prussian Council that its mission was to
lead Germany and that Austria stood in its way of doing so. Bismarck
had met Napoleon III at Biarritz in 1865 and was confident that the
French would not support Austria in any future war. There is also little
doubt that Bismarck was preparing for war when Prussian troops were
mobilised in April.

What is less clear is whether Bismarck expected a short war with Austria. Austrian armies had endured heavy losses in Italy in 1859 and fought well in Denmark. Also, Austria had the support of most of Germany and interior lines of communication, whereas the Prussian forces had to be split to get to Austria by rail. There was little indication that Austria was economically weak; furthermore, industrial capacity was not a significant factor in a war that lasted only seven weeks. The Prussians had the breech-loading needle gun, while the Austrians had rifled artillery that was more accurate and had a longer range. However, Austrian shock tactics of rapid frontal assaults were ineffective when faced with the rapid-firing breech-loading Prussian rifles. Yet the key element was Austria's inferior military leadership and organisation. Ludwig von Benedek, the Austrian military commander, allowed Austria to be attacked on high ground at Sadowa. He mismanaged the battle and gave Prussia too many chances to use their superior rifles.

While the Prussian army's rapid victory against Austria justified Bismarck's dedicated anti-Austrian policy, the outcome of the battle was unexpected.

Figure 6.3: Lithograph of 1866 showing the Battle of Sadowa

The counter-view

Some historians argue that, even after the joint control of the duchies, Prussia's war with Austria was not inevitable or planned:

> **SOURCE 6.9**
>
> There was no reason to suppose that joint control of the duchies would necessarily lead to a quarrel. Powers usually learn from working together how to work together…Why should not Schelswig and Holstein be the cement of a new…partnership?
>
> *Taylor, A. J. P. 1958.* **Bismarck: The Man and the Statesman.** *London. Hamish Hamilton. pp. 73–74.*

In Taylor's view, Bismarck and the Austrian leader Rechberg came close to an agreement on Prussian annexation of the duchies. However, could Austria have accepted any solution that left Prussia in complete control of the duchies without substantial compensation – and would Bismarck have offered anything meaningful?

The key question here is: did Bismarck simply deal with the duchies when the issue arose in 1863 and then, once he had ensured a Prussian military presence there, move on to getting Austria out of both the duchies and Germany; or did he have a long-term intention to fight Austria and simply needed a valid excuse?

> **ACTIVITY**
>
> In a group, produce two posters: one supporting the view that Bismarck planned the war with Austria and one arguing that he did not. State your arguments clearly – posters are hard to read with too much detail, but try to make a strong case. Display the posters and hold a class vote on which is more convincing.

The results of the war of 1866

Prussia was now dominant in Germany. The other German states had backed the losing side in Austria and had to accept what Prussia demanded:

- Austria was forced back on its homeland and, in 1867, made an agreement with the largest of its eastern possessions, Hungary, for joint rule called Ausgleich. This created the Austro–Hungarian empire. The new empire gave up any attempt to dominate Germany.

- The North German Confederation was created in 1867. This established a federal north Germany with Prussia in charge.
    ◦ King Wilhelm I of Prussia was the overall ruler of the Confederation.
    ◦ Bismarck ran the new federal government as well as the Prussian government.
    ◦ Bismarck gave every adult male the right to vote (universal male suffrage) for the new parliament of the Confederation. He trusted the mass of the Prussian people to support him because they had been so enthusiastic about the war against Austria. He thought ordinary Prussians were conservative and monarchist at heart.
    ◦ Prussia annexed some German states and allowed others to be part of the Confederation and run their own affairs, but Bismarck controlled the army and foreign policy. This maintained Prussia's power and his own influence.
- The liberals ended their opposition to Bismarck, and the National Liberals became his greatest supporters in the new parliament.
- The military budget was now out of parliament's control and the prestige and special position of the Prussian army was elevated. In alliance with the great armaments firm of Krupp, Prussia built up its weapons, especially rifled artillery. There were other military developments, including the setting up of a general staff and military planning that made particular use of the railway system that had proved so instrumental in the victory of 1866.

It was clear that the new Germany was a major European power that was financially and economically strong, well-supported by German nationalist opinion and led by a successful minister.

Who lost from the events of 1866–67?

There were various losers from the events of 1866–67:

- The liberals, who wanted peace and a new Germany that was not based on Prussian military strength, viewed Bismarck as a cynic who sought to undermine true parliamentary rule.
- Independent states lost land and independence – for instance, Hanover was annexed by Prussia, and Saxony lost substantial lands to Prussia.
- Württemberg, Baden and the southern states of Bavaria kept their right of self-government, but were forced into military alliances with Prussia that compromised their independence. They showed their

resentment by voting against Prussia in the Zoll parliament – the assembly that ran the Zollverein, which continued after the war. These largely Catholic states resented the Austrian defeat.

- The greatest loser, however, was France. The opportunities for France to be the main power in Europe were much reduced. The Prussian army, rather than the French army, was now seen to be dominant.

Opinion in France became more and more anti-Prussian. It was unlikely that France would form any alliance with Russia, and Austria had been removed as an effective ally. Indeed, France now had little to offer to Prussia as an ally. Napoleon III was increasingly isolated while Bismarck became the up-and-coming statesman of Europe.

> **KEY CONCEPTS QUESTION**
>
> **Consequence:** Who won and who lost as a result of the war of 1866? In groups, each person takes a winner or loser and explains to the class the feelings of that person regarding the events of 1866. Make it as personal as possible; for example, give the views of Napoleon III rather than those of France.

6.5 Why was there war between Prussia and France in 1870–71?

The first indications of major tensions between Napoleon III and Bismarck came in 1867 with the Luxembourg crisis.

The Luxembourg crisis

Given his neutrality in the war of 1866, Napoleon III expected some support for the French acquisition of Luxembourg. The duchy of Luxembourg was owned by the Dutch king, though garrisoned by Prussia. Its people were French-speaking and it had little strategic significance.

In 1866, Bismarck hinted to the German ambassador that there would be 'no obstacles in the way of French expansion on the basis of French nationality'. Luxembourg was not included in the North German Confederation, and in 1867 Napoleon III was negotiating with the king to gain it for France. He thought that Bismarck would agree.

However, when Bismarck told the German public about Napoleon III's ambitions in 1867, it resulted in a wave of national outrage in Germany and international concerns about French expansion. This meant that Bismarck could no longer support French claims on Luxembourg, despite his earlier suggestions to the contrary.

The Dutch king now broke off negotiations with Napoleon, his decision influenced by Bismarck's publication of secret military agreements with the south German states. Prussia would oppose the French acquisition of Luxembourg and provide military support in the event of a French invasion. There was now a threat of war if Napoleon acquired the duchy. To resolve the crisis, an international conference was held in London to guarantee Luxembourg's independence.

The French thought they had been misled and made to appear foolish. The Luxembourg crisis had almost caused a war.

Spain's revolutionary government

In 1868, Queen **Isabella II** was overthrown by a revolutionary government in Madrid.

Isabella II (1830–1904):

Isabella came to the throne as an infant in 1830. Her reign was marked by internal conflict and wars when more liberal elements (Carlists) fought to overthrow her and her reactionary advisers. In the 'Glorious Revolution' of 1868, the liberals forced her off the throne and she formally abdicated in 1870. Her son succeeded her in 1874.

Spain's new revolutionary government needed a head of state. It was not unusual to ask a foreign royal family to provide a ruler, and one candidate for this was Prince Leopold von Hohenzollern-Simaringen.

Leopold was nephew to the king of Prussia and was married to a Portuguese princess, so he had connections with Iberia. Bismarck urged the prince to agree to rule, but it was not until July 1870 that his candidacy was announced. This caused uproar in France, as it seemed that France would now be encircled by Prussia.

The French ambassador, Vincent de Benedetti, visited Wilhelm I at Bad Ems to put forward the French point of view. Wilhelm had been pressed to accept Prince Leopold by Bismarck, but agreed to withdraw the candidature without ill will.

The French pressed their advantage, sending Benedetti back to get a promise that it would not happen again, which Wilhelm could not agree to. The meeting was not angry as both men were embarrassed. Wilhelm sent a telegram explaining the meeting.

However, Bismarck edited the telegram to suggest a more acrimonious refusal by the king. There were storms of outrage in Paris, and France mobilised for war.

Debate: did Bismarck plan a war with France?

There is disagreement among historians about whether Bismarck planned the war with France, as Sources 6.8 and 6.9 show.

QUESTION

How far do Sources 6.10, 6.11 and 6.12 agree or disagree that Bismarck had no plans to go to war against France?

SOURCE 6.10

It would be...an exaggeration to say that Bismarck 'planned' the war with France. Bismarck was not an advocate of preventive war. It was, as he once remarked, equivalent to shooting yourself in the head because you were afraid to die. On the other hand, war with France was on his menu of options.

Clark, C. 2006. Iron Kingdom. London. Allen Lane. p. 549.

SOURCE 6.11

[Bismarck] had neither planned war, not even foreseen it. But he claimed it as his own once it became inevitable…Attention had to be diverted from his carelessness in giving France an opportunity to humiliate Prussia…Against all previous statements war had to appear necessary and inevitable.

Taylor, A. J. P. 1958. **Bismarck: The Man and the Statesman**. *London. Hamish Hamilton. p. 121.*

SOURCE 6.12

It was not enough to hem France in [by alliances with the southern states]. She must be coerced or lured into declaring war. The war could then be proclaimed a defensive one on behalf of German honour, security and independence, public opinion must be influenced to demand the chastisement of France. The Bismarckian version [of the Ems telegram] gladdened the gloomy hearts of Roon and Moltke. On July 19 1870, France declared war. Bismarck had won.

Grant Robertson, C. 1919. **Bismarck**. *London. Constable. pp. 232–34.*

Checking the evidence: the Ems Telegram

SOURCE 6.13

Ems, July 13, 1870.

To THE FEDERAL CHANCELLOR, COUNT BISMARCK, No. 61 EOD. 3:10 P.M. (STATION EMS: RUSH!)

His Majesty the King writes to me: 'M. Benedetti intercepted me on the Promenade in order to demand of me most insistently that I should authorize him to telegraph immediately to Paris that I shall obligate myself for all future time never again to give my approval to the candidacy of the Hohenzollerns should it be renewed. I refused to agree to this, the last time somewhat severely, informing him that one dare not and cannot assume such obligations *à tout jamais*. Naturally, I informed him that I had received no news as yet, and since he had been informed earlier than I by way of Paris and Madrid he could easily understand that my Government was once again out of the matter.'

Since then His Majesty has received a dispatch from the Prince [Karl Anton]. As His Majesty informed Count Benedetti that he was expecting news from the Prince, His Majesty himself, in view of the above-mentioned demand and in consonance with the advice of Count Eulenburg and myself, decided not to receive the French envoy again but to inform him through an adjutant that His Majesty had now received from the Prince confirmation of the news which Benedetti had already received from Paris, and that he had nothing further to say to the Ambassador. His Majesty leaves it to the judgment of Your Excellency whether or not to communicate at once the new demand by Benedetti and its rejection to our ambassadors and to the press. [Signed]

The original text of the Ems Telegram, July 1870; it was written by the diplomat Heinrich Abeken under Kaiser Wilhelm's instruction to Bismarck.

SOURCE 6.14

After the reports of the renunciation by the hereditary Prince of Hohenzollern had been officially transmitted by the Royal Government of Spain to the Imperial Government to the Imperial Government of France, the French Ambassador presented to His Majesty the King at Ems the demand to authorize him to telegraph to Paris that His Majesty the King would obligate himself for all future time never again to give his approval to the candidacy of the Hohenzollerns should it be renewed.

His Majesty the King thereupon refused to receive the French envoy again and informed him through an adjutant that His Majesty has nothing further to say to the Ambassador.

Bismarck's edited version of the Ems Telegram, which was made public.

QUESTION

How does Bismarck's edited version of the Ems Telegram (Source 6.14) give a different impression from the original (Source 6.13)?

The arguments turn on why Bismarck seemed so keen to promote the candidature of Prince Leopold.

Did Bismarck intend to go to war with France in 1870?

View A

One view is that Bismarck felt war with France was inevitable from 1866 and therefore wanted an excuse for war that would put France in the wrong. France was a threat, especially as the south German states were hostile to Prussia. At any time there might be an alliance between France, Catholic south Germany and Austria, who were far from reconciled to their defeat against Prussia.

After the Luxembourg crisis (see 6.5, The Luxembourg crisis), it did not seem possible to be on good terms with France, so the Spanish candidature was intended to provoke France. Bismarck expected that Prussia's stronger army, with its efficient railway system, improved artillery, needle guns and high morale, would win a war against France. This would solve the south German problem and complete the unification of Germany.

In this view, Bismarck's editing of the Ems Telegram was a clear indication of his plans for war.

View B

Another view is that because Bismarck liked to have various alternatives and possible diplomatic weapons at his disposal, his intention in supporting Leopold's candidate was to stir up French feeling and increase Bismarck's popularity at home. Bismarck also recognised that this might also be useful in building a case for war against France. However, he underestimated the reaction. The strength of popular opinion in France in turn stirred up Germany and left Bismarck with no option but to go to war.

According to this view, the war with France was not planned for 1870, nor was it expected at the start of the year. Bismarck did not particularly want to add millions of Catholic subjects and potential opponents to the enlarged Prussia, nor could he be certain of defeating France.

Problems in accepting View A

Supporters of View A need to be confident that Bismarck could foresee victory, when French equipment and military reputation were highly thought of in Europe. France had already defeated Austria and had large forces equipped with the superior Chassepot rifle. There was also the danger that Austria would intervene to support France against Prussia.

In the event, Russian threats prevented Austrian action, but Russia might have backed down if France had begun to win battles. Bismarck, too, needed to be confident in the support from Germany as a whole. German contributions to Austria's war in 1866 had been poor. Would German national feeling withstand defeats by France? Also, given Bismarck's views on national unification, did he really aim for greater unity at the cost of war?

As for the Ems Telegram, Bismarck altered only a few words and added nothing. The vital element was French insistence on a humiliating declaration rather than the way that Bismarck presented it. On 11 January 1869, Bismarck wrote to his envoy in Bavaria:

SOURCE 6.15

I think it probable that German unity would be advanced by violent events. But it is quite another matter to assume responsibility for bringing about a violent catastrophe…It is obvious that German unity is not a ripe fruit.

Letter of 11 January 1869 from Bismarck to his Bavarian envoy.

Bismarck's letter appears to confirm that it was not his deliberate and premeditated policy to bring about German unity by war with France. The key phrase is 'It is obvious that German unity is not a ripe fruit' – here Bismarck means that Germany was not ready yet for unification.

Bismarck's problem was that the Catholic south German states would need to be included in the new Germany, and France was a constant danger. The events of 1866 had stirred up powerful national feelings in Germany. Also, German military growth, especially in terms of new heavy artillery, had created the opportunity to have a final confrontation with France and take over the south German states. Despite Bismarck's assurances to Bavaria, it was probably a matter of when there would be another war and further unification rather than if.

Problems in accepting View B

Supporters of the second view need to consider whether Bismarck could truly not foresee the impact of his support of the Spanish candidature on French opinion. Given the way he had provoked France over Luxembourg, the continuing expansion of the German army, and the hostility to him in south Germany that might easily have led to an alliance with France, was his support of Leopold's candidature really only a scheme for some future action or negotiation?

Why was Bismarck so angry when King Wilhelm refused to support the candidature? Wilhelm had been against the idea, fearing that Leopold would be overthrown because of the unsettled political situation in Spain. He did not see the force of Bismarck's diplomatic arguments, but was more concerned for the safety of his nephew. Bismarck was deeply upset and he wrote to his friend Delbrück:

SOURCE 6.16

The Spanish affair has taken a miserable turn. The undoubted reasons of state have been subordinated to princely interests. My annoyance about this has burdened my nerves for weeks.

Letter from Bismarck to Delbrück, dated 13 May 1870.

Why, if no war was envisaged, was Moltke able to mobilise so quickly and assure Bismarck that the army was ready? The editing of the Ems Telegram needs explaining if Bismarck really did not want war.

The war with France

The French forces were slow to prepare. Moltke brought three armies to the frontier rapidly by train and over 300 000 troops were stationed at the front within days of the war beginning on 28 July 1870. The campaign did not go with the same clockwork precision as the mobilisation. There were heavy German losses at Worth on 5 August, and at Spicheren on 6 August. However, the Germans had superior artillery. The French decided to withdraw to their fortifications and attempted to move from Metz to Verdun, but were attacked on the way. There were again heavy Prussian losses at Gravelotte on 18 August, and at St Privat-la-Montagne, when the Prussian troops attacked prematurely. French marshal Bazaine failed to counter-attack and, despite their losses, the Germans contained the French army at Metz.

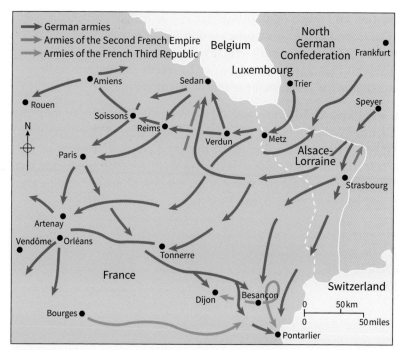

Figure 6.4: The movement of troops in the Franco–Prussian War of 1870–71

A French relief army under McMahon pushed towards Metz to relieve Bazaine. His army was attacked and driven into the frontier fortress of Sedan, to which Moltke brought 150 000 men in a rapid march of 50 miles through the Ardennes forest in three days. King Wilhelm, the officials of the North German Confederation and Bismarck himself watched the assault on Sedan on 1 September 1870. The German Krupps artillery was too powerful – in a bloody battle, the French lost 17 000 to the German's 9000 men and Napoleon III was taken prisoner.

Napoleon went into captivity, but the war continued. Bazaine did not surrender Metz for another seven weeks and a new government of national defence was formed in Paris. The German armies surrounded the French capital on 19 September.

Bismarck wanted to negotiate a quick peace; however, the army did not. The French began a sort of guerrilla resistance, to which the Germans responded brutally with executions and by burning villages. The French war leader Léon Gambetta escaped from Paris in a balloon and set about raising an army. The Germans then narrowly avoided defeat by a large French force at St Quentin in January 1871, and there was a bitter three-day battle in the Vosges.

Figure 6.5: Bismarck and Napoleon III after France's surrender in the Franco–Prussian War at Sedan in 1870

The war dragged on until the veteran French statesman Adolphe Thiers was chosen as head of the provisional government in Bordeaux, and negotiated with Bismarck. In return for Belfort, Bismarck acquired Strasbourg and Metz and the provinces of Alsace and Lorraine. France was to pay an indemnity of 5 billion francs. The terms agreed by Bismarck were formalised in the Treaty of Frankfurt.

After the peace, there was revolution in Paris, with the emergence of a revolutionary Commune. This revolution was deeply opposed by the new government of the French Republic, led by the conservative politician Adolphe Thiers. French forces bombarded Paris and then took it by storm. German troops looked on as the armies of Thiers and the new republic attacked its own people.

The war with France of 1870–71 lasted longer than the war of 1866. It was also more costly. Casualties were high and aspects of German leadership were poor. Bismarck generally seemed to lose control of the military, and it was with difficulty that he negotiated peace terms.

Bismarck knew that he could not afford to make such a lenient peace with France as he had done in 1866. There were good strategic reasons for Prussia taking Alsace and Lorraine, but by doing so, Bismarck made good relations with France impossible. Here, the basis was laid for the next war with France – the First World War of 1914–18.

The biggest change resulting from the war with France of 1870–71 was the creation of the German empire. It was proclaimed by the princes and offered in the way of a gift to the German people in a military ceremony at Versailles in January 1871. The German empire had indeed come about by 'blood and iron', as Bismarck had predicted.

Figure 6.6: The princes proclaim the empire, 1871; Bismarck stands centre right and wears a lighter uniform; Wilhelm I stands on the stage (second from right); Crown Prince Wilhelm (bearded) watches from the left of Wilhelm I

6.6 What was the nature of the German empire of 1871?

The new constitution of the German empire was based on that of the North German Confederation, but included the south German states:

- It was a federal constitution in which power was shared between a central Reich (empire) government and the local government of the states (Länder).
- The German emperor was Wilhelm I, the king of Prussia, and this was a hereditary title.
- The emperor chose Bismarck as Reichskanzler (imperial chancellor), a position he held until 1890.
- The imperial ministers were not elected but were chosen by the chancellor and were responsible to the emperor.
- There was a Reichstag – an imperial parliament elected by all men over 25 years. The individual states kept their own assemblies. The largest was the Prussian Landtag, which was elected on a reactionary three-tier voting system until 1918. Internal matters were the responsibilities of the states.
- There was also a Bundesrat – a council representing the governments of the individual states. Prussia was able to dominate this council as it was the largest state and made up two-thirds of the new Reich.
- The Reichstag and Bundesrat could pass legislation for the whole of Germany, and there was a federal budget that had to be voted by the parliament. However, the largest item was defence and the army budget was voted on for seven years at a time, not annually.
- The chancellor and the ministers addressed the Reichstag but were not responsible to them. A vote against the chancellor did not mean resignation. Only the king-emperor could dismiss the government.
- Foreign affairs were the direct responsibility of the chancellor and not a matter for discussion.

This new constitution was decided by King Wilhelm of Prussia and the princes as a result of war. It was declared in a palace in a conquered country. Germany was already a militarised state led by an aristocrat who had ignored parliament and was devoted to the interests of the monarchy.

Figure 6.7: The progressive unification of Germany, 1815–71

6.7 'How did Bismarck do it?'

This question was raised by the historian Jonathan Steinberg in the magazine *History Today* (February 2011). However, another question is: 'Did Bismarck do it at all?' The debate is between those who see unification as the result of one man's brilliant manipulation of circumstances and those who see the key factors as circumstances and developments that were largely independent of Bismarck.

Biographers such as Alan Palmer and Edward Crankshaw put Bismarck at the centre of events. However, writers on Germany such as David Blackbourn tend to consider the context more:

SOURCE 6.17

Prussia was always likely to come out on top. Austria not only had chronic financial problems and non-German distractions; it also lagged behind Prussia in economic development.

Blackbourn, D. 1997. **The Fontana History of Germany 1780–1918: The Long Nineteenth Century.** *London. Fontana Press.*

Certainly, Austria suffered defeats in Italy in 1859 and experienced a loss of prestige. Austria had also lost the support of Russia by sympathising with Russia's enemies in the Crimean War. However, actual failure to enter the war alienated Britain and France. This isolation was a key factor in enabling Prussia to defeat Austria.

Prussia's military developments, supported by financial surpluses from the growth of Prussian trade and industry, were a huge advantage. Though Bismarck encouraged army reforms, the developments in weaponry, railways and organisation had little to do with him and would have ensured Prussian victory sooner or later. Military historians such as John Gooch, writing in *Armies in Europe* (Routledge, 1980), stress these factors – although detailed military studies do show that Prussian victories were neither effortless nor inevitable. Nevertheless, Prussia's weaponry and military skill were key aspects of its victories against Denmark, Austria and France.

Economic unity and growth are also seen as key factors. The Zollverein – independently from Bismarck – established the idea of unity under Prussian leadership, and arguably created conditions for prosperity (see Chapter 5). The most enthusiastic supporter of the view that economic growth, rather than Bismarck, made unification possible is Helmut Böhme (*Foundation of the German Empire*, Oxford University Press, 1971).

Last but not least, although Bismarck did not admire German national feeling, it is difficult to see how his policies could have succeeded without it. While the National Association of 1859 restricted membership and met with little public enthusiasm, it spread the idea of a greater Germany. There were also wider underlying forces, such as an improved railway system, better roads and cultural developments in German literature and music, that encouraged greater unity.

Certainly the factors described above contributed to Bismarck's success. Yet while it is possible that another statesman might have achieved similar results, not every statesman had the sheer will power of Bismarck or commanded the same respect. Bismarck was able to exploit diplomatic opportunities after the Crimean War and made critical decisions – for instance, to go to war with Denmark in 1864. Military developments were important, but the Prussian army was an instrument used by Bismarck and could not have achieved major change independent of his decisions.

6

Italy (1815–1871) and Germany (1815–1890)

The Zollverein provided a model for German unity, but all except one of its members fought for Austria and not Prussia in 1866. Also, its economic importance may well have been exaggerated. James Sheehan, writing in *German History, 1770–1866* (Oxford University Press, 1989) argues that the main purpose of the Zollverein was to raise taxes and it had limited impact on actual economic growth or political unity.

Was Bismarck the man who made opportunities or the man who reacted to them; the master planner or the master improviser; the lone genius or someone who took advantage of the developments of his time; the man who moved purposefully towards unification or the man who made his share of mistakes, often uncertain of what to do next? While there can be no certain judgements about Bismarck, the fact remains that the new Germany was the most important development in European history. It overturned the European balance of power that had existed since 1815, and its creation led eventually to two world wars.

KEY CONCEPTS QUESTIONS

Consequence: Do you think that German Unification was possible only because of the weakness of Austria?

Significance: Do you think that Bismarck played a crucial role in German unification?

Paper 3 exam practice

Question

Evaluate the importance of Bismarck's role in establishing a united Germany by 1871. **[15 marks]**

Skill

Avoiding a narrative-based answer

Examiner's tips

Even once you have read the question carefully (and so avoided the temptation of including irrelevant material), produced your plan and written your introductory paragraph, it is still possible to go wrong.

By 'writing a narrative answer', history examiners mean providing supporting knowledge that is relevant (and may well be very precise and accurate) **but** which is not clearly linked to the question. Instead of answering the question, it merely **describes** what happened.

The main body of your essay/argument needs to be **analytical**. It must not simply be an 'answer' in which you just 'tell the story'. Your essay must **address the demands/key words of the question**. Ideally, this should be done consistently throughout your essay, by linking each paragraph to the previous one in order to produce a clear 'joined-up' answer.

You are especially likely to lapse into a narrative answer when answering your final question – and even more so if you are getting short of time. The 'error' here is that, despite all your good work at the start of the exam, you will lose sight of the question and just produce an *account*, as opposed to an analysis. Even if you are short of time, try to write several analytical paragraphs.

Note that a question that asks you the extent to which you agree with a statement expects you to come to judgements about success/failure or the relative importance of a factor/individual, or the accuracy of a statement. You need to provide a judgement on the views expressed in the statement. Very often, such a question gives you the opportunity to refer to different historians' views (see Chapter 7, End of chapter activities for more on this).

A good way of avoiding a narrative approach is to refer back to the question continually, and even to mention it now and again in your answer. That should help you to produce an answer that is focused on the specific aspects of the question – rather than just giving information about the broad topic or period.

For this question, you will need to cover the following aspects of Bismarck's policies which led to his success in increasing Prussia's power:

- his aims in overcoming the obstacles to greater unification

- his policy of building up the army and getting diplomatic support for Prussia

- his policy towards Denmark

- how he achieved the isolation and defeat of Austria

- how he enlarged Prussian influence and territory in 1867

- how he used war to unify Germany in 1870

- the economic factors which made this possible and which he used

- the military factors that made this possible and which he recognised and used

- the diplomatic factors that made this possible and which he used to his advantage.

You will then need to make a judgement in your concluding paragraph about the extent to which Bismarck succeeded or failed.

You should also refer back to the advice in Chapter 4 (writing an introductory paragraph) to help you define what is meant by success and failure.

Common mistakes

Every year, even candidates who have clearly revised well, and therefore have a good knowledge of the topic and of any historical debate surrounding it, still end up producing a mainly narrative-based or descriptive answer. Very often, this is the result of not having drawn up a proper plan.

The extracts of the student's answer show an approach that essentially just describes Bismarck's policies, without any analysis of the aims, degree of success/failure or his relative importance compared with other factors.

This example shows what examiners mean by a narrative answer – it is something you should **not** copy!

Sample paragraphs of narrative-based approach

Bismarck became Minister-President of Prussia in 1862 and supported the growth of the army by defending Roon's military reforms against the Landtag, which did not wish to see an expansion of the professional Prussian army. Bismarck, however, knew that the army would be important if Prussia were to go to war to defeat Austrian influence.

Bismarck was very unpopular, but he knew that any success would be rewarded by more support. He also knew that it was important to get Russia on his side so he sent General Alvensleben to give Russia support against the Polish rebellion, which had broken out in 1863. Poland had been divided up in the 18th century between Russia, Austria and Prussia and the Poles wanted their freedom. They had revolted in 1830 and 1848 and again in 1863.

In 1863 another major crisis arose over Denmark when the Danish king died. This affected Germany because of two provinces, Schleswig and Holstein…

[The rest of the essay continues in the same way – there are plenty of accurate/relevant facts about Bismarck's main policies/actions and the situations he faced, but there is no attempt to answer the question by addressing relative importance.]

Activity

In this chapter, the focus is on **avoiding** writing narrative-based answers. Using the information from this chapter, and any other sources of information available to you, try to answer one of the following Paper 3 practice questions in a way that avoids simply describing what happened.

Remember to refer to the simplified Paper 3 mark scheme in Chapter 9.

6   Italy (1815–1871) and Germany (1815–1890)

Paper 3 practice questions

1 'Economic factors were the most significant reason for the achievement of German unification by 1871'. To what extent do you agree with this statement?

2 Compare and contrast Cavour and Bismarck as statesmen who brought about greater unification of their countries.

3 Compare and contrast the roles of political leadership and national feeling in the unification of either Germany or Italy?

4 To what extent was the weakness of Austria important in German and Italian unification?

5 Discuss the view that the greatness of Bismarck's statesmanship before 1871 been exaggerated?

6 Evaluate the factors that brought about German unification by 1871.

Germany under Bismarck: domestic policies 1871–90

7

7

Italy (1815–1871) and Germany (1815–1890)

Introduction

This chapter deals with the main elements in Bismarck's domestic policy, in particular the Kulturkampf and the threat of socialism. German unification brought considerable problems as well as opportunities. It had come about by wars, not by peaceful discussion and agreement. There were many, both within Germany and in other countries, who saw the rise of Germany as dangerous. At home, he faced the rise of working–class discontent and socialism, the challenge of making a new constitution work, and opposition from Catholic subjects who had formed a separate political party. The new Germany was a large state in the centre of Europe with no natural boundaries. This new nation had to be made secure and it needed to accommodate economic and social change.

TIMELINE

1870   Vatican Council issues doctrine of Papal Infallibility

1871   **Jan:** Proclamation of German empire

        May: Treaty of Frankfurt; Germany gains Alsace-Lorraine

        Adalbert Falk appointed as Prussian Minister of Religion

        Jul: Abolition of Roman Catholic Bureau in Prussian Ministry of Culture

        Nov: Priests banned from making political statements from the pulpit

1872   Kulturkampf starts throughout Germany as Bismarck condemns Catholic Church over Papal infallibility and intolerance

        Mar: Catholic schools brought under state control

        Jesuits forbidden to forbidden to set up establishments in Germany

1873   **May:** May Laws

1874   Obligatory civil marriage introduced into Prussia

1878   **May:** Assassination attempt on Wilhelm I

        Oct: Anti-socialist laws

1879   **Jul:** Tariff Law

1882   Triple Alliance

1883   Health Insurance Law

1884   Accident Insurance Act

1885	**May:** German colonial expansion
1885–86	Expulsion of Poles and Jews from eastern Prussia
1889	Old-age pensions introduced
1890	**Mar:** Bismarck resigns

KEY QUESTIONS

- How liberal was the German empire under Bismarck?
- What were the challenges to Bismarck's Germany and how serious were they?
- What was the situation by 1890?

Overview

- The new German constitution contained both liberal and authoritarian elements. There is debate about the extent to which the new Germany was a true parliamentary state or an absolute monarchy with some liberal elements.
- Much of the 1870s was dominated by Bismarck's clash with the Catholic Church, the Kulturkampf. Bismarck's main concern in this period was to unite the country and he perceived that many who were opposed to the new Reich were Catholic.
- Bismarck saw the rise of new socialist and liberal political movements as a threat to the new Germany. He dealt with this threat by introducing new powers of repression.
- After 1879, Bismarck's regime became more conservative by introducing tariffs and aligning with the Conservative and Catholic parties against the left.
- Bismarck encouraged colonial expansion in the 1880s but he did not sustain this policy.
- By 1890, Bismarck's internal position was weakened by disputes with the new emperor, Wilhelm II, and it was clear that his foreign policy could not be maintained.

7.1 How liberal was the German empire under Bismarck?

The constitution of 1871: liberalism and absolutism

The German constitution of 1871 had both liberal and absolutist elements in it. The constitution was federal and the individual states had the right to determine their own affairs. As there was a strong liberal tradition in some states, this meant there were local liberal regimes.

The whole idea of a nation state was something that liberals had wanted. The new Germany was not simply a version of Prussia – there was a new national currency, national weights and measures, and customs barriers were eliminated. Businesses were supported by a national railway network and German business laws. Specialist legislation freed businesses from state control. Laws made bills of exchange legal and it became easier to borrow money. Though a national flag did not emerge for over twenty years, there was the feeling a new country had emerged from a period of modernisation. Money was raised for new buildings and there was investment in industry and trade. The sort of economic growth that liberals had hoped for with unification now occurred, and until 1879 the government continued its policies of free trade with low customs barriers.

The major political party – the National Liberals – were the main supporters of Bismarck in the Reichstag. They approved not only unification, free trade and economic growth, but also Bismarck's campaign against the Catholic Church (see 7.1 The Kulturkampf, 1871–87).

The Reichstag was elected by universal adult male suffrage – all men over 25 years. Having a wide electorate meant that political parties had to campaign for votes. Evidence of modern liberal politics was seen in the existence of national political parties, a Reichstag in which important policies were discussed, and voting by deputies on non-military elements of the federal budget. Bismarck saw the importance of gaining the Reichstag's support for the smooth running of the federal government – it demonstrated to foreign countries that the government represented Germany.

The less liberal aspects of the new German nation derived partly from the constitution and partly from developments after it formed. A crucial weakness of the new constitution was the Reichstag's lack of control over the all-important military budget.

Bismarck had funded army reforms between 1862 and 1866 without consulting the Prussian parliament (see Section 6.3). There was also no elected body that had control of the German army, and yet the army's support was critical – indeed, the nation had come about because of the military.

In the war of 1870–71, the Prussian generals were unwilling to accept civilian control. In the new empire, the German army grew increasingly independent and military values became widespread. Officers asserted their superiority over civilians and military parades were a spectacle similar to religious processions. The army planned ceaselessly for new wars and the court became militarised. Bismarck himself adopted military dress.

After 1888, German militarism became even more pronounced with the arrival of Kaiser Wilhelm II, but its roots lay in the earlier period.

Prussia and the Bundesrat

The Bundesrat (Federal Council) had 43 seats, of which Prussia – because of its size – had 17 seats, giving it dominance. The emperor was Prussian; the army was largely led by Prussian generals; the administration was on Prussian lines; the chancellor was the Prussian minister-president. The Prussian parliament, sitting in a building in Berlin separate from the Reichstag, was clearly biased in its voting system, using the old three-tier franchise in which nobles and the rich got more votes. Foreign policy was Prussian. This imbalance undermined the federal system, and Prussian dominance undermined the liberalism of the new Germany.

Reichstag deputies could speak freely, but the restriction on the military budget and the state's heavy reliance on indirect taxes, especially after 1879, meant that they did not have the sort of financial control of the government that their British or American counterparts held. (Because so much government income came from customs duties, there was less need for direct taxes, which could be controlled by the Reichstag.)

The Reichstag was also unable to bring down governments by voting against them, and there was no government party. Bismarck was not responsible to parliament but to the king-emperor.

The way the parliament was set out in a large semi-circle (see Figure 7.1) is indicative of this: Bismarck lectured or criticised the Reichstag, but he was not part of it. The ministers, who were also not members of political parties, addressed the Reichstag from the front.

Figure 7.1: The Reichstag in 1889; Bismarck (wearing uniform and sitting in the centre of the bench) is addressing the assembly, not really part of it

In 1874, a new press law authorised the imprisonment of newspaper editors who published sensitive information. This marked the start of a new era for the Reichstag as a tool of political suppression.

The historical debate

Hans Ulrich Wehler, writing in *The German Empire, 1871–1918* (Berg Publishers, 1985), describes Germany after 1871 as set on a 'special way' (Sonderweg). The growth of railways and industry from the 1850s allowed Prussia to develop large military forces. After 1871, economic growth and militarism continued, but political development lagged behind. In this way, Germany came to admire power more than democracy. There was contempt for freedom and individual rights, a trend that accelerated during the First World War. Bismarck's parliament was a meaningless pretence that eroded respect for genuine liberal values. The result was the rise of Hitler and another major war ending in catastrophe and division for Germany.

An alternative view is to see Bismarck not as a forerunner of Hitler, but as a man of the 19th century. This is the view of Lothar Gall in *Bismarck: The White Revolutionary* (Allen & Unwin, 1986). Gall argues that while Bismarck may have disliked liberalism, he was willing to work with it. He was open to new ideas and enjoyed parliamentary debate; he was democratic in extending the right to vote and introducing social reforms later in his career.

Not all historians see the empire as using liberal institutions such as the Reichstag as 'the fig leaf of absolutism' (that is, a token gesture to parliamentary rule while the real power lay with the emperor and his government). The historian Geoffrey Barraclough (1946) expresses a widely accepted view that the Constitution of 1871 was 'a veiled form of monarchical absolutism'.

This was because Bismarck was not responsible to the Reichstag and Prussia had the right of veto in the Bundesrat. If Prussian members opposed a measure, then they could prevent it passing because of the number of representatives Prussia had.

Yet, Eric Dorn Brose, in *German History, 1789–1871* (Berghahn Books, 1997) argues that the new German constitution allowed individual states the freedom to look after their own affairs, and that in the states outside Prussia, liberal and progressive forces flourished. More people voted in Germany than in contemporary Britain. Bismarck allowed a federal structure; there was no need for it. He also saw the Reichstag as important enough to spend considerable time building majorities there. Germany had a working parliamentary system and was not strictly absolutist, even if the system could not actually overturn chancellors or vote on key areas of defence and foreign policy.

What emerged after 1871 was a distinctive German culture focused on economic and technological developments and military power, and which contained increasingly illiberal elements. Germany in 1871 could have developed into a more liberal parliamentary state, but it was some way from becoming a full democracy.

7.2 What were the challenges to Bismarck's Germany and how serious were they?

There were a number of key political developments after 1871 which appeared to challenge Bismarck's vision for the new Germany. This section will examine those challenges and analyse how serious a threat they were to the new state.

The Centre Party

First, there was the development of the Centre (Zentrum) Party, founded in December 1870. There was not a strong tradition of distinct parties in Germany. The Centre Party combined the promotion of a special interest – that of Catholics in the German empire – with elements of a popular political party organised to mobilise opinion and win votes. The Centre Party owed much to the work of Ludwig Windthorst (1812–91), a Catholic lawyer from Hanover who had a strong dislike of Bismarck.

Windthorst deeply resented the annexation of his home state by Prussia in 1866. He was elected deputy of both the Prussian Landtag and the new Reichstag. He brought together Catholic deputies who also opposed Bismarck. In 1874, he led a new popular organisation named the Centre Party. (The name did not reflect the Party's moderate views, but rather their seating position in the Reichstag.)

The Centre Party backed the opposition of the Pope and the Catholic Church to developments in Italy and Germany, which were seen as against Catholic interests. The Pope condemned nationalism and democracy as 'errors' in a pronouncement in 1864 called the 'Syllabus of Errors'. Then, in an attempt to enforce his authority in 1870, he confirmed papal infallibility (the doctrine that the Pope's official pronouncements are free from error) as a set belief of the Church.

The Catholic Centre party in the north joined with other Catholics in south Germany, Poland and those in Alsace-Lorraine, with the result that by 1871 it had become the second largest party in the Reichstag as the table below shows. This was a major concern for Bismarck as the party favoured greater self-rule for the states of the Empire and did not want the state to interfere in issues such as education. Bismarck therefore viewed the party with suspicion.

Party	1871	1874	1877	1878	1881	1884	1887	1890
National Liberals	125	155	128	99	47	51	99	42
Centre Party	58	91	93	94	100	99	98	106
Social Democratic Party	2	9	12	9	12	24	11	35
German Conservative Party	57	22	40	59	50	78	80	73
Free Conservatives	37	33	38	57	28	28	41	20
Progressives	47	50	52	39	115	74	32	76
National Groups	14	30	30	30	35	32	29	27
Guelphs	9	4	10	4	10	11	4	11

Table 7.1: German political parties and their number of seats in the Reichstag, 1871–90

ACTIVITY

Research what each of the political parties stood for.

The Kulturkampf, 1871–87

The biggest political change of the 1870s was a struggle between the Prussian state and the Catholic Church. It was termed the Kulturkampf, meaning a 'struggle of cultures' in the sense of opposing outlooks and philosophies. The focus of this particular Kulturkampf was Catholic tradition versus liberal modernisation.

Liberals had begun passing laws against the Catholic Church in the southern German states in the 1860s, in an attempt to limit the influence of church education. In the new German empire, the supporters of unification also urged restrictions on the Church. The issue arose when some German Catholics rejected the Pope's doctrine of papal infallibility and queried the Pope's jurisdiction over them. The National Liberals sought the introduction of anti-clerical measures, and liberals in Hesse and Baden agreed. Bismarck decided to lend his support to the movement.

Figure 7.2: A cartoon of 1875 in which the Kulturkampf appears as a chess game – rather than as a titanic struggle – between Bismarck (left) and Pius IX (right). 'Between Berlin and Rome', with Bismarck on the left and the Pope on the right, from the German satirical magazine Kladderadatsch, 1875. Pope: "Admittedly, the last move was unpleasant for me; but the game still isn't lost. I still have a very beautiful secret move." Bismarck: "That will also be the last one, and then you'll be mated in a few moves — at least in Germany."

What were Bismarck's motives for the Kulturkampf?

In the 1870s, the internal policies of the Reich were dominated by a bizarre religious battle that seems more fitting to the 16th century and the Reformation than the 19th century. Germany was divided religiously with some two thirds of the population, mostly in Prussia, Protestant, while the other third, largely in the south, were Catholic. There had been a series of clashes between the Catholic church and other states in the mid and later 19th century, as described in the previous section, over the question of papal infallibility. This doctrine had laid down the belief that papal pronouncements on morals and faith could not be challenged. This was seen by some liberals in Germany as a direct challenge to the state, with the Church likely to interfere in domestic issues and give its support to reactionary issues. Such an attitude worried the main party, the National Liberals, who believed that freedom was at stake. As a result, it brought the National Liberals and Bismarck closer, and some have suggested that this was the true motivation behind Bismarck's actions. Bismarck wanted neither a liberal Germany nor to give the Reichstag any real power, but he could appear to be 'liberal' by supporting anti-Catholic legislation, which would give him the support of the largest party in the Reichstag (see Table 7.1) and put him at the head of a popular protestant crusade. Hans Ulrich Wehler, writing in *The German Empire, 1871–1918* (Berg Publishers, 1985) supports this theory. He argues that to avoid concessions in other areas, Bismarck used the Catholic problem to side with the liberals and gain their support.

The alternative view is that Bismarck had genuine fears that German unity was threatened by the Pope and the loyalty of his Catholic followers. The Catholics of south Germany voiced anti-Prussian views before the war, and there was opposition to Prussian control from Ludwig Windthorst and Prussia's Polish population in its eastern provinces, which was mostly Catholic.

Poland was divided between Russia, Austria and Prussia at the end of the 18th century, and Prussia had annexed two largely Catholic provinces in the west – Alsace and Lorraine. Would Catholic politics in these key border areas undermine German security? The success of the Catholic party in the 1871 election to the Reichstag appeared to suggest that it was a distinct possibility.

A campaign against Catholic extremism, exemplified by the self-serving decrees of an embittered pope, might prove successful. Was Bismarck taking war to a prospective domestic enemy in the same way that he taken war to Austria and France? David Williamson points to a revealing speech made by Bismarck on 10 February 1872:

SOURCE 7.1

The Roman Catholic clergy is national in all other lands. Only Germany is an exception. The Polish clergy align with the Polish national cause, the Italian clergy to the Italian national cause. Only in Germany is there the particular phenomenon that the clergy has a more international character. The Catholic Church even when it obstructs the development of Germany is closer to the heart of the clergy than the development of the German empire.

Speech given by Bismarck to the Reichstag, 10 February 1872.

The historian A.J.P. Taylor (1958) views Bismarck as determined to 'strangle the Centre in the cradle' – that is, to destroy this new political party entirely. If so, this dispute was as much about the new politics that Bismarck had introduced through universal male suffrage as it was about religion. Bismarck feared that the new Centre Party would become a focus for all the discontents of the Reich, especially in sensitive border areas – the eastern frontier areas with a Polish population subdued by Prussian conquest, and the western frontiers with newly conquered Alsace-Lorraine and a largely Catholic Rhineland, who were determined to destroy the new state. This view appeared to have some credibility as the party became a rallying point for those who opposed the new Empire. Perhaps Bismarck's plan was to stir up events to see how he could take advantage of them – part of what Otto Pflanze describes as a 'strategy of alternatives' in *Bismarck and the Development of Germany* (Princeton University Press, 1963).

Bismarck was given his opportunity to act by the action of some 5000 Catholics, known as 'Old Catholics', who broke with the Church over the doctrine of papal infallibility. These 'old Catholics' were dismissed as teachers and professors by the Church and this gave Bismarck the opportunity to start his attack on the Catholic church, arguing that he was defending religious toleration.

Bismarck started his campaign with a series of newspaper articles in 1872. The campaign that followed was directed against Catholics in Poland and the Rhineland, but its impact was felt throughout Germany. Legislation was passed in Prussia against Catholics and this was soon repeated across the country.

KEY CONCEPTS ACTIVITY

Causation: As this section has shown, there is much debate surrounding the reasons why Bismarck introduced the Kulturkampf. Using the information above, complete the chart below to help you summarise the reasons for its introduction:

Motive for the Kulturkampf	Evidence
Bismarck wanted to win popular Protestant support	
The Catholic Church was a threat to the unity of the state	
Bismarck wanted to destroy the Centre party	

Having completed the chart, decide which you think is the most important reason and write a paragraph justifying your choice.

In 1871, Bismarck had appointed a strict anti-clerical liberal called **Adalbert Falk** as Prussian minister of religion.

Adalbert Falk (1827–1900):

Falk was a liberal lawyer from Silesia. He initially worked as a public prosecutor before being elected as a liberal deputy in the Prussian parliament in 1858. He was later made Prussian Minister of Religion by Bismarck. He resigned in 1879 but continued to work in the Prussian civil service.

This was soon followed by attacks on Catholicism:

- The Roman Catholic Bureau within the Prussian Ministry of Culture was abolished in July 1871.
- Priests were banned from making political comments from the pulpit in November 1871.
- Catholic schools were placed under state supervision in March 1872.

- Lay inspectors were appointed for all church schools.
- The Jesuits, who had supported papal authority, were forbidden from setting up establishments in Germany.

Then in 1873, Falk introduced a series of measures called the May Laws:

- The Prussian state became responsible for priests' education, so priests had to have a secular education.
- A royal tribunal for Ecclesiastical Affairs was set up by the state to undermine the Church's jurisdiction over its own members, meaning religious appointments had to be approved by the state.
- Provincial governors were allowed to veto clerical appointments.
- In 1874, priests lost their endowments (the lands or assets of individual Catholic parishes on which the Church depended for money).
- The Jesuits, the main Catholic teaching and preaching order, were expelled from Germany.
- Priests were forbidden to discuss or preach about 'politics'.
- A civil marriage was made compulsory for all couples wishing to marry.

The effects of the Kulturkampf

Over 240 priests were fined or imprisoned in the early part of 1875, and over 1000 parishes were left without a priest. In all, 2412 Catholic clergy were arrested or imprisoned. By 1876 only two Prussian bishops were not in exile or under house arrest. Despite the penalties, only 30 priests agreed to submit to the new laws. At the same time as this attack on their religion, Poles in Prussia and French-speakers in Alsace and Lorraine were forced to accept German as the language in schools.

Bismarck's natural allies – the conservatives – were disgusted by this religious attack on Catholics and the dishonour suffered by respectable Catholic clergy and bishops. Bismarck's response was to denounce these conservative critics and draw closer to the National Liberals, who were offering enthusiastic support for his religious policies.

Bismarck's attempt to kill off the Catholic Centre Party by labelling its members 'Reichsfeinde' (enemies of the Reich) failed – the Party actually increased its seats in 1874 from 61 to 95. Thus, the persecution of German Catholics brought about the very result it was attempting to prevent – a mass party that united those elements in Germany who were hostile to Bismarck. Even some Protestants were opposed to the policy as it limited their influence on education as well. Bismarck's anti-religious campaign also damaged relations with the emperor and gave a poor image of the new Germany to foreign powers.

As a result, by 1878 Bismarck acknowledged that his policy had failed and that he had actually increased disunity within the state. Given that Bismarck believed that there was an even greater threat to the state, the socialists, he ended the Kulturkampf. This was made possible because of the death of Pope Pius IX in 1878 and his successor, Leo XIII, who was conciliatory. As a result, Falk was dismissed from his post in 1879 and some of the laws were repealed, however some remained in place:

- Jesuits were still prevented from entering Germany.
- Civil marriage remained compulsory.
- The state still oversaw Church appointments.

The socialists

Bismarck was anxious about another popular mass party – the socialists. They had been founded in 1875 when moderate and revolutionary socialists had joined together to form the Social Democratic Party, or SPD. Their aim was to overthrow the existing order, but only by legal means, and they had been able to gain support because of the German economic downturn of 1873, which caused unemployment and discontent. As a result, Bismarck was worried about the spread of radical ideas in industrial and urban areas, both of which grew rapidly after 1871 as Germany became increasingly industrialised. He saw socialism as revolutionary and a direct threat to the type of society he wanted to establish.

Figure 7.3: The Krupps factories at Essen; large-scale industrialisation was changing Germany and increasing the appeal of socialism

The National Liberals opposed Bismarck's attempts to suppress socialism in 1875, and Bismarck was beginning to see that he was allied with the wrong political party. He started moving towards another type of policy altogether. Convinced of the need to break ties with the liberals, Bismarck now aimed to re-establish his links with the Conservative groups, improve his relationship with the emperor and restore Germany's reputation abroad. Doing so would ensure that France could not exploit the failures of Bismarck's Catholic policy – for example, by allying with another Catholic country such as Austria.

Economic developments and changes in politics

After 1876, farmers and tradesmen feared foreign competition, particularly Russian food imports and British industrial products. Many supporters of the Centre party had economic as well as religious interests. The Conservatives, landowners and large-scale industrialists sought an end to free trade and the introduction of tariffs.

Free trade was the major policy of the National Liberals. Bismarck decided that he needed to abandon free trade and the persecution of the Church, and instead concentrate on protecting the rights of industrial workers. Socialism, with its atheistic ideas, was not favoured by the Catholic Centre politicians or their supporters, who were mainly from farms and small towns. A union of the Centre and the Conservatives was more to Bismarck's taste: it would please the king, allow for an agreement with Austria and undermine the socialist's cause. It would also end Bismarck's dependence on the middle-class National Liberals, who he was finding restricting and tiresome. This development was therefore one reason why the Kulturkampf ended and Falk was dismissed on 13 July 1879. As historian Alan Palmer notes (1976), Bismarck introduced a new tariff – a customs duty on imported goods – two days later.

As we have seen, from 1880 to 1883, Prussia amended much of the anti-clerical legislation and the Catholic Church regained some of its freedom. The Kulturkampf was an unpleasant episode driven by hatred more than any constructive political or philosophical aim. Bismarck told friends in late January 1875:

SOURCE 7.2

Hatred is no less a spur than love. My life is kept going by two things – my wife and Windthorst – the love for the one and the hatred for the other.

Bismarck speaking in 1875.

The Kulturkampf episode was linked to many other factors, but it did herald future campaigns of hatred against groups labelled 'enemies'. It is hard to grasp that educated, enlightened liberal academics and politicians saw Bismarck as a true progressive, given the persecutions. The extreme persecution of the Catholic Church and the negative cynicism of Bismarck suggested that the new Germany had limited claim to be seen as liberal.

The end of the Kulturkampf, a new tariff policy, the nationalisation of German railways and Bismarck's alliance with the Reichstag conservatives was confirmed by an alliance with Austria in 1879, and the secret Reinsurance Treaty with Russia of 1887 (see page 195). Bismarck was now eager to deal with another unintended result of his policies – the rise of socialism.

KEY CONCEPTS ACTIVITY

Perspectives: Assess the significance of the Kulturkampf on Germany. In groups, write an article that might have appeared in:

- A Catholic newspaper in 1879, commenting on the events of the Kulturkampf since 1873 and expressing an opinion about them.
- A liberal newspaper commenting on the same events, expressing the views of the National Liberals.
- A conservative newspaper expressing the views of landowners and Junkers.

How would a modern historian writing about Germany after Bismarck see the significance of this episode?

German socialism

Socialism was a particularly German phenomenon. **Karl Marx** gave ideas on social justice a pseudo-scientific framework by arguing that there were laws of human development that made revolution inevitable.

> **Karl Marx (1818–83):**
>
> Marx was a radical journalist from the Rhineland who was forced to live in exile for much of his life because of his ideals. *The Communist Manifesto* (written with Friedrich Engels in 1848) and *Das Kapital* (1867) were among his most influential books. His attempts to form International Workers' Associations met with limited success, but his ideas are among the most important in world history.

Marx saw capitalism as deeply flawed and believed that class conflict was inevitable. He argued that industrial workers would eventually stage a revolution with the aim of establishing a classless society where all were truly free to live by the principle 'from each according to his or her ability, to each according to his or her need'. If this happened, Marx argued that the existing state would wither away. Marx and his collaborator, Friedrich Engels, provide vast volumes of 'proof', so this socialist ideal was seen as not merely a sought-after dream but a clear historical process supported by scientific evidence.

There were common intellectual roots between Marxism and Prussian theories of state building. Both were opposed to liberal individualism. Indeed, Bismarck met with the German socialist **Ferdinand Lassalle**, having an amicable discussion with him in 1863 and later passing laws to help German workers. Yet Bismarck became increasingly concerned when working-class socialist groups were established in Germany. With the development of new industries and urban centres, these groups soon attracted the support of German workers. Marxism had nothing to offer peasants, but it offered state control to the working classes.

> **Ferdinand Lassalle (1825–64):**
>
> Lassalle was a Jewish lawyer who was influenced by the ideas of Marx, but believed that the national state would be able to promote democracy and workers' rights. After discussing reforms with Bismarck in 1862, he founded the German Workers' Association in 1863. He was killed in a duel in 1864.

Socialism spread with the development of the mass electorate and modern communications. It presented Bismarck with another united party that could never be integrated into his system.

Repression and its failure

Bismarck responded to the rise of socialism with another policy of repression, initially in 1876 trying to ban socialist propaganda, but his liberal allies did not want to violate freedoms of speech and opinion. Although socialists were permitted in the Reichstag, the socialist press was suppressed, local socialist organisations were broken up and raided by the police, and socialist clubs and trade unions were banned.

Bismarck's proposals to ban the Socialist Party were accepted after two attempts on the emperor's life in May 1878 – first by Karl Nobiling and then by Max Hödel. It did not matter that these attempts were by anarchists; in the popular mind, and that of Bismarck's there was no distinction between anarchism and socialism, even though the would-be assassins had no links to socialism. In June 1878, Bismarck dissolved the Reichstag, and he and his allies started a frenzied campaign against socialism, arguing that that there was a 'red conspiracy' which threatened the state. The attempt to pass a bill against socialism initially failed as the National Liberals were concerned about civil liberties. However, the second attempt on William led to criticism of the National Liberals for not passing a bill that might have protected him. Bismarck used the backlash to dissolve the Reichstag and call fresh elections, in which given the circumstances it is understandable that the SPD vote fell from 493 000 in 1877 to 312 000, and the National Liberal vote also fell and they lost 29 seats (see Table 7.1).

Bismarck's actions against Socialism

The new Reichstag was only too willing to pass anti-socialist legislation and in October 1878, with the support of Conservatives and many National Liberals, an anti-socialist bill was passed and the following restrictions were imposed:

- Socialist publications were banned.
- Socialist meetings were banned and broken up.
- Socialist organisations, including trade unions, were banned.

Although some socialists were imprisoned and others left the country, Bismarck's persecution proved ineffective – by suppressing socialism he only succeeded in creating heroes and martyrs, and the movement went underground. The law was also interpreted differently in the various states and it did not prevent SPD members from standing for election to state parliaments or the Reichstag. With industry continuing to grow, and poor working and living conditions, there was growing support for a well-organised socialist party. It is therefore easy to explain why by 1890 the SPD won 35 seats and polled over a million voters.

Reforms intended to reduce the appeal of socialism

In the 1880s, Bismarck tried a new approach. He abandoned total persecution and tried 'killing socialism by kindness'. By offering a series of reforms and welfare measures Bismarck hoped to lessen the appeal of socialism to the working class. Some have argued that Bismarck was simply being cynical in his approach, but others have suggested that his Christian beliefs may have led him to believe that he had a moral obligation to help those in poor conditions.

The German government introduced a series of social reforms, sometimes called 'state socialism', that were a considerable political innovation. They had significant effects on political expectations in Germany and in other countries such as Britain, where the changes were copied. They included the emergence of a 'welfare state', in which the state takes responsibility for the well-being of its citizens and recognises the needs of a modern industrial society. This was a political change of enormous consequence.

The Reichstag passed a number of schemes in the period from 1883 to 1889, of which the most important were:

- The Sickness Insurance Act, 1883. This gave low paid workers medical treatment and up to 13 weeks' sick pay. It was a contributory scheme, with employees paying two-thirds and employers one third of the contribution.
- The Accident Insurance Act, 1884. This gave protection to workers who were permanently disabled or sick for more than the thirteen weeks covered by the previous act.
- The Old Age and Disability Act, 1889. This gave pensions to those over 70 and disability pensions to those who were younger. It was paid for by workers, employers and the state.

The social reforms reflected the 'fatherly' concern for workers shown on many Junker estates and the pride of the Prussian civil service in overseeing complex projects. They also represented a total break with the liberal politicians of the 1870s, who preferred individual responsibility and no state interference. By modern standards, the reforms were forward-looking and humane. Yet they were intended to reduce and weaken working-class aspirations for political power.

Theodor Lohman, the Prussian civil servant who developed the reforms, made a revealing comment (see Source 7.3).

SOURCE 7.3

Social discontent is not rooted in material grievances, but in working-class demands for real equality before the law and a share in the achievements of modern culture.

Theodor Lohman, a Prussian civil servant, speaking in 1889.

Despite these measures, many workers were not won over and socialism continued to grow; many workers did not trust Bismarck as trade unions were still banned. Working conditions did not really improve and many worked for long hours in poor conditions. Bismarck was unwilling to take state action on these issues, which meant that the SPD would continue to gain support. However, in judging the reforms it should be remembered that Bismarck did put down the foundations for the welfare state in Germany and that such reforms were the first in the world.

Analysis

Here is the root of the problem of the Bismarck political system – there were too many elements that did not share in its aspirations and general culture:

- The workers were cut off from the state and had little loyalty to it, with the Socialist Party (SPD) providing a sort of alternative government. The SPD provided support such as welfare schemes, help in times of hardship and political guidance.

- Other groups remained separate – for example, the two million Poles living in the east. Bismarck feared and resented them, and was concerned about their rising birth rate. In 1885, he ordered that any Poles and Jews of Russian nationality be expelled from the country. This brutal 'ethnic cleansing' caused considerable distress. There was certainly no question of integration.
- Similarly, there was little success in integrating the Danes of Schleswig or the French speakers of Alsace and Lorraine into the Reich.
- Catholics were never truly integrated, as a result of the campaign against them at a crucial period in the early years of the empire.

By the time of his fall in 1890, Bismarck was contemplating the launch of a full-scale attack on socialism, even if it meant changing the constitution and re-modelling parliament.

ACTIVITY

Read Sources 7.4 and 7.5. How do these views differ? Which seems more convincing, and why? Start by reading the passages aloud, then summarise them. What knowledge would you use to judge which view was the more correct?

SOURCE 7.4

Unification has often been presented as a willing surrender by the liberals. But that is one-sided and ignores those aspects of the process that liberals could welcome. After all, anything disliked by Catholics and extreme conservatives was bound to have positive features in their eyes. Unification produced a new constitution and a defined national state. The new Germany had much that was important to the liberals; the rule of law, freedom of movement and a liberal commercial code. They did not choose unity over freedom, but looked to extend freedom through unity.

Blackbourn, D. 1997. **The Fontana History of Germany 1780–1918: The Long Nineteenth Century.** Blackwell. London. Fontana Press. p. 158.

SOURCE 7.5

Bismarck always insisted that Germany remained 'a confederation of principalities' but the constitutional promise of the federal Council was never fulfilled. The most important reason for this was simply the overwhelming primacy, in military and political terms, of Prussia. Within the federation, the state of Prussia – with 65% of the surface area and 62% of the population – enjoyed de facto hegemony [domination]. The Prussian army dwarfed the south German forces. The primacy of Prussia was further assured by the weakness of imperial administrative institutions. Prussia's bureaucracy was larger than that of the Reich and most of the imperial officials were Prussian. The Prussian system became the conservative anchor within the German system, just as Bismarck intended.

Christopher C. 2006. **The Iron Kingdom**. *London. Allen Lane. p. 55.*

Theory of Knowledge

The limits of liberalism:

To what extent can liberalism oppose those who deny freedom, without itself becoming illiberal? This was the dilemma facing the German liberals, since the Catholic Church was seen as repressive and preventing free thought. Should historians 'take sides' here?

Foreign policy, colonialism and national unity

Italy had used foreign and colonial policy after 1871 to help unify the state and try to show its people that it was a great power in the hope of winning further support. The same was not true of Germany. The creation of the new German state had changed the 'balance of power' in Europe as the new state was one of the, if not the most, powerful nation in Europe. As a result other powers were frightened by its emergence and concerned that, as it had done to achieve unification, it would use force to assert its power. Therefore, Bismarck was determined to allay such fears and show that Germany had no territorial desires. Far from following an aggressive policy to win support, Bismarck pursued a policy of remaining on good terms with both Austria and Russia, aware that France would not be able to mount a challenge or seek revenge for its defeat in 1870. His policy of maintaining alliances with Austria and Russia was therefore scarcely one around which the new nation could rally.

Bismarck had stated in 1881 that 'so long as I am Chancellor we shall pursue no colonial policy'. This was again in contrast to Italy, and the situation under Kaiser Wilhelm II, who hoped to use colonial expansion to unite the nation. However, in 1884–85 it appeared as if Bismarck had changed his policy. The change was due, at least in part, to the political situation and designed to win popular support because:

- Pressure groups, such as the German Colonial Union founded in 1882, had won public support and Bismarck hoped to win over these supporters, particularly as an election was due in 1884.
- Gaining colonies would provide a market for German goods which, with economic problems and the policy of protectionism, would win support from industrialists.
- He hoped to ally himself with patriotic support, as had been attempted in Italy, particularly at the time of elections.

During this period Germany acquired German South-West Africa, Togoland, Cameroons and German East Africa, as well as some Pacific Islands. However, the policy was short-lived and was used only briefly as a rallying point for the nation as Bismarck was more concerned to avoid conflict with Britain over imperial developments.

7.3 What was the situation by 1890?

The arrival of the young **Wilhelm II** on the German throne in 1888 transformed the situation. Bismarck had been expecting to disagree with **Frederick II**.

Wilhelm II of Germany (1859–1941):

Wilhelm was born in 1859, the son of Frederick II and Victoria, the daughter of Queen Victoria of Britain. He was born with a withered arm and was determined to overcome his disability by every show of manliness. Neurotic and aggressive, he resented British naval power, was hostile to Jews, Catholics, France and Russia, and distrusted parliament. He dismissed Bismarck in 1890 and his erratic policies helped to lead Germany to war in 1914. He abdicated after Germany's military failures in 1918. He died in Holland in 1941.

Figure 7.4: Wilhelm II

Frederick II (1831–88):

Frederick was born in 1831, the only son of Wilhelm I. Despite being brought up with a military background and being praised for his leadership during both the Austro-Prussian and Franco-Prussian wars, he developed liberal tendencies, in part through his marriage to Victoria, the daughter of Queen Victoria and the links it brought with Britain. It was this link with progressive politics that worried Bismarck. However, suffering with cancer, he died after only 90 days on the throne.

7

However, the more liberal Frederick died soon after coming to the throne in 1888 and was succeeded by his young, neurotic and unstable son, Emperor Wilhelm II. Relations between the older and younger men deteriorated quickly. By March 1890, they were no longer on speaking terms. Bismarck seemed remote and inaccessible and spent more and more time away from Berlin. The emperor wanted to promote the power of Germany on the international stage and nationalistic feeling in Germany. Neither of these ideas met with Bismarck's approval.

The 1890 elections were a disaster for the group of conservative parties who supported Bismarck, called the Cartel. The Socialist Party of Germany (SPD) increased their seats and votes, as did the Centre Party and the Progressive Party opposed to Bismarck. In all, Bismarck's 'enemies of the Reich' took 207 out of 397 seats. In response, Bismarck called for a severe anti-socialist law in which 'agitators' would be exiled and a new electoral law that would end universal suffrage.

Bismarck's fall

By this point in 1890, Bismarck had lost the support of the Kaiser and the entire cabinet – even his conservative supporters had lost faith in him. The Kaiser insisted on removing the rule that no other minister could visit the emperor without the chancellor – Bismarck – being present. Yet the German public and the German political and military establishment did not rally round Bismarck in the quarrel. By 1890, even the unstable young emperor was more popular than Bismarck, whose resignation was received by the Reichstag 'in icy silence'.

Bismarck retired to his estates full of resentment and anger. He wrote his memoirs – a highly dubious work of self-justification – and, though highly praised, remained out of power until his death in 1898.

In one of the most famous political cartoons of all time, the British magazine *Punch* showed Emperor Wilhelm II as the captain of a ship 'dropping the pilot'.

Figure 7.5: Punch cartoon of 22 October 1890, 'The old man leaves the ship of state to be guided by the inexperienced youth'

Devise your own cartoon to comment on Bismarck's fall from power.

Change: In what ways do think that Germany changed in the period from 1871–90?

Perspective: To what extent would Catholics have thought that they suffered more in Germany than Socialists in this period?

Paper 3 exam practice

Question

Evaluate the reasons why Bismarck introduced the Kulturkampf.
[15 marks]

Skill

Using your own knowledge analytically and combining it with
awareness of historical debate

Examiner's tips

Always remember that historical knowledge and analysis should be the
core of your answer – aspects of historical debate are desirable extras.
However, where it is relevant, the integration of relevant knowledge about
historical debates and/or interpretations, with reference to individual
historians, will help push your answer up into the higher bands.

Assuming that you have read the question carefully, drawn up a
plan, worked out your line of argument/approach and written your
introductory paragraph, you should be able to avoid both irrelevant
material and simple narrative. Your task now is to follow your plan
by writing a series of linked paragraphs that contain relevant analysis,
precise supporting own knowledge and, where relevant, brief references
to historical debate interpretations.

For this question, you will need to:

* **consider Bismarck's motives** – motives cannot exist
  independently of what problems he faced or his ambitions

* **supply a brief explanation of their historical context** –
  the situation in 1871; the danger from the Catholic Church and
  Catholics within Germany

* **outline what actually happened** – describe what the main
  elements of policy were, but link these to his motives; what measures
  Bismarck took to weaken the Catholic church in Germany

* **provide a consistently analytical examination** – describe the
  reasons for the introduction, course and development of these events.

Such a topic, which has been the subject of much historical debate, will give you the chance to refer to different historians' views.

Common mistakes

Some students, being aware of an existing historical debate (and knowing that extra marks can be gained by showing this), simply write: 'Historian X says…, and historian Y says…' However, they make no attempt to **evaluate** the different views (for example, has one historian had access to more/better information than another, perhaps because he/she was writing at a later date?); nor is this information **integrated** into their answer by being pinned to the question. Another weak use of historical debate is to write things like: 'Historian X is biased because she is American.' Such comments will not be given credit.

Remember to refer to the simplified Paper 3 mark scheme in Chapter 9.

Sample paragraph containing analysis and historical debate

The clash with the Catholic Church dominated Bismarck's domestic policy for much of the 1870s. There were a number of possible reasons for this clash, but most importantly Bismarck hoped to take advantage of the religious division between Protestants and Catholics within Germany. With some two thirds of Germany Protestant it made sense to ally with the Protestant cause and, as Hans Ulrich Wehler has argued, use the problem of a Catholic church that wanted to interfere in domestic issues and follow an illiberal policy after the pronouncement of papal infallibility, to win the support of the National Liberals and increase Bismarck's strength in the Reichstag as the National Liberals were the largest party. An anti-Catholic policy would also have much appeal to the National Liberals, who were seen as defenders of freedom and by pursuing such a policy it would bring them closer to Bismarck. It would also give the impression that Bismarck was more liberal in his policies and help to lessen the image that he wanted to limit the power of the Reichstag, further supporting the view of Wehler. It would also, according to Wehler's view, mean that Bismarck would not be forced into making concessions in other areas and therefore by exploiting the idea of a protestant crusade, Bismarck was able to gain popular support. However, it is possible, as Pflanze has suggested, that Bismarck had no idea how such a policy would develop and was simply waiting to see how, having stirred up the situation, events unfolded before deciding on his exact policy towards the Catholic church.

Activity

In this chapter, the focus is on writing an answer that is analytical, and well-supported by precise own knowledge, and one which – where relevant – refers to historical interpretations/debates. Using the information from this chapter, and any other sources of information available to you, try to answer **one** of the following Paper 3 practice questions using these skills.

Paper 3 practice questions

1 'The internal problems of Germany were successfully tackled by their rulers by 1890.' To what extent do you agree with this statement?

2 To what extent was the German empire liberal between 1870 and 1890?

3 Compare and contrast the Catholic and Socialist threat to Germany in the period from 1870 to 1890.

4 Discuss the view that, in Germany in the period from 1870 to 1890, the threat from the Socialists was greater than that presented by the Catholics.

5 Examine the extent of Bismarck's control of policy in Germany after 1871.

6 Evaluate the reasons why Bismarck was unable to prevent the growth in socialism.

Analysis: an overview of Italian and German unification

8

8 Italy (1815–1871) and Germany (1815–1890)

The aim of this chapter is to offer some analysis, exercises and additional source material to help you compare Italian and German unification. It also looks forward to consider the impact of German and Italian unification on the emergence of fascism and Nazism in the 20th century.

KEY QUESTIONS

- What were the similarities and differences between Italian and German unification?
- What were the roles of individuals and nationalism?
- How far did the experience of unification lead to fascism and Nazism in the following century?

Overview

This chapter will help you reflect on some of the themes in the earlier chapters and think about the unification of central Europe as whole. Though there were similarities between the way that Italy and Germany were united, there were also key differences. For instance, the successes of unification were different: in Italy, when the north took control of the south, unification was experienced as an intense upheaval, while unification resulted in Germany becoming a great industrial power. The role played by individual leaders in the unification of both countries was extremely important. It led to an over-reliance on nationalist leaders in the following century. The ideas and dictatorial rule of Benito Mussolini in Italy and Adolf Hitler in Germany were far more extreme than those of Cavour, Garibaldi and Bismarck.

8.1 What were the similarities and differences between Italian and German unification?

There was no unity of aim

There were supporters of nationalism in both Italy and Germany after 1815, but they lacked a united aim. Some looked for complete union of all 'Italians' or 'Germans', while others had more limited goals. In Germany, there was a distinction between the supporters of a greater Germany (Grossdeutschland) and a smaller Germany (Kleindeutschland). In Italy, there was a deep north–south divide; many in the north felt that the south should play no part in a progressive new Italy. Before 1848, some Italians looked to the kingdom of Piedmont to unite Italy, some looked to the Pope, and others hoped for a popular republican movement.

Regional traditions

Both Germany and Italy had very strong regional traditions. In Germany, there were also religious differences between a mainly Protestant north and east and a more Catholic south and west. In Italy, there were more obvious cultural, economic and linguistic differences between the north and south. In Germany, there was no equivalent of the mezzogiorno – the deprived south with its mass poverty and illiteracy. There were more linguistic differences in Italy, even though Germany had various dialects.

Two dominant states

In both Germany and Italy, the country was led towards unification by its dominant state. Piedmont and Prussia were richer and more advanced in terms of industry than other parts of their respective countries. Both states developed considerably after 1815. The role of parliament was important in both Piedmont and Prussia, and both states had strong and ambitious prime ministers.

8

Nationalism and the impact of Napoleon on Italy and Germany

The Napoleonic Wars changed the extent of national feeling in both Italy and Germany. French rule resulted in a greater sense of national unity and people saw that it was possible to build a more unified and modern state. There was the introduction of modern systems of administration and new legal codes based on the French model. As French ideas seemed progressive and forward-looking, and replaced old traditions and divisions, they were attractive to the educated Italian middle classes. Even though these people were a minority, the French looked to them for support. This class was to provide the core of later nationalist feeling in Italy. They supported Napoleon's wars through heavy taxation and conscription.

In both Italy and Germany, there were attempts to return to the old ways of the *Ancien Régime* after the Revolutionary and Napoleonic Wars. The Church had suffered under the French Revolution and opposed nationalism and reform. The old rulers wanted to repress national feeling and liberal and reforming ideas. In both Italy and Germany, Austria fought to maintain its dominance and the Austrian foreign minister, Metternich, suppressed opposition.

Unrest after 1815

Both Italy and Germany experienced unrest after 1815, though there was more sustained nationalist activity in Italy than in Germany. In Italy, the revolutions of 1848–49 produced more heroic nationalist figures, such as Manin and Garibaldi, yet they were rarely successful. In Germany, there was no equivalent to the determined and fanatical Mazzini. While there were student movements and secret societies in both countries, the German students were less rowdy than the Carbonari. Nevertheless, both Italy and Germany experienced widespread unrest and calls for national unity in 1848.

In Italy, the revolts were fragmented and did not lead to a national parliament as they did in Germany. In Italy, there was more fighting and bloodshed and more savage counter-revolution. In neither country did the rulers of the leading state call for a national revolution, despite nationalists' hopes that they would do so. Carlo Alberto went to war with Austria in order to win lands and power for Piedmont; unification was not his ambition. Frederick Wilhelm IV of Prussia disliked nationalism and refused to accept popular rule. In neither country did the rural population show much enthusiasm for unification.

The hostility of the Catholic Church to revolution was more pronounced in Italy, where the Pope was forced to crown Napoleon and became a virtual prisoner. The ideas of the revolutionaries were often anti-clerical, so many priests supported France's enemies – especially in Naples and Sicily. In Germany, there was less religious opposition. For instance, German Protestants did not oppose nationalism very much.

The armed forces of both Italy and Germany were loyal to their Austrian rulers and defended Austria against revolution. The fact that no revolutionary movement succeeded in Austria was significant. The conservative ruling classes in both Italy and Germany, with the backing of their armies, took advantage of divisions in the revolutionary cause; for example, divisions between radicals such as Mazzini, supporters of a papal-led union and those who favoured rule by Piedmont. In Germany, there were divisions between conservative nationalists and those who sought greater democracy, as well between supporters of Grossdeutchland and Kleindeutschland. In Italy, the middle classes were enthusiastic for change and played a significant role in the revolts, but this was not the case in Germany.

In both countries, some form of constitutional government remained after unification. Piedmont's constitution continued although its role was limited, and the Prussians retained their Diet. Austria was able to impose its authority in both countries, and both Prussia and Piedmont suffered humiliation at Austrian hands – Piedmont was defeated by Austrian armies, and Prussia was not allowed to form a new union at Erfurt.

Reforms

There were internal reforms in both Italy and Germany. In Piedmont, the reforms were administrative and economic; in Prussia, there were army reforms and the Zollverein. It was clear in both countries that the dominant state – Piedmont and Prussia – would have to take the lead if unification were to be successful. For both states, this success was also dependent on careful diplomacy to secure the support or the neutrality of foreign powers.

8

Leaders

Unification of both Germany and Italy depended on the policies of its strong national leaders, Bismarck and Cavour. However, neither Cavour nor Bismarck was a true nationalist. Cavour never visited many parts of Italy and had little interest in including the backward agricultural and feudal areas in a progressive north Italian state. Bismarck had little enthusiasm for nationalism, which he thought of as a 'swindle', and certainly had no interest in strengthening the association of German nations – the Bund.

The true Italian national idealist and leader was Garibaldi, and there was no German equivalent: the hard-headed Prussian generals who did the fighting for Bismarck were not remotely like the dashing and impulsive Garibaldi.

Both Cavour and Bismarck were essentially diplomats who worked hard to take advantage of circumstances and saw very clearly what the end of Austrian domination would involve. For Cavour, the support of France was vital to ending Austrian rule. Unlike Prussia, Piedmont did not have an army capable of defeating Austria, so it relied on French forces and the neutrality of Britain and Russia. For Bismarck, there was no need for assistance from a foreign military force, but it was essential to secure the neutrality of France, Russia and Britain. Therefore, Bismarck's diplomacy was crucial. Both Cavour and Bismarck made deals with Napoleon III – the offer of Nice and Savoy in Cavour's case, and Bismarck initially supported French claims on Luxembourg, although this support was later withdrawn (see Chapter 7). Both men achieved their aims in part due to a favourable diplomatic situation.

ACTIVITY

Draw up a list of similarities and differences between Cavour and Bismarck as men and statesmen. You could present your list as a poster. Think about the men's background and early lives, how they came to power, their domestic policies and attitudes to national unity, their diplomacy and what they achieved. Do you think there are more similarities than differences between them?

The impact of foreign powers

Austria opposed Russia and sympathised with France and Britain during the Crimean War of 1853–56, but it did not commit forces.

Austria's actions alienated Russia, and so Russia did not support Austria when war broke out with Piedmont in 1859 and then Prussia in 1866. Likewise, because France and Britain did not receive military support from Austria during the Crimean War, they owed no debt of military support in 1859 and 1866. Britain, in any case, sympathised with the aspirations of Italian nationalism and had cultural and royal links with Germany. Thus, the attitude of foreign powers was crucial to Italian unification, and in this the diplomacy of Cavour and Bismarck played a key role. Cavour recognised the wisdom of sending Piedmont's troops to fight on the French and British side in the Crimean War, while Bismarck sought Russia's friendship. At meetings at Plombières and Biarritz respectively, Cavour and Bismarck made the most of Napoleon III's territorial greed and desire for an empire. Napoleon III let Cavour down – the casualties at Magenta and Solferino were too much for the French emperor and he made a separate peace with Austria in 1859. Bismarck, on the other hand, let Napoleon III down – his victories in 1866 left him without any need for the French emperor and he abandoned their agreement. In the end, Napoleon III fought Austria for Italy and Bismarck fought Napoleon III to protect and extend Germany.

Both Italy and Germany were united more by military force than national feeling. It is likely that the final form that unification took in both countries was more than their leaders hoped for. Cavour was forced to accept Garibaldi's successful revolution in the south and step in to prevent a more radical unification and ensure control by Piedmont. Bismarck may well have been happier with the North German Confederation, but events resulted in a larger German nation.

The weaknesses of Austria

The defeat of Austria in war was essential to both Italian and German unification. This might never have happened had Austrian diplomacy been more skillful and its military stronger.

When Austria won its struggle against the revolutionaries in 1849, it was aided by powerful armies and an alliance with Russia. Austria was able to re-establish control over its empire and defeat Piedmont. Austria was also powerful enough to prevent Prussia from establishing a union to rival the Austrian-controlled Bund.

Although Austria began to develop economically before 1810, the Austrian empire remained largely agricultural and its agricultural practices were not modernised in the way that Britain's and Prussia's were. Austria's per capita production of grain fell by 17% in the period 1810–1913. Furthermore, Austria's production did not rise as quickly as its population grew, so its productivity fell behind that of other European powers. Austria's technological developments were inferior to those of Britain, Germany and the USA; for example, its railway system was poor in comparison to Germany's. Austria's capital growth and industrial development were also limited. The Austrian ruling classes did not invest in industry, nor did they value entrepreneurs in the way that the other western powers did. While parts of the Austrian empire experienced some industrial growth, this was often dependent on direct state intervention and Austria had many regions of considerable economic backwardness. Consequently, the need to maintain a large army and bureaucracy was a drain on the empire's resources and Austrian struggled to maintain its great power status.

The strain on Austria's economy meant there was a lack of military investment. Prussia defeated Austria in 1866 because Prussian weaponry was superior. There was also a decline in Austria's military leadership. The military defeats of 1859 and 1866 were in part due to Austria's weak generals and poor military strategy. At key times, the Austrian armies were not able to move fast enough – for example, French forces mobilised more quickly in 1859. This is not to say that the Austrian army was entirely weak. The French army suffered heavy casualties in 1859, and Austrian artillery proved superior to Prussia's in 1865. Yet, the Austrian army's leadership, logistical organisation, transport, training and rifles were inferior to Prussia's. These military weaknesses reflected a lack of economic and social modernisation in the Austrian empire. Austria was too reliant on its aristocratic leaders; its factories could not supply enough war materials; vital railway links were not built; its people were not sufficiently united by education or industry.

Austria's diplomatic errors also contributed to the empire's loss of power. The scale of Austria's possessions meant that it was threatened by Russian ambitions in the Balkans, yet Austria's rivalry with Russia undermined a vital friendship that had proved essential to its victory against France and Piedmont in 1849. Austria did not provide military support to France, Britain and Turkey in the Crimean War, and yet gained from Russia's defeat. Subsequently, Austria lost the support of France and Britain on the one hand and Russia on the other.

This meant there was no help from any of Europe's great powers when Austria went to war with Piedmont and France in 1850 and Prussia in 1866. By allowing Austria's relations with the other European powers to deteriorate in this way, Austrian statesmen showed poor judgement.

Austria's main problem was that it was overstretched. Its large empire included several different nationalities and areas of varying economic and social development. To defend the empire against both the internal pressures of different national groups wanting self-government and the external threats from abroad, Austria needed considerable economic and military resources. While Italy and Germany produced outstanding leaders that had widespread public support, Austria produced – after Metternich – no leader of brilliance. After the Holy Roman Empire ended, Austria's ability to defeat France depended on alliances with Britain and Russia. There was internal revolt in 1848, and in 1867 Austria was forced to enter into equal partnership with Hungary – a powerful and restless province. Whereas national feeling led Italy and Germany forward towards unification, it contributed to Austria's decline.

Theory of Knowledge

History and comparison:

Italy and Germany were both unified at the same time in the mid 19th century. The methods and factors influencing their unification were often similar. However, given that countries have different political, economic and cultural backgrounds and development consider the following:

- How valuable is a comparative study of similar events in different countries?
- In what ways does a comparative study give us a better/clearer understanding of the events?
- What are the advantages and disadvantages of such comparative studies?
- Can you think of other examples from history where comparative studies would help our understanding of events?

The limits of unification

Following unification in both Italy and Germany, many Italians remained under Austrian rule and many German speakers lived outside the Reich. There was no national language in either country, nor was there complete parliamentary rule. Germany had a federal structure, although it appeared more democratic that it really was. In Italy, the regions were ruled by Piedmont directly and this led to a bitter civil war.

In both countries, the monarchy of the dominant state became the monarchy of the new country. Cavour died and was not able to see the longer-term impact of unification, as Bismarck was. 'National unity' was not fully achieved in either nation. Regional loyalties persisted in Italy to a greater degree than in Germany. In Germany, improved education and communications, greater national feeling and the sheer size of Prussia contributed to a stronger sense of national identity. In both nations, the period after unification saw considerable disunity. In Italy in the 1860s there was the peasants' war; in Germany there was the Kulturkampf.

Constitutional rule

Constitutionalism did not work well in either country. In Italy, a small electorate and lack of political tradition resulted in corrupt and ineffective parliaments. In Germany, despite a large electorate, Prussia's dominance and Bismarck's hostile campaigns against political groups hindered the growth of democracy. In both Italy and Germany, economic growth contributed to social discontent and colonial expansion achieved little. Both countries feared isolation and sought protection against France through alliance systems. Bismarck created the Dual then Triple Alliance, which Italy joined.

Both Italy and Germany suffered heavy casualties in the First World War (1914–18) and neither country gained what they wanted. The post-war period in each nation was marked by considerable political unrest and deep political divisions between right and left. In both, there was the rise of paramilitary mass parties led by charismatic dictators – Adolf Hitler in Germany and Benito Mussolini in Italy. Both Italy and Germany followed a policy of aggressive territorial expansion in the 1930s and were defeated in the Second World War (1939–45). Germany was then politically and geographically divided until the end of the Cold War. Today, both nations are democratic parliamentary states.

KEY CONCEPTS ACTIVITY

Cause and consequence: Were there more differences than similarities between the causes, course and results of unification in Germany and Italy? Using material from this chapter and the other chapters you have read, draw up two lists. Which list seems more convincing?

Similarities	Differences

8.2 What were the roles of individuals and nationalism?

KEY CONCEPTS QUESTION

Significance: How much did Italian and German unification owe to the leadership and inspiration of individuals?

ACTIVITY

Read interpretations A, B and C below. They focus on the role of key individuals in Italian and German unification. Do you agree with the views presented about these people, or do you think they should be challenged?

Topics

Interpretation A: Garibaldi and Mazzini

For Italy, Garibaldi is the ultimate hero. Not only did he take a leading and inspiring role in attempting to sustain the revolutions of 1848, but he was the key reason why Italian unification was not simply a matter for the more developed north of Italy. His daring expedition led to Sicily falling to the nationalists, the invasion of Naples and the historic meeting with Vittore Emanuele. Without this expedition, there would have been no Italy. Indeed, the story of Garibaldi's life was so rich that biographers turned to it as an exciting and inspirational story.

Garibaldi was the doer, the soldier, the man of action. However, for him to achieve his aims, his supporters needed motivation and here the great writer, thinker and theorist Mazzini fits into another biographical category. Inspired by a vision of moral rebirth through the nation, he is the true soul of the Italian *Risorgimento*.

Both Garibaldi and Mazzini were idealists and neither had the responsibility of power.

Interpretation B: Cavour

Cavour was an aristocratic, rational and deeply thoughtful statesman who recognised the causes of the failures of 1848. He saw the need for patient diplomacy – to make Europe aware of the Italian Question, to enlist the aid of foreign powers, to provoke Austria into a war, to ensure that Piedmont had an excuse to ask for French help and then had the opportunity to move into the duchies. Cavour did not see a completely united Italy, but once Garibaldi's expedition had proved successful, he moved in a clear and sure-footed way to take control and ensure complete unity under Piedmont's rule. He was also able to hold on to the support of foreign powers and keep the revolution moderate.

Interpretation C: Bismarck

Bismarck did not have the idealistic passion of Mazzini, nor the colourful, romantic popularity of Garibaldi, but he had an overwhelming sense of realism, vision and timing that made him a genius. He saw the obstacles to a Prussian-led, united Germany and dealt with them by shrewd diplomacy. His support of army reforms and his friendship with Von Roon and Von Moltke ensured that he could make the most of the superb Prussian army, and he secured the friendship of Russia. He lured Austria into a war against Denmark and then used the acquisitions of that war to ensure that a quarrel with Austria happened at the right time. He was generous to Austria after it lost against Prussia, knowing that he would need Austrian neutrality in the forthcoming war with France. His clever diplomacy kept France neutral in 1866, but he knew that France could not stand by and see a new Germany emerge. He also knew that a war against France would complete the unification of Germany that was so necessary. He cleverly provoked France into declaring war – ending any hope that France had of getting sympathy and support from any other power in Europe – and defeated it rapidly. Out of the patriotism of war came the new German empire, which was proclaimed in 1871 and owed all to this statesman of genius.

KEY CONCEPTS ACTIVITY

Significance: In a group, choose whether to focus on Garibaldi and Mazzini, Cavour or Bismarck. You need to decide how valid the interpretation is of the role they played in Italian or German unification. For example, have some elements been overlooked or are too many assumptions made? Aim to be critical by looking at the evidence given. Present your findings to the class.

DISCUSSION POINT

In a class discussion or balloon debate, argue the case for and against Garibaldi, Mazzini, Cavour and Bismarck. Come to a class decision – it need not be 'for' or 'against' the importance of each person's contribution, but it could bring together different arguments and offer a synthesis or compromise.

The extent and influence of nationalism

This issue is discussed in the preceding chapters, but the sources below take a more general view. They also introduce some contemporary ideas of the importance of nationalism.

QUESTION

Why do you think the idea of nationalism was so powerful? Who did nationalism most appeal to? Was nationalism a key reason for the unification of either Germany or Italy?

ACTIVITY

In a group, choose one of the following sources. Consider who wrote the source (research this if necessary) and how this influences what they say about nationalism.

SOURCE 8.1

Nature brings forth families; the most natural state therefore is also one people, with a national character of its own. For thousands of years this character preserves itself within the people and, if the native princes concern themselves with it, it can be cultivated in the most natural way: for a people is as much a plant of nature as is a family, except that it has more branches. Nothing therefore seems more contradictory to the true end of governments than the endless expansion of states, the wild confusion of races and nations under one sceptre. An empire made up of a hundred peoples and 120 provinces which have been forced together is a monstrosity, not a state-body.

Von Herder, J.G. 1784. **Materials for the Philosophy of the History of Mankind**.

SOURCE 8.2

Those who speak the same language are joined to each other by a multitude of invisible bonds by nature herself, long before any human art begins; they understand each other and have the power of continuing to make themselves understood more and more clearly; they belong together and are by nature one and an inseparable whole. Such a whole, if it wishes to absorb and mingle with itself any other people of different descent and language, cannot do so without itself becoming confused, in the beginning at any rate, and violently disturbing the even progress of its culture. From this internal boundary, which is drawn by the spiritual nature of man himself, the marking of the external boundary by dwelling place results as a consequence; and in the natural view of things it is not because men dwell between certain mountains and rivers that they are a people, but, on the contrary, men dwell together – and, if their luck has so arranged it, are protected by rivers and mountains – because they were a people already by a law of nature which is much higher.

Thus was the German nation placed – sufficiently united within itself by a common language and a common way of thinking, and sharply enough severed from the other peoples – in the middle of Europe, as a wall to divide races.

Fichte, J. G. 1806. **To the German Nation**.

Figure 8.1: The 'Cafe Della Concordia' at Genoa, the principal meeting place of the friends and sympathisers of Garibaldi

SOURCE 8.3

Young Italy is a brotherhood of Italians who believe in a law of Progress and Duty, and are convinced that Italy is destined to become one nation – convinced also that she possesses sufficient strength within herself to become one, and that the ill success of her former efforts is to be attributed not to the weakness, but to the misdirection of the revolutionary elements within her – that the secret of force lies in constancy and unity of effort. They join this association in the firm intent of consecrating both thought and action to the great aim of re-constituting Italy as one independent sovereign nation of free men and equals…National unity, as understood by Young Italy, does not imply the despotism of any, but the association and concord of all. The life inherent in each locality is sacred. Young Italy would have the administrative organization designed upon a broad basis of religious respect for the liberty of each commune, but the political organization, destined to represent the nation in Europe, should be one and central. Without unity of religious belief, and unity of social pact; without unity of civil, political, and penal legislation, there is no true nation.

Mazzini's instructions to those joining Young Italy, 1831.

257

SOURCE 8.4

The history of every age proves that no people can attain a high degree of intelligence and morality unless its feeling of nationality is strongly developed. This noteworthy fact is an inevitable consequence of the laws that rule human nature…Therefore, if we so ardently desire the emancipation of Italy – if we declare that in the face of this great question all the petty questions that divide us must be silenced – it is not only that we may see our country glorious and powerful but that above all we may elevate her in intelligence and moral development up to the plane of the most civilized nations…This union we preach with such ardour is not so difficult to obtain as one might suppose if one judged only by exterior appearances or if one were preoccupied with our unhappy divisions. Nationalism has become general; it grows daily; and it has already grown strong enough to keep all parts of Italy united despite the differences that distinguish them.

The Programme of Count Cavour, 1846.

SOURCE 8.5

Where is the German's fatherland?
Then name, oh, name the mighty land!
Wherever is heard the German tongue,
And German hymns to God are sung!
This is the land, thy Hermann's land;
This, German, is thy fatherland.
This is the German's fatherland,
Where faith is in the plighted hand,
Where truth lives in each eye of blue,
And every heart is staunch and true.
This is the land, the honest land,
The honest German's fatherland.
This is the land, the one true land,
O God, to aid be thou at hand!
And fire each heart, and nerve each arm,
To shield our German homes from harm,
To shield the land, the one true land,
One Deutschland and one fatherland!

Ernst Moritz Arndt, 'The German Fatherland' (1806)

Causation: Consider the factors that brought about the unification of Italy and Germany. Explain the importance of each factor in a few sentences. Rank the factors in order of importance by giving each a score out of 10. Compare your results in a group.

Factor	Explanation	Mark
National feeling		
Economic unity		
Leadership		
Foreign support		
Weakness of opponents		
Military power		

8.3 How far did the experience of unification lead to fascism and Nazism in the following century?

Direct links between unification and later extremism

It can be argued that there are direct links between the unification experience and later extremism:

- Unification in both Germany and Italy was achieved by military force rather than democratic voting; this meant that military force was a key element in control of the state.
- Unification increased national feeling, and this contributed to colonialism and a desire for national (territorial) expansion.

Both of these elements were important in the Nazi and fascist dictatorships of Hitler and Mussolini.

8 Italy (1815–1871) and Germany (1815–1890)

The men who led both Germany and Italy towards unification came to be seen as heroic. Their leadership was associated with elements of despotism.

- Garibaldi organised an illegal nationalist paramilitary force with a distinctive uniform of red shirts. His invasion of Sicily and Naples was unlawful. Only when he was victorious did Vittore Emanuele II and Cavour legitimise his actions and annex the lands he had conquered. Garibaldi ruled Sicily briefly as dictator and asked Cavour and the king of Piedmont for dictatorial powers over Naples. He can be seen as the forerunner of Mussolini, who in 1922 chose dictatorship over kingship.

Figure 8.2: Garibaldi and his 'red shirts' land at Marsala, Sicily, 11 May 1860

Figure 8.3: Mussolini's 'black shirts' in front of the Royal Palace in Rome, November 1922

- In Germany, Bismarck was not a dictator. However, from 1852 to 1866 he reformed and strengthened Prussia's army without parliamentary approval. He also deliberately provoked Austria and France into war with Prussia. His 'blood and iron' speech championed the use of military force, and Prussia's army inflicted cruel punishments on French civilians who were suspected of opposition. Elements of Bismarck's militarism can be found in the arguments the Nazis used to justify their policies of aggressive territorial expansion and racial 'purification'.

In Italy, there was severe repression during the peasants' war and Piedmont used military force to impose its rule on other Italian states. This mirrors Mussolini's Fascist control of the regions in the 1920s and 1930s. The suppression of 'enemies of the Reich' by Bismarck anticipates Nazi repression and dictatorship. Benito Mussolini and Adolf Hitler continued to call parliaments although they had lost any real power – as Bismarck did in order to disguise Prussia's dominance of Germany.

Both Mussolini and Hitler wanted total devotion to the state. They viewed local liberties and traditions as encouraging independence, and therefore a threat to national unity. This view is suggested in the way Piedmont imposed control on the other areas of Italy. Bismarck ensured that Prussia dominated Germany and saw local rights as secondary to national unity.

Extremism was not the obvious consequence of unification

It can also be argued that fascism and Nazism were not the obvious consequence of Italian and German unification.

- Fascism and Nazism developed from the militarism and mass mobilisation of the First World War, not the 19th century. They were also, to a large extent, reactions against socialism and communism.
- In both Italy and Germany in the 19th century, there were parliamentary institutions; in neither was there a police state on anything like the scale of Fascist Italy or Nazi Germany.
- Though there was strong national feeling in Italy and Germany in the period of unification, this was very different to the intensity of national feeling seen in Nazi Germany and Fascist Italy.
- In Italy and Germany after unification, there was no attempt to control every aspect of citizens' lives. Cavour and his successors were

liberals, and Bismarck sought loyalty rather than total obedience. There was nothing like the brutal oppression of Fascist Italy and Nazi Germany, with state spies and secret police.

- Following unification, power was shared among political parties. There was not one all-powerful party as there was in Mussolini's Italy and Hitler's Germany.
- Though there was some anti-Semitism in Bismarck's Germany, it was far more widespread in Germany after the First World War and in Italy in the 1930s.

The economic and social control established under Nazism and fascism was not seen in the previous century. The Fascist organisation 'Dopolavoro' and the Nazi organisation 'Strength Through Joy' set up elaborate welfare schemes that were very different to Bismarck's welfare state, and there was nothing like this in 19th-century Italy.

Historians at the University of Bielefeld in the 1960s and 1970s saw unification as leading to contempt for freedom and military authoritarianism; they argue this put Germany on a Sonderweg ('special way') to later dictatorship. This argument has been firmly rejected by historians such as Thomas Nipperdey, writing in *German History 1866 to 1918* (1990), who see Bismarck's Germany as having liberal elements. Bismarck's attempts to crush socialism were not widely supported. Furthermore, repression in 19th-century Germany was minimal when compared with that experienced during the dictatorships of Adolf Hitler and Benito Mussolini.

KEY CONCEPTS QUESTIONS

Perspective: Do you think the people of Italy gained more from Unification than the people of Germany?

Significance: What was the role of individuals in the Unification of Italy and Germany?

Paper 3 exam practice

Question

Compare the reasons for the success of German and Italian unification by 1871. **[15 Marks]**

Skill

Writing a conclusion to your essay

Examiner's tips

Provided you have carried out all the steps recommended so far, it should be relatively easy to write one or two concluding paragraphs.

For this question, you will need to cover the following possible reasons:

- the role of leaders – Bismarck and Cavour

- the role of economic factors

- the role of foreign powers

- the role of national feeling and idealism

- the importance of the changes in the international situation.

With general questions that ask for comparison, you have to avoid telling two separate 'stories' – Italy's and Germany's – and think in terms of themes and explanations.

This question requires you to consider a **range** of different reasons/factors, and to support your analysis with **precise** and **specific** supporting knowledge – so you need to avoid generalisations.

Also, such a question, which is asking for an analysis of several reasons, implicitly expects you to come to some kind of **judgement** about which reason(s) was/were most important.

Common mistakes

Sometimes, candidates simply rehash in their conclusion what they have written earlier – making the examiner read the same thing twice!

8

Italy (1815–1871) and Germany (1815–1890)

Generally, concluding paragraphs should be relatively short. The aim should be to come to a judgement/conclusion that is clearly based on what has already been written. If possible, a short but relevant quotation is a good way to round off an argument.

Remember to refer to the simplified Paper 3 mark scheme in Chapter 9.

Sample student conclusion

Thus there were similar elements in the success of both unifications, but on the whole the differences were greater. The role of the Prussian state, its army and organisation and its economic power were greater than the role of Piedmont's. There was no Prussian equivalent of Garibaldi and his heroic volunteers. Another major difference was the role of France. Prussia did not need the considerable military assistance of another power to unify Germany in the way that Cavour relied on French armies. The power of Piedmont's military did not approach that of Prussia's army, as shown by the poor contribution made by Italian forces in 1866. Superficially there were similarities, and both countries were able to take advantage of the weaknesses of Austria. However, the heroic idealism of the Risorgimento gave Italian unification a unique character, far removed from the disciplined militarism of the imposition of Prussian rule on Germany.

EXAMINER COMMENT

This is a good conclusion because it briefly pulls together the main threads of the argument (without simply repeating or summarising them), and then also makes a clear judgement. In addition, there is an intelligent final comment that rounds off the whole conclusion – and the core of the essay – in a memorable way.

Activity

In this chapter, the focus is on writing a useful conclusion. Using the information from this chapter, and any other sources of information available to you, write concluding paragraphs for **at least two** of the following Paper 3 practice questions. Remember: to do this, you will need to do full plans for the questions you choose.

Paper 3 practice questions

1 To what extent did either Italian or German unification bring long-term benefits to the people?

2 'German and Italian unification was less about popular feeling, and more about military power.' To what extent do you agree with this statement?

3 Evaluate the view that Italian and German unification was only possible because of Austrian weakness.

4 To what extent was Cavour a greater statesman than Bismarck?

5 Compare and contrast the reasons for the growth of national feeling in Germany and Italy after 1815.

6 Examine the role of foreign powers in the unification of Italy and Germany.

9 Exam practice

Introduction

You have now completed your study of the main events and developments in the unification of Italy (1815–1871) and Germany (1815–1890). You have also had a chance to examine the various historical debates and differing historical interpretations that surround some of these developments.

In the earlier chapters, you encountered examples of Paper 3-type essay questions, with examiner's tips. You have also had some basic practice in answering such questions. In this chapter, these tips and skills will be developed in more depth. Longer examples of possible student answers are provided. These are accompanied by examiner's comments that should increase your understanding of what examiners are looking for when they mark your essays. Following each question and answer, you will find tasks to give you further practice in the skills needed to gain the higher marks in this exam.

IB History Paper 3 exam questions and skills

Those of you following HL Option 4 – *History of Europe* – will have studied in depth three of the 18 sections available for this HL Option. *Italy 1815–1871 and Germany 1815–1890* is one of those sections. For Paper 3, two questions are set from each of the 18 sections, giving 36 questions in total; and you have to answer three of these.

Each question has a specific mark scheme. However the 'generic' mark scheme in the *IB History Guide* gives you a good general idea of what examiners are looking for in order to be able to put answers into the higher bands. In particular, you will need to acquire reasonably precise historical knowledge so that you can address issues such as cause and effect, and change and continuity. You will need this knowledge in order to explain historical developments in a clear, coherent, well-supported and relevant way. You will also need to understand relevant historical debates and interpretations, and be able to refer to these and critically evaluate them.

Essay planning

Make sure you read each question **carefully**, noting all the important key or 'command' words. You might find it useful to highlight them on your question paper. You can then produce a rough plan (for example, a spider diagram) of **each** of the three essays you intend to attempt, *before* you start to write your answers. That way, you will soon know whether you have enough own knowledge to answer them adequately. Next, refer back to the wording of each question. This will help you see whether or not you are responding to **all** its various demands/aspects. In addition, if you run short of time towards the end of your exam, you will at least be able to write some brief condensed sentences to show the key issues/points and arguments you would have presented. It is thus far better to do the planning at the **start** of the exam; that is, **before** you panic, should you suddenly realise you haven't time to finish your last essay.

Relevance to the question

Remember, too, to keep your answers relevant and focused on the question. Don't go outside the dates mentioned in the question, or write answers on subjects not identified in that question. Also, don't just describe the events or developments. Sometimes students just focus on one key word, date or individual, and then write down everything they know about it. Instead, select your own knowledge carefully, and pin the relevant information to the key features raised by the question. Finally, if the question asks for 'causes/reasons' and 'results', 'continuity and change', 'successes and failures', or 'nature and development', make sure you deal with **all** the parts of the question. Otherwise, you will limit yourself to half marks at best.

Examiner's tips

For Paper 3 answers, examiners are looking for well-structured arguments that:

- are consistently relevant/linked to the question
- offer clear/precise analysis
- are supported by accurate, precise and relevant own knowledge
- offer a balanced judgement
- refer to different historical debates/interpretations or to relevant historians and, where relevant, offer some critical evaluation of these.

Simplified mark scheme

Band		Marks
1	Consistently clear understanding of and focus on the question, with all main aspects addressed. Answer is fully analytical, balanced and well-structured/organised. Own knowledge is detailed, accurate and relevant, with events placed in their historical context. There is developed critical analysis, and sound understanding of historical concepts. Examples used are relevant, and used effectively to support analysis/evaluation. The answer also integrates evaluation of different historical debates/perspectives. All/almost all of the main points are substantiated, and the answer reaches a clear/reasoned/consistent judgement/conclusion.	13–15
2	Clear understanding of the question, and most of its main aspects are addressed. Answer is mostly well-structured and developed, though, with some repetition/lack of clarity in places. Supporting own knowledge mostly relevant/accurate, and events are placed in their historical context. The answer is mainly analytical, with relevant examples used to support critical analysis/evaluation. There is some understanding/evaluation of historical concepts and debates/perspectives. Most of the main points are substantiated, and the answer offers a consistent conclusion.	10–12
3	Demands of the question are understood – but some aspects not fully developed/addressed. Mostly relevant/accurate supporting own knowledge, and events generally placed in their historical context. Some attempts at analysis/evaluation but these are limited/not sustained/inconsistent.	7–9

Band		Marks
4	**Some understanding** of the question. **Some relevant own knowledge**, with some factors identified – but with **limited explanation**. **Some attempts at analysis**, but answer **lacks clarity/coherence, and is mainly description/ narrative.**	4–6
5	**Limited understanding of/focus on the question. Short/generalised answer**, with very **little accurate/relevant own knowledge.** Some **unsupported assertions**, with **no real analysis.**	0–3

Student answers

The following extracts from student answers have brief examiner's comments in the margins, and a longer overall comment at the end. Those parts of student answers that are particularly strong and well-focused (such as demonstrations of precise and relevant own knowledge, or examination of historical interpretations) will be *highlighted in red*. Errors/confusions/irrelevance/loss of focus will be *highlighted in blue*. In this way, students should find it easier to follow why marks were awarded or withheld.

Question 1

'Military factors were the most important cause of the unification of Germany by 1871.'To what extent do you agree with this statement? **[15 marks]**

Skills

- factual knowledge and understanding
- structured, analytical and **balanced** argument
- awareness/understanding/evaluation of historical interpretations
- clear and balanced judgement.

Examiner's tips

Look carefully at the wording of this question, which asks you to consider how important military factors are. This is different from explaining why they were important, and requires you to weigh them against other factors. So, when you start to think about the different elements in unification, you should remember to compare them with the key factor in the question. Don't just explain the wars.

Student answer

German unification came about in 1871 as a result of a war with France. Since 1862 there had been three major wars. The first was against Denmark in 1864, and the second was between Prussia and Austria in 1866. These wars were won by Prussia's superior military forces and weapons. So war was at the heart of Prussia's growth.

However, war alone did not unify Germany. There were other factors. There had been the growth of German national feeling. The diplomacy of Bismarck was very important in preventing other nations helping Prussia's enemies, and Prussia's economic development made the state very important within Germany. Therefore, military factors alone did not unify Germany, but they were of considerable importance.

EXAMINER COMMENT

This is a clear and well-focused introduction, showing accurate knowledge of the topic and a good understanding of several of the general factors contributing to unification. The answer now needs to develop a judgement about the importance of each of these factors.

Unification had been attempted before in 1848 and had failed. This was because the army remained loyal to the kings, and other powers – such as Austria and Russia, with their large armies – opposed revolution. Prussia built up its army because of the humiliation it faced when the Austrians prevented it from forming a new union of Erfurt. The army reforms of von Roon were crucial in making Prussia stronger. With a better army, weapons such as the Needle Gun, and good planning and railways, Prussia was able to defeat Austria and France, so the army was extremely important.

In 1862, Bismarck became the Minister-President of Prussia and supported the army reforms against the opposition of the Prussian parliament. He knew how important the army was to be and spoke of 'blood and iron' unifying Prussia. In 1863 a quarrel arose between Germany and Denmark over two provinces, Schleswig and Holstein. Bismarck was prepared to use Prussia's army against Denmark and he negotiated joint action with Austria which led to war in 1864.

Prussian forces did well and this helped to increase Prussia's prestige. The Danes were forced to give up the provinces and they were ruled by Austria and Prussia, a result of the Convention of Gastein. The two countries then quarrelled and Bismarck used this quarrel to start a war against Austria. The Austrians had big forces but the Prussians were better organised.

[There follows an account of the war.]

EXAMINER COMMENT

Although there is some accurate own knowledge, this is mostly **descriptive** material, and so is **not** explicitly linked to the demands of the question. The reader is left to judge the importance of all this for unification, and it becomes an account of what happened.

In fact, there are several different theories about whether Bismarck planned the wars or merely took advantage of events. Historians like Taylor see Bismarck as just an opportunist, not having a clear idea beyond the general aim of reducing the power of Austria and promoting the power of Prussia. Others like Seaman see Bismarck planning to gain Russian friendship and to provoke a war with Austria. When the quarrel over Schleswig and Holstein came about, he already knew that he must use it to start a war with Austria, even if he did not know when.

EXAMINER COMMENT

This paragraph shows awareness of an aspect of historical debate, although these different interpretations are merely mentioned, with no attempt to **evaluate** them. However, the overriding point is that all this information is largely irrelevant – and so will not score any marks. The candidate is thus wasting time, when he/she should be writing about the importance of military factors, not answering a question about what Bismarck did or did not plan.

Bismarck's use of the army meant that military victory was a key factor. Without the war with Denmark, Bismarck could not have undermined the Bund, which was ignored, and so weakened Austria. Without war, Bismarck could not have ended Austrian power in Germany. Bismarck then had to face the problem of France, which was jealous of Bismarck's success in defeating Austria and setting up a new North German Confederation. France was seen as the greatest military power, but Prussia armies defeated France in 1870. This war brought in the southern German states to ally with Prussia, and completed unification. Thus, war was an important unifying factor. It also brought about a wave of national feeling.

The war went on longer than Bismarck wanted. There were early victories and the French emperor was captured at Sedan in September 1870, but the French fought on under a new government. Also, the peace treaty was delayed by a revolution in Paris. The Prussian army waited while the French fought a civil war, and it was not until March 1871 that a peace treaty was finally signed that gave Germany Alsace and Lorraine and a new German empire. The new empire was proclaimed in January 1871, and the king of Prussia became the new Kaiser of Germany with Bismarck as chancellor.

EXAMINER COMMENT

Again, there is accurate own knowledge in this paragraph – but this is not what the question requires. While the opening sentence shows the correct focus, the candidate goes on to produce more narrative that does not weigh up military factors.

Thus, wars had brought unification but there were other factors at work. The first was the greater economic unity and growth of Germany. After 1818, there was also the Zollverein – an economic union to promote free trade. There was also the development of railways, which brought about more trade. By gaining lands in the Rhine in 1815 with coal and ore, Prussia became stronger and this helped it. Prussia's industries, especially iron and steel, grew.

There was also Bismarck's diplomacy. This was important – in 1862, Bismarck had become prime minister of Prussia. In 1863, he signed the Alvensleben Convention with Russia. This was important in gaining Russian friendship. In 1863, a quarrel arose with Denmark…

[There then follow several more paragraphs giving detailed and accurate accounts of different elements including nationalism and the weaknesses of Austria.]

Therefore, many factors brought about German unification. The wars and Prussia's military power ended the ability of Austria and France to prevent unification. The war in 1870 also brought the southern German states into alliance with Prussia, and helped bring them into the empire in 1871. The military successes were linked to Prussia's economic growth as they needed good weapons like the needle gun and the heavy artillery which defeated France. The growth of railways helped Prussia's armies. However, unless Bismarck had led Germany well, this would not have brought about unification. Bismarck had to decide when to go to war and he had to know that his enemies could be defeated. He took a risk that Austria could be defeated before the other German states that supported Austria could raise many troops, and before other nations could interfere. So it was not purely military factors but also Bismarck's genius, as he ensured that Austria and France would not have any allies by his clever treaties – for example, with Italy.

EXAMINER COMMENT

There is some relevant focus on the demands of the question – and some relevant discussion of the relative importance of different elements.

In conclusion, I think that military factors, while important, are not the key to German unification. Nationalism had grown since before 1815 and there was increasing economic unity. The wars speeded up a process that would have happened anyway.

EXAMINER COMMENT

This brief conclusion makes a valid judgement. Unfortunately, this is not a supported judgement and comes rather suddenly as an assertion – there has not been much consideration of nationalism, and there is not a sustained analysis of the relative importance of different factors.

Overall examiner's comments

There is plentiful and accurate own knowledge – unfortunately, it is **mostly irrelevant**. While there are some hints of analysis, the answer is mostly descriptive, so it is not really focused on the demands of the question. However, brief sections **are** relevant, so the answer is probably good enough to gain a mark in Band 4 – 6 marks. What was needed was an answer that focused more on explaining how different factors linked with unification, and compared these with the impact of military factors.

Activity

Look again at the simplified mark scheme, and the student answer. Now try to draw up a plan focused on the demands of the question. Then try to write several paragraphs that will be good enough to get into Band 1, and so obtain the full 15 marks. As well as making sure you address **all** aspects of the question, try to integrate into your answer some references **and** evaluation of relevant historians/historical interpretations.

Question 2

Compare and contrast Cavour and Bismarck as 'architects of national unity'. **[15 marks]**

Skills

- factual knowledge and understanding
- structured, analytical and **balanced** argument
- awareness/understanding/evaluation of historical interpretations.

Examiner's tips

Look carefully at the wording of this question, which asks you to compare and contrast the leadership of Cavour and Bismarck. Questions such as this show how important it is to study **all** the bullet points in the sections you study. If you only select a few of the named individuals for detailed study, you could seriously limit your options in the exam. To answer questions such as this in the most effective way, it is best to structure your answer so that the comparisons/contrasts are brought out **explicitly**. In other words, draw up a rough plan with headings for *'comparisons'* and *'contrasts'* – then jot down where aspects of their policies were similar under *'comparisons'*, and where/how they were different under *'contrasts'*. Remember: don't just **describe** what their policies were; what's needed is explicit focus on similarities **and** differences.

Student answer

Although Bismarck and Cavour were very different personalities, they were similar in the way in which they were architects of unity – they both wanted to use diplomacy to expand their countries and they both had to defeat Austria to achieve their aims. To show this, I shall start by examining Cavour's policies, before moving on to look at Bismarck's policies.

EXAMINER COMMENT

This introduction starts in a generally promising way. However, the final sentence in this paragraph is **very** worrying. This is because such an approach will almost certainly result in a **narrative** of the two sets of policies with, at best, only some kind of **implicit** comparison/contrast. As has been seen in previous answers, a narrative account without clear focus on the demands of the question is unlikely to get beyond Band 4–6 marks.

Italy (1815–1871) and Germany (1815–1890)

Cavour saw that if Piedmont were to expand and become the leading power of a more united Italy, he had to build its economy and ensure that it was recognised as an important European power. The situation when Cavour became the prime minister of Piedmont was not very promising. Italy was a country with many linguistic and political differences. The south, ruled by the King of Naples and Sicily, was economically and socially underdeveloped and there was illiteracy and poverty. The centre of Italy was still ruled by the Pope directly. The Austrians controlled Lombardy and Venetia with the big cities of Milan and Venice. Attempts to bring more unity in 1848–49 had failed. The Kingdom of Piedmont had emerged under its king, Carlo Alberto, as the leading power, but defeats by Austria had prevented any increase in Italian unity. Piedmont had kept its constitution and Cavour had led modernising measures in the 1850s that reduced the power of the Church, introduced free trade and built up railways.

EXAMINER COMMENT

This paragraph contains a lot of very precise information, and is clearly the result of solid revision. However, it is mainly background material – **there is little on his actual policies**.

Cavour understood that 1848 had failed because of the power of Austria and the support of other powers such as France and Russia for the existing regimes in Italy. He saw that Piedmont would not be strong enough to defeat Austria alone, but needed allies. In 1854 the Crimean War broke out and this gave Cavour his opportunity to increase Piedmont's standing in Europe and get support. He joined the war on the side of France and Britain against Russia, and some of Piedmont's troops took part in the fighting.

This gave Cavour a place in the peace negotiations, and he used this to raise the issue of Italy. Britain was quite sympathetic to the Italian cause, and the French saw that the peace could be used to benefit France. The Crimean War had worsened relations between Austria and Russia, so Russia would not necessarily help Austria. It had also worsened the relations between Austria and France and Britain, as Austria had not joined them in the fighting but had benefitted from Russia's defeat. Cavour managed to use this situation by getting an agreement with Napoleon III of France to support Piedmont against Italy in return for getting Nice and Savoy. This Pact of Plombières led to a war in 1859, in which France defeated Austria.

EXAMINER COMMENT

Again, there is a lot of accurate own knowledge – this time, some of it **is** relevant, as it deals with Cavour's diplomacy and the international situation which he used. However, so far, this answer seems to be turning into a descriptive account of what Cavour did. There has, as yet, been no attempt to address the **key** issue of similarities/differences. This is the danger with such a 'one by one' approach to questions like this.

Cavour's diplomatic policies had been successful up to a point, and Austria's defeat had opened up the chance for Piedmont to expand into Lombardy. This would have been impossible without French help. However, France withdrew after the heavy losses in the fighting at Solferino and Austria ceded Lombardy to France, who passed it to Piedmont. However, Cavour encouraged agitation in other areas of northern Italy. His aim was not to create a great united Italy but rather to create a prosperous northern kingdom dominated by Piedmont, and this is what emerged as a result of risings in Piedmont's favour. However, Cavour was faced by the danger of a revolt in the south. Despite his efforts, a radical nationalist force under Garibaldi set sail to support a rising in Sicily. Cavour saw he had to act once Garibaldi had taken Sicily and crossed into Naples. He was decisive in taking control of the nationalist rising by sending forces into the Papal States and Naples. Thus it was not Garibaldi who took control of the south and central Italy, but Piedmont. Cavour responded to events and maintained Piedmont's influence.

EXAMINER COMMENT

Again, there is plenty of accurate own knowledge and explanation, some of which supports the political policies Cavour followed. However – as in the previous paragraphs – no comparisons/contrasts with Bismarck's political style and policies have been made.

Bismarck used diplomacy, too, by getting the support of Russia in 1863. There was a revolt in Poland and he co-operated with Russia. This encouraged Russia to stand aside during the unification of Germany. Bismarck went to war against Denmark in 1864 and then used the outcome of the war to start a war against Austria and create a new state. He then went to war against France, so like Cavour he depended on war and diplomacy. He really wanted only a larger Prussia, just as Cavour wanted a larger Piedmont.

> ## EXAMINER COMMENT
> This is a good conclusion – brief and to the point. However, it is not a supported judgement or conclusion, as there is nothing about Bismarck's policies in the body of the essay. The only real reference to him comes here in the conclusion.

Overall examiner's comments

Though there is precise and accurate own knowledge, the essay is basically about Cavour and Piedmont. If the candidate had also written about Bismarck in the same way, then the answer would have been awarded Band 4 – 6 marks – even though it hasn't really addressed the demands of the question.

However, because it almost **only** deals with Cavour, it can only be awarded Band 5 – which would be 3 marks at most. To reach Band 3 and higher, the answer would need some **explicit and well-structured treatment of comparisons and contrasts, with consistent analysis of both similarities and differences**.

Activity

Look again at the simplified mark scheme, and the student answer. Now try to draw up a plan, with a structure focused on the demands of the question. Then try to write your own answer, making sure you consistently make comparisons and contrasts – so that the answer can get into Band 1 and obtain the full 15 marks.

Question 3

To what extent was Italy a united country by 1871? **[15 marks]**

Skills

- factual knowledge and understanding
- structured, analytical and **balanced** argument
- awareness/understanding/evaluation of historical interpretations.

Look carefully at the wording of this question, which asks the degree of unity to be assessed. This may involve considering different sorts of unity – political and territorial, as well as economic and cultural. The word 'unity' has to be broken down. Remember: don't just describe what happened. What is needed is explicit analysis and explanation, with precise supporting own knowledge.

Student answer

The Kingdom of Italy, established in 1861, gave Italy more unity than it had at any time since the Napoleonic wars. There was a common monarch, constitution and government. However, not all Italians were in the new kingdom and not all regions accepted the new state. Thus, Italy was still not 'complete' and the divisions between different areas were still strong. By 1871, there had been some progress to unity but not all the problems in establishing genuine unity had been resolved. There were social and economic divisions between north and south and cultural differences, but there was greater political and territorial unity.

EXAMINER COMMENT

This is a clear and well-focused introduction, showing a good appreciation of all the demands of the question, and indicating that an analytical approach is likely to be followed. This is a good start. A distinction is made between different sorts of unity and a clear point of view is established.

In many ways, it is difficult to justify the use of the term 'unity' when looking at Italy in the 1860s. For instance, the south resented the imposition of what they saw as 'foreign' rule and especially military service and new taxation by Piedmont. There was no attempt at a federal rule in which the different regions had their own local institutions. Instead, Piedmont's laws, administration and government were imposed. This led to a large-scale rebellion by many areas of southern Italy, which the north referred to as 'the Brigands' War', but more recent research indicates this was a popular uprising similar to a civil war. Thousands of troops were engaged in suppressing the rising, which left resentment that has lasted to the present day. Thus, the unity that idealists had hoped for did not always come about.

EXAMINER COMMENT

There is some accurate supporting own knowledge, explicitly linked to the question's issue of unity, and this is a well-focused section.

Regional resentment of Piedmont's rule was a strong feature of the 1860s, but there was also the limitation of the unity achieved by Cavour and Garibaldi. Venice and the Venetia remained under Austrian control. Nice and Savoy remained French as a result of the bargain struck with Napoleon III. Rome continued to be garrisoned and protected by French troops. There was little the Italian state could do about this. Though armed forces were built up, Piedmont was still militarily weaker than Austria and France. It was only because of an alliance with Prussia that Italy got Venice in 1866 after Prussia defeated Austria and gave it to her. There were still substantial areas in the north that Austria retained – Istria, Trieste, Trentino, and the South Tyrol. The war between France and Prussia allowed Italy to take Rome in 1870, leaving the Pope only the small independent area of the Vatican City. Previous attempts to seize Rome by Garibaldi were put down by the Italian government for fear of upsetting France. Thus, by 1870 there was more territorial unity, but this had not been achieved by united efforts by the Italian people but by circumstances of foreign wars, and still Italy was not completely united.

EXAMINER COMMENT

Again, this is a well-focused paragraph, with some initial analysis of why there was increasing but limited unity. So far, there is reasonable supporting own knowledge with some good detail.

Politically, there was greater unity in the sense of new national instructions. There was a national monarchy, but Vittore Emanuele's heart really lay in Piedmont rather than Italy as a whole. The monarchs took their title from Piedmont, so Vittore Emanuele was not Vittore Emanuele I of Italy, but rather Vittore Emanuele II of Piedmont who became king of Italy. The same is true of the parliament and electoral system. The narrow, property-based franchise of Piedmont was applied to the rest of Italy. The army was generally led by Piedmontese officers. The tax system and the parliamentary system was also based on Piedmont's statutuo. The official language of the new Italian state was the classic Italian of northern Italy. All this did give Italy a greater sense of unity, but it was imposed rather than coming from genuine integration.

EXAMINER COMMENT

This is a very relevant paragraph that focuses on how the political domination of Italy by Piedmont could be seen as unifying, but at a deeper level it meant that the unity was superficial.

[There then follow several paragraphs – with detailed supporting own knowledge – analysing social and economic unity and suggesting that the development of a more flexible political system might have increased unity. However, there is no mention or evaluation of different historians' views.]

In conclusion, there were clear signs of greater unity after 1861 and by 1871 Italy had broken down some of the internal resistance and developed a political system in which localism was starting to be better accommodated. Common institutions, currency, laws, administration and symbols were starting to establish a greater sense of national unity. However, the scars of the conflicts of the 1860s were still there; economic disparity between the more industrial and commercial north and the predominantly agricultural and increasingly over-populated south was still a barrier to true social unity. Greater education had broken down some linguistic and cultural barriers, but not completely, and there remained – despite increases in railways, literacy and migration from north to south – considerable differences between the regions that still persist today.

EXAMINER COMMENT
The conclusion is thoughtful and well-focused, and ends a well-focused and analytical argument.

Overall examiner's comments
This is a good, well-focused and analytical answer, with some precise and accurate own knowledge to support the points made. The answer is thus certainly good enough to be awarded a mark in Band 2. To get into Band 1, the candidate needed to provide some reference to historians' views/historical interpretations, and some critical evaluation of these interpretations.

Activity
Look again at the simplified mark scheme, and the student answer. Now try to write your own answer to the question, and attempt to make it good enough to get into Band 1 and so obtain the full 15 marks. In particular, make sure you are aware of the main historical debates about this topic – and incorporate some critical evaluation of them in your answer.

Further reading

Italy

Beales, D. and Biagini, E. 2002. *The Risorgimento and the Unification of Italy*. London. Longman.

Clark, M. 2009. *Italian Risorgimento*. London. Longmans Seminar.

Davis, J. 2000. *Italy in the Nineteenth Century*. Oxford. Oxford University Press.

Duggan, C. 2007. *The Force of Destiny: A History of Italy since 1796*. London. Penguin.

Gooch, J. 1986. *The Unification of Italy*. London. Routledge.

Hearder, H. 1983. *Italy in the Age of the Risorgimento*. London. Longman.

Hearder, H. 1984. *Cavour (Profiles in Power)*. London. Longman.

Mack Smith, D. 1985. *Garibaldi*. London. Littlehampton Book Services.

Mack Smith, D. 1996. *Mazzini*. London. Yale University Press.

Mack Smith, D. 1997. *Modern Italy: A Political History*. London. Yale University Press.

Pearce, R. and Stiles, A. 2006. *The Unification of Italy*. London. Hodder.

Riall, L. 2009. *Risorgimento: The History of Italy from Napoleon to Nation State*. London. Palgrave Macmillan.

Riall, L. 2009. *Garibaldi: Invention of a Hero*. London. Yale University Press.

Germany

Blackbourn, D. 1997. *The Fontana History of Germany 1780–1918: The Long Nineteenth Century*. London. Blackwell.

Breuilly, J. 1996. *The Formation of the First German Nation-State*. London. Palgrave.

Clarke, C. 2006. *The Iron Kingdom: The Rise and Downfall of Prussia 1600–1947*. London. Allen Lane.

Craig, G. 1980. *Germany 1866–1945*. Oxford. Oxford University Press.

Eyck, E. 1964. *Bismarck and the German Empire*. London. Norton.

Feuchtwanger, E. 2002. *Bismarck*. London. Routledge.

Fulbrook, M. 2004. A *Concise History of Germany*. Cambridge. Cambridge University Press.

Kitchen, M. 2011. *A History of Modern Germany: 1800 to the Present*. Oxford. Wiley-Blackwell.

Schulze, H. 1991. *The Course of German Nationalism*. Cambridge. Cambridge University Press.

Schulze, H. 2001. *Germany: A New History*. London. Harvard University Press.

Steinberg, J. 2011. *Bismarck: A Life*. Oxford. Oxford University Press.

Taylor, A.J.P. 1958. *Bismarck: The Man and the Statesman*. London. Hamish Hamilton.

Wells, M. 2004. *Bismarck*. London. Collins.

Williamson, D.G. 2011. *Bismarck and Germany: 1862–1890*. London. Longmans Seminar.

Further information

Sources and quotations in this book have been taken from the following publications.

Barraclough, G. 1946. *Factors in German History*. Oxford. Blackwell.

Blackbourn, D. 1997. *The Fontana History of Germany 1780–1918: The Long Nineteenth Century*. London. Blackwell.

Blumberg, A. 1990. *A Carefully Planned Accident: The Italian War of 1859*. Delaware. Associated University Press.

Brook Shepherd, G. 1997. *The Austrians*. London. HarperCollins.

Clarke, C. 2006. *The Iron Kingdom: The Rise and Downfall of Prussia 1600–1947*. London. Allen Lane.

Crankshaw, E. 1981. *Bismarck*. London. Macmillan.

Duggan, C. 2007. *The Force of Destiny: A History of Italy since 1796*. London. Penguin.

Feuchtwanger, E. 2002. *Bismarck*. London. Routledge.

Fichte, J. G. 1806. *To the German Nation*.

Fisher, H.A.L. 1935. *A History of Europe*. London. Eyre & Spottiswood.

Grant Robertson, C. 1919. *Bismarck*. London. Constable.

Hearder, H. 1983. *Italy in the Age of the Risorgimento*. London. Longman.

Hobsbawm, E.J. 1959. *Primitive Rebels: Studies in Archaic Forms of Social Movement in the 19th and 20th Centuries*. Manchester. Manchester University Press.

Kissinger, H. 1994. *Diplomacy*. New York. Simon & Schuster.

Marriott, J.A.R. 1945. *A History of Europe from 1815 to 1939*. London. Methuen.

Mazzini, G. 1864. *Life and writings of Mazzini*. London.

Palmer, A. 1976. *Bismarck*. London. Littlehampton Book Services.

Procacci, G. 1970. *History of the Italian People*. London. Weidenfeld & Nicolson.

Schroder, P. 2000. *Short Oxford History of Modern Europe*. Oxford. Oxford University Press.

Smith, M. 1968. *The Making of Italy 1796–1870*. London. Macmillan.

Steinberg, J. 2011. *Bismarck: A Life*. Oxford. Oxford University Press.

Taylor, A.J.P. 1958. *Bismarck: The Man and the Statesman*. London. Hamish Hamilton.

Thayer, W.R. 1911. *Life and Times of Cavour*. London. Constable.

Thompson, D. 1957. *Europe Since Napoleon*. London. Longman.

Von Herder, J.G. 1784. *Materials for the Philosophy of the History of Mankind*.

Wells, M. 2004. *Bismarck*. London. Collins.

Williamson, D.G. 2011. *Bismarck and Germany 1862–1890*. London. Longmans Seminar.

Index

Index

Index

Index

Acknowledgements

The authors and publishers acknowledge the following sources of copyright material and are grateful for the permissions granted. While every effort has been made, it has not always been possible to identify the sources of all the material used, or to trace all copyright holders. If any omissions are brought to our notice, we will be happy to include the appropriate acknowledgements on reprinting.

Cover DEA/G. DAGLI ORTI/Getty Images; Figure 2.2. DEA/G. DAGLI ORTI/Getty Images; Figure 2.4. Alinari Archives/Getty Images; Figure 2.5. Print Collector/Getty Images; Figure 2.6. Mary Evans Picture Library; Figure 3.1. Mayer & Pierson/Stringer/Getty Images; Figure 3.2. DeAgostini/Getty Images; Figure 3.4. Roger-Viollet/ TopFoto; Figure 3.6. Iberfoto/Mary Evans Picture Library; Figure 3.8. Stefano Bianchetti/Getty Images; Figure 4.1. Art Media/Print Collection/Getty Images; Figure 4.3. Hulton Royals Collection/Getty Images; Figure 5.2. Nellmac/Getty Images; Figure 5.5. ullsteinbild/Getty Images; Figure 5.6. INTERFOTO/A. Koch/Getty Images; Figure 5.7. INTERFOTO/Sammlung Rauch/Mary Evans Picture Library; Figure 5.8. Hulton Deutsch/Getty Images; Figure 5.9. Bildagentur-online/ Getty Images; Figure 5.10. ullstein bild/ullstein bild via Getty Images; Figure 6.1. Fine Art Images/Heritage Images/Getty Images; Figure 6.2. Henry Guttmann/Getty Images; Figure 6.3. Bettmann/Getty Images; Figure 6.5. Hulton Archive/Getty Images; Figure 6.6. Chronicle/ Alamy Stock Photo; Figure 7.1. Weltbild APA/Press Association Images/ PA Photos; Figure 7.2. Universal Images Group/Getty Images; Figure 7.3. The Granger Collection/TopFoto; Figure 7.4. Universal History Archive/Getty Images; Figure 7.5. BISMARCK/DROPPING PILOT Cartoon by Tenniel in Punch 29 March 1890, pp150-1/Mary Evans Picture Library; Figure 8.1. Cartoon - The 'Cafe Della Concordia,' at Genoa, the principal meeting place of the friends and sympathizers of Garibaldi, Nast, Thomas/Cartoonstock; Figure 8.2. Pictorial Press/ Alamy Stock Photo; Figure 8.3. Topham Picturepoint/TopFoto